Marxism in Britain

Marxism in Britain has declined, almost to the point of oblivion, since the Second World War. The Communist Party of Great Britain had more than 50,000 members in the early 1940s, but fewer than 5,000 when it disbanded in 1991. Dissenting and Trotskyite organisations experienced a very similar decline, although there has been a late flowering of Marxism in Scotland.

Based on the Communist Party archives at Manchester, *Marxism in Britain* examines the decline over the last sixty years. The book deals with the impact of the Cold War upon British Marxism, looking at how international events such as the Soviet invasions of Hungary and Czechoslovakia affected the Communist Party of Great Britain. The issues of Marxism and Britain's withdrawal from the Empire are also addressed, as are the Marxist influence upon British industrial relations and its involvement in the feminist movement. Keith Laybourn focuses very much on the current debate in British Marxist history which divides historians over the influence of Moscow and Stalinism on the Communist Party, and he explores the ways in which this undermined Marxism in Britain.

Keith Laybourn is Professor of History at the University of Huddersfield. He has written extensively on British labour history, British social policy and women in twentieth-century Britain.

Routledge Studies in Modern British History

1 Violence and Crime in Nineteenth-Century England
   The shadow of our refinement
   J. Carter Wood

2 Revolutionary Refugees
   German socialism in Britain, 1840–60
   Christine Lattek

3 Marxism in Britain
   Dissent, decline and re-emergence 1945–*c*.2000
   Keith Laybourn

Marxism in Britain

Dissent, decline and re-emergence
1945–*c.*2000

Keith Laybourn

LONDON AND NEW YORK

First published 2006
by Routledge
2 Park Square, Milton Park, Abingdon, Oxfordshire OX14 4RN

Simultaneously published in the USA and Canada
by Routledge
711 Third Avenue, New York, NY 10017

First issued in paperback 2015

Routledge is an imprint of the Taylor and Francis Group, an informa business

© 2006 Keith Laybourn

Typeset in Garamond by
Newgen Imaging Systems (P) Ltd, Chennai, India

All rights reserved. No part of this book may be reprinted or
reproduced or utilised in any form or by any electronic,
mechanical, or other means, now known or hereafter
invented, including photocopying and recording, or in any
information storage or retrieval system, without permission in
writing from the publishers.

British Library Cataloguing in Publication Data
A catalogue record for this book is available from the British Library

Library of Congress Cataloging in Publication Data
A catalog record for this book has been requested

ISBN 13: 978-0-415-75867-3 (pbk)
ISBN 13: 978-0-415-32287-4 (hbk)

To
Julia Mary Laybourn, Independence Serhish Watson
and Hayden Orien Bunning

Contents

Acknowledgements		ix
List of abbreviations		xi
	Introduction to British Marxism since 1945	1
1	The Communist Party of Great Britain during the emergence of the Cold War 1945–56	11
2	The emergence of the Broad Left 1957–70	57
3	The Red Seventies: industrial conflict and the emergence of Eurocommunism 1971–9	81
4	The challenge of Thatcherism, the triumph of Eurocommunism and the collapse of 'Stalinism', 1980–91	114
5	Postscript: the re-emergence and reconstruction of Marxism in Britain or 'All dressed up with nowhere to go?'	148
	Conclusion	170
	Notes	173
	Bibliography	192
	Index	199

Acknowledgements

Many people have helped in the research which has led to this book. In many ways, the formative influence has been Jack Reynolds (1915–88), who first pointed me in the direction of British labour history in the 1960s. I was also greatly influenced by David Wright (1937–95). Over the years I have benefited greatly from discussions with a wide variety of historians, including Professor Chris Wrigley, Professor Maggie Walsh, Paul Ward, Alan Campbell, John McIlroy, Christine Collette and Professor John Shepherd who have helped shape my opinions. I would like to thank them all for their support. I would also like to thank the staff of The Labour History Archives and Study Centre: John Rylands University Library, the University of Manchester, soon to be the National Museum of Labour History, for their help and guidance in providing access and permission to use the Communist Party archives and the papers of Marxists which they have in their collection. In this respect I am greatly appreciative of Steven Bird, the Archivist, Janette Martin, the Assistant Archivist and the many other members of staff who have assisted me over the years, including Darren. Finally, I would like to apologise for any inadvertent infringement of copyright.

Abbreviations

AEU	Amalgamated Engineering Union
AITUC	All-India Trades Union Congress
ASLEF	Associated Society of Locomotive Engineers and Firemen
ASSET	Association of Supervisory Staffs and Executive Technicians
CND	Campaign for Nuclear Disarmament
CPB	Communist Party of Britain
CPGB	Communist Party of Great Britain
CPI	Communist Party of India
CPSU	Communist Party of the Soviet Union
CWU	Communication Workers' Union
DL	Democratic Left
DLS	Democratic Left Scotland
EC	Executive Committee (of the Communist Party of Great Britain)
ESA	English Socialist Alliance
ETU	Electrical Trade Union
GLA	Greater London Authority
GLC	Great London Council
ICBH	Institute for Contemporary British History
IG	International Group
ILP	Independent Labour Party
IMG	International Marxist Group
IPDC	Inner Party Democracy Commission
IS	International Socialists
ISFI	International Secretariat of the Fourth International
LCDTU	Liaison Committee for the Defence of Trade Unions
LPYS	Labour Party Young Socialists
MSF	Manufacturing, Science and Finance union
MSP	Member of the Scottish Parliament
MT	Militant Tendency
NALGO	National and Local Government Officers Association
NATFHE	National Association of Teachers in Further and Higher Education
NATO	North Atlantic Treaty Organisation
NCB	National Court Board

NCP	New Communist Party
NEC	National Executive Committee (of Labour Party)
NHS	National Health Service
NIRC	National Industrial Relations Court
NPN	New Politics Network
NUM	National Union of Mineworkers
NUR	National Union of Railwaymen
NUS	National Union of Seamen
NUT	National Union of Teachers
OWAAD	Organisation of Women of African and Asian Descent
PCE	Spanish Communist Party
PCF	French Communist Party
PCI	Italian Communist Party
PPPS	People's Press Printing Society
RCP	Revolutionary Communist Party
RCPB (ML)	Revolutionary Communist Party of Britain (Marxist–Leninist)
RMT	(National Union of) Rail, Maritime and Transport workers
RSL	Revolutionary Socialist League
RWP	Revolutionary Workers' Party
SLL	Socialist Labour League
SLP	Socialist Labour Party
SNP	Scottish National Party
SOGAT	Society of Graphical and Allied Trades
SPGB	Socialist Party of Great Britain
SRSM	Scottish Republican Socialist Movement
SRSP	Scottish Republican Socialist Party
SSA	Scottish Socialist Alliance
SSP	Scottish Socialist Party
SWP	Socialist Workers' Party
TASS	Telegrafnoe Agentsvo Sovietskovo Soyuza – Telegraph Agency of the Soviet Union
TGWU	Transport and General Workers' Union
TUC	Trades Union Congress
UDM	Union of Democratic Mineworkers
WAPC	Women Against Pit Closures
WIL	Workers' International League
WLM	Women's Liberation Movement
WRP	Workers' Revolutionary Party
WSA	Welsh Socialist Alliance
YCL	Young Communist League

Introduction to British Marxism since 1945

Marxism in Britain has declined rapidly since the Second World War. Indeed, the membership of the Communist Party of Great Britain (CPGB), the largest Marxist organisation in Britain, fell from a wartime peak of 56,000 in 1942 to 45,000 in 1945, and further, to a mere 4,750 by the time of its dissolution in November 1991. Also, many of those groups who splintered from it in the post-war years, along with the numerous 'Trotskyite' organisations, experienced a similar fate.

The prime aim of this book is to examine, record and explain this post-war decline of British Marxism, in all its various forms, through a study of its interaction with the national and international politics of the period. However, one must be mindful that since the late 1990s there has been a revival and re-emergence of Marxism, although there is little evidence of this late flowering achieving even the modest glories of the past except perhaps in Scotland where the Scottish Socialist Party (SSP) has emerged to win seats in the Scottish Parliament on behalf of the Socialist Alliance movement.

The post-war decline of Marxism in Britain may have been inevitable. Its main growth was achieved in the late 1930s and during the Second World War, particularly after the CPGB declared its opposition to Hitler in 1941, after Stalin's entry into the war against Germany, which earned the CPGB unprecedented popularity. Yet, it declined in the post-war years for a variety of reasons, not least because of the international political situation, the Cold War and the continuing influence of Moscow, at least until the late 1970s or early 1980s. Indeed, the continued post-war decline of the CPGB, and British Marxism more generally, has helped to provoke a wide-ranging and heated debate about the extent of the influence Moscow wielded over the CPGB. Was it, or was it not, Stalinism and Bolshevism which prevented the CPGB flourishing in Britain, imposing as it often did, the need to follow its exigent policies?

There is no doubt that Stalinism and the domination of Moscow were impediments to Party growth up to the 1970s even before it turned in upon itself with the wrangling over Eurocommunism. Neither the influence from without, nor the conflict within the Party helped to maintain a consistent and effective presence in the post-war years, either before or after the late 1970s. As a result, membership generally continued to decline, the CPGB's policies on women and trade unions, in particular, languished, and its influence in other spheres diminished. With the decline in Soviet and Eastern European Communism, and the international context within which the

CPGB continued to operate even in the 1980s, the Party's eventual demise was almost inevitable by the late 1980s and early 1990s. Yet, it is likely that British Marxism would have declined in any case, having never established a strong base within the British political system when it was reshaped during and after the First World War. The short-time factors were mere political eddies operating in a system which made it difficult for Marxism to operate at a mass level. The associational and structural links in society may well have, as Ross McKibbin suggests in his article 'Why was there no Marxism in Britain?', made it impossible for Marxism to thrive in Britain.[1]

International politics, Eurocommunism, empire, trade unionism and women

The international politics of Marxism has indeed been vital in producing many points of conflict and change along the route of the overall decline of Stalinism and British Marxism since the Second World War. The events in Yugoslavia and Eastern Europe in the late 1940s and the early 1950s, the Soviet invasion of Hungary in 1956, China's Great Leap Forward in 1958 and the events in Czechoslovakia in 1968 all produced division, dissent and fragmentation. In most cases the CPGB lost support but regrouped and, in the wake of Hungary, even recaptured some of its lost membership. However, the most serious challenges to British Marxism began to occur in the 1970s and 1980s. There were particularly serious tensions within the CPGB as Eurocommunism, which rejected the idea of basing Marxism upon the old Stalinist and Soviet models and stressed the need to work within the political, social and economic climate of Britain, began to emerge. These ideas were encouraged by the writings of Santiago Carrillo, most obviously in his book *Eurocommunism and the State*, and F. Claudin, in *Eurocommunism and Socialism*.[2] This led to the secession of a number of organisations from the CPGB, some described as old 'Stalinist' organisations, and, most obviously, the New Communist Party (NCP) in 1977. By the mid-1980s, when the Eurocommunists became the dominant force in British Marxism, the CPGB was deeply divided and expelled many of the more pre-Moscow members who fought against change and allied themselves to the Communist Campaign Group. The splintering of the CPGB and British Marxism continued in the 1980s and culminated in the collapse of the CPGB in 1991, although the partial collapse of international Marxism at this time determined its demise. Thereafter the Democratic Left (DL) emerged as a replacement for the CPGB, although it ceased in 1999, and was then re-formed as the New Politics Network (NPN), which now openly rejects its Marxist tradition on its websites.[3]

The DL records are now deposited in the John Rylands Labour Archive and Study Centre, Manchester, along with those of the CPGB which were deposited earlier in the 1990s. The CPGB records now allow us to view the extent of Moscow's influence as against that of the individuals who made up the CPGB, and can be viewed alongside the records in the Moscow archives which were also opened up in the 1990s. In contrast, the majority of the records of the DL are not yet open to public gaze. The trail of their failure will have to be examined by a future generation of historians who use the Manchester archives.

Yet, despite the decline of the DL, other Marxist organisations have proliferated. Scottish dissidents published their own bulletin entitled *Alert Scotland*. Stan Kelsey of the Communist Party of Britain (CPB) stood for Bethnal Green in the 1992 general election, whilst Mark Fischer represented the organisation in London North East during the 1994 European Election. Fischer was in fact, at the time, the National Organiser of the CPB and was a regular contributor to its organ *The Weekly Worker*. This organisation claimed to be the real heir of the CPGB. In opposition, the International Communist Party of the Fourth International, a Trotskyite organisation, which has suggested that it is Stalinism, not Marxism, which collapsed in the Soviet Union in 1991, re-emerged when Anthony Hyland contested for the seat of London North East in the European Election of 1994. In other words, Marxism in all its forms, remained active in the 1990s, despite its much-reduced influence. More recently, the SSP, formed in 1998 from the Scottish Socialist Alliance (SSA) in 1996, has had significant success in the Scottish Parliament, although the English and Welsh Socialist alliances have made only limited progress. Whether or not such developments could lead to the formation of a viable British Marxist movement is still doubtful if open to question.

Clearly the decline and partial re-emergence of Marxism in Britain has much to do with international politics. The actions of Moscow dictated many of British Marxism's conflicts and the dissolving of the Soviet Union in the early 1990s may have sealed the CPGB's fate in the early 1990s. However, British Marxism was also interested in other international issues as well, which reflected its peculiar interests combined with its concerns for creating new, independent, possibly even Marxist, states. This was most evident in the case of India.

Given the influence of Rajani Palme Dutt in the CPGB, the issue of Indian independence and the partition of the Indian sub-continent in the late 1940s was very important during the Cold War isolation of British Marxism and the Soviet Union. The CPGB and other Marxist groups were particularly concerned about the independence of nations that were part of the British Empire and issues such as the partition of India in the late 1940s. As a result, Empire was an important element in British Marxist thinking as indicated in the CPGB's Empire Conference in 1947 where there was a concern to maintain the unity of India, the newly emerging independent Commonwealth states and the colonial independence movements.

The marginal importance of all forms of Marxism in Britain since the Second World War, and its almost continuous decline, raises particular issues about its relationship with the trade unions. It has been argued that the CPGB was 'nearly in control of the trade union movement in 1945'.[4] Indeed, it has also been suggested that, of the seventeen largest trade unions, the CPGB had control of four unions and significant influence over six others.[5] More recently, Nina Fishman has made much the same claim for the influence of the CPGB.[6] If this was the case in 1945, it was certainly not so in the 1960s, and for good reasons.

The Labour Party and Labour Governments fought against the way in which communists used trade unions towards their own political ends, largely on the grounds that this was their domain. They attacked Communist influence during the Dock Strike of 1951, the Electrical Trade Union's ballot-rigging activities in the early 1960s and the Seamen's strike of 1966. The Labour Party has also sought to keep the CPGB and Marxist influences at bay, from the days when Morgan Phillips kept his 'Lost Sheep' files in the 1930s and 1940s to Labour's fight against entrism in the 1970s and the 1980s.

Marxist decline has also to be set against its effectiveness in developing a relationship with women's groups. The CPGB was deeply involved in the activities of the National Assembly of Women, founded by the International Women's Day Committee, in the early 1950s, the national conferences of Communist women, the first of which was held in 1951, and the Women Against Pit Closures (WAPC) miners' wives groups in the mid-1980s, where there was conflict between the CPGB and the WAPC about the way in which the movement was 'hijacked' by Ann Scargill and Betty Heathfield. Indeed, women's groups became increasingly influential Marxist organisations. The National Women's Advisory Committee of the CPGB produced Women in Action leaflets between 1965 and 1969, dealing with issues such as peace in Vietnam, rents, prices, and moves towards 'second-wave feminism', with attempts to change the position of women within society, is evident in *Link*, a more substantial publication. *Link* produced 44 issues between 1973 and 1984, including articles from a wide variety of socialist writers. However, the CPGB's women's section never fully came to terms with the 'third-wave feminism' of the 1980s with its emphasis upon the diversity of experiences of women and its fate was largely sealed by the declining fortunes of the CPGB.

The influence of Moscow

Inevitably, the decline of Marxism raises the vital and contentious issue of the relationship between the Soviet Union and the CPGB. A recent article, entitled 'A Peripheral Vision', written by John McIlroy and Alan Campbell, and to be published in *American Communist Review*, offers a timely and much needed critical summative review of the recent debate that has consumed the writing of some historians of British Communist history most bitterly, through the pages of *Labour History Review*.[7] It presents a powerful argument for reuniting the role of the Russian leadership, and Stalinism, with work on the British party leadership and the rank-and-file activists within any future histories of British Communism. The vital point of the McIlroy and Campbell article is that the new revisionist history which has emerged in Britain since the 1980s has sought to remove, or at least play down greatly, the Stalinism and the Russian leadership as one of the factors, and the primary one, in the evolution and development of the CPGB.[8] Although there may be many forces shaping the revisionist, grass-roots approach to the history of the CPGB, it is partly rooted in the fact that one of its leading exponents, Nina Fishman, was associated with the Eurocommunist section of the Party and its successors, who have emphasised the break with Moscow.

The revisionist writers have rejected the Communist history writings of Henry Pelling, Walter Kendall and L. J. Macfarlane, who are criticised for believing that the CPGB was almost robotic in its acceptance of the doctrines and influence of Moscow.[9] In contrast, McIlroy and Campbell are adamant that only a re-instatement of the importance of Bolshevism and Stalinism for the history of the CPGB until the 1970s, or even the 1980s, will allow a full and accurate picture to be presented. Indeed, they conclude by suggesting that the political and Soviet dimensions are not peripheral matters: 'They go to the root of the experience of Communism and they remain fundamental to its history.'[10]

They present three, interrelated, points. First, they imply that neither the traditionalist approach nor the new revisionist approaches are sufficient in themselves for a full and accurate picture of events to emerge. Second, they indicate that the revisionist approach, which has been influenced by the study of American Communism, has been used to neglect, suppress and distort events. Third, and consequently, they suggest that only a full account of events re-incorporating a study of the Russian influence alongside the activism of the CPGB will allow the historical record to be complete and that then, and only then, can genuine historical interpretation take place. They place their hope and faith in a younger, or newer, generation of historians, such as David Renton and James Eadon, to do this work.[11]

Although the issues and tensions raised by McIlroy and Campbell are well rooted in the long-standing conflict between British Communism and British Trotskyism, it is only in the last 5 or 6 years that the debate has become particularly heated. McIlroy and Campbell began to distil their particular approach in 1999, but the catalyst for the heightening of this debate was Nina Fishman's article on 'Essentialists and realists' in *Communist History Network Newsletter*, published in 2001.[12] In this, she suggested that 'essentialists' who believed in the domination of the Russian leadership were wrong, and that the 'realists', including herself, were right in maintaining that the CPGB relied upon their 'individual judgements' and that in this respect 'there simply was no bolshevisation of the CPGB'.[13] This had been prompted by her earlier adoption of this nomenclature at the April 2001 conference in Manchester, 'People of a Special Mould?', organised by Kevin Morgan, partly in response to the challenges of McIlroy and Campbell.[14]

Fishman's 'Essentialist and realist' article appeared at a time when McIlroy and Campbell had gained acceptance of the idea of producing a Special Issue of *Labour History Review* on International Communism. In the autumn of 2001, Fishman swept in to an ill-attended Advisory Editorial Board of *Labour History Review* held in Manchester, and attempted to prevent the publication of the Special Issue of *Labour History Review*, which McIlroy and Campbell were editing, on the grounds that 'they [the editors and the contributors] are all essentialists'. Her efforts were deflected with the offer of a right of reply. A few months later, in February 2002, a conference on communism held by the Institute of Contemporary British History saw Fishman press forward with her 'essentialist' and 'realist' ideas in, what proved to be a contentious conference which McIlroy and Campbell did not attend, the report of which was to lead to further debate.

Fishman's action in opposing the Special Issue was unsuccessful, but the tensions it produced were evident at the next meeting of the Advisory Editorial Board of *Labour History Review*, also held at Manchester, in the spring of 2002. Nevertheless, the Special Issue in International Communism was published a year later, in April 2003, and McIlroy and Campbell, in their editorial on 'New Directions in International Communist Historiography' explained their position:

> While our views were far from uniform, we were all uncomfortable with the 'history from below' paradigm which obscured, neglected or marginalized the typically decisive influence of what were centralist parties, sections of a centralized world party whose politics were finally forged in Moscow, on their members. We all questioned an approach which focussed on the activities of Communists in industry and the community; but which often failed to relate them to disturbing factors such as espionage, Moscow gold and the tyrannical turn of society and politics in the Soviet Union, the political and spiritual home of these activists.[15]

Their own particular contribution was an examination of the development of the historiography on British communism, with an appeal for a more balanced approach to the study than what the 'history from below' approach had produced in recent years. In response to Fishman's terminology they wrote that '... we do not subscribe to the crude essentialism which asserts that Bolshevism automatically led to Stalinism. Rather, we see Bolshevism as a complex politics which held the potential for different political paths. Stalinism constituted only one such path'.[16]

In the meantime, as mentioned, a conference had been held at the Institute of Contemporary British History, Institute of Historical Research, on 20 February 2002. It provided the basis for further conflict and confusion about the 'essentialist' and 'realist' positions. Harriet Jones produced a report of this meeting for *Labour History Review* in December 2002.[17] In effect, the report presented the 'realist' side of the debate and rejected the 'essentialist' position. According to Jones:

> Fishman's own characterization of the divide was unrepentant. In her words, 'the essentialists ... are the people who consider everything the British Party did was determined by Moscow full stop ... the realists are the people who say "of course Moscow is important, but you also need to look at what is happening on the ground"'.[18]

Jones adds, in connection with the comments of Donald Sassoon on Italian communism, that 'Scholars by definition tend to fall into the realist camp...'.[19] This statement seems to have been broadened out and applied to the larger debate.

The Jones report earned a vigorous riposte from McIlroy and Campbell in the December 2003 issue of *Labour History Review* and it may be that even more detailed discussion will be published.[20] What McIlroy and Jones revealed was the absurdity of Fishman's division in a section entitled 'You're *really* an essentialist, No I'm *essentially* a realist', which points to the almost meaningless nature of Fishman's division. Indeed, if one examines the conference report being criticised, as well as the condemnation of it by Campbell and McIlroy, it becomes clear that Eric Hobsbawm and Willie Thompson, both apparently linked to the 'realist' camp accept, the primary determinant of the CPGB's policy was the Russian party. As Thompson said,

'...if Moscow wanted something done it was done, however reluctantly'.[21] The discussion at the Institute for Contemporary British History (ICBH) conference was then more about areas of Moscow intervention – whether or not Moscow felt the need to intervene with a small party it felt was unlikely ever to be a mass party, the fluctuating attitudes of the Comintern, and the conservatism of the CPGB in the post-Comintern period – but this was still within the confines of Moscow's gift.

The debate continues and grows with recent articles in the German journal *Mitteilungsblatt* and in forthcoming issues of *Labour History Review* and *American Communist Review*.[22] Undoubtedly new angles will develop.

Much of this recent debate has, however, been fought over the events of 1920–45 and little has been said of the history of the CPGB since the Second World War. Nevertheless, the debate is relevant to any discussion of the policies of the CPGB and particularly to events of worldwide importance, such as the position of the CPGB on Tito's Yugoslavia and to the Soviet invasions of Hungary and Czechoslovakia in 1956 and 1968, respectively. The remarkable loyalty shown to the Soviet Union by many of the CPGB members calls into question the relationship between the CPGB and the Soviet Union, for even when they gained some freedom from the demands of Moscow, Stalinism and Bolshevism, they were often conservative in the way that they used their independence. One is reminded of this by Brian Behan, a member of the Executive Committee (EC) of the CPGB in the early and mid 1950s, who, having written of Pollitt's refusal to accept the Stalin–Hitler Pact of 1939 in *Labour History Review*, and with a view to the future, asked:

> Why then did Party virtually vanish? When I sat on the EC it was a powerful body with most of the trade union general secretaries sitting with me. Why is the Communist Party the largest ex-party in England? Tens of thousands of people leaving through disappointment. It could have been so different. If only Pollitt had said to hell with democratic centralism. Let us be a truly democratic. Let us adopt the Swiss system of referendum with everything. Democratic centralism gave us the same structure as the Catholic Church complete with Pope Stalin. Submission of the lower to the higher meant stifling thought. [He gives two examples and writes the following on the second.] Again when the Russians invaded Hungary I moved another resolution demanding the withdrawal of the troops. Vote thirty-three to one. So we missed another opportunity and broke the heart of thousands of devoted comrades.[23]

It is true that Behan was an isolated member of the EC, but his views were supported by many in the Party – 7,000 or so of the 33,000 Party members taking the very extreme measure of resigning – and are reflected in *The Reasoner* debate of 1956, which is discussed in the next chapter. In the same volume of *Labour History Review*, Monty Johnstone, also in a letter to the editors, stresses the problems of James Klugmann, a leading Communist historian, dealing with the possible fudging of the Cetnik/Partisan activity in Yugoslavia and his change of attitude on the position of Yugoslavia after its split with the Soviet Union. Apparently Klugmann deeply regretted the fact that he allowed his faith in the Soviet leadership to obscure his critical judgement but Monty Johnstone felt that:

> To reduce the whole matter, as Walter Kendall does, to demands to brand Klugmann as a conscious liar shows a penchant for demonology. He totally fails to grasp the problem of Stalinism's hold on the minds of many decent, idealistic and intelligent people, leading them to justify (first of all for themselves) the unjustifiable.[24]

This is a revealing quote from a pro-CPGB historian who is in effect saying that loyalty to Stalin blinded many CPGB members such as Klugmann, to making a critical judgement about the truth of the situation. Similar comments about the conservatism and loyalty of CPGB members has also been remarked upon frequently by grass roots of the Party. There can surely be no doubt about the power and persuasion of Stalinism in the early post-war years of the CPGB and, indeed, the slowness to throw off the dominance of Moscow even after the revelations on Stalin were made in 1956. Indeed, E. P. Thompson and many other members were on their way out of the Party in 1956 as a result of its lack of open discussion before the Soviet invasion of Hungary. Indeed, McIlroy and Campbell have noted, in affirming that British radicalism was 'a distinct radicalism with roots outside Britain' that:

> The national terrain required accommodation and tactical adaptation. Yet what is remarkable and primary is the fact that at the heart of the British empire men and women placed the cause and policies of the USSR at the heart of their own lives and their own politics. How this happened, its causes and its consequences, remains a central issue for historians of the British labour movement.[25]

The challenge raised in the last sentence is partly what this book is about, for it seeks to examine both the national and international roots of the CPGB and its supporters for the post-1945 years, based essentially upon the Manchester CPGB archives, some of which have been retrieved from Moscow.

The Communist Party of Great Britain and Trotskyism

The 'essentialist' versus 'realist' debate raises the whole issue of the relationship between the CPGB and the alternative 'Trotskyite' Marxist movements. This book will examine the developments of alternative Marxist ideas in the late 1940s and early 1950s, the events following the Third World Congress of the Fourth International in 1951, the activities of John Lawrence and Gerry Healy in the early 1950s, and the resurgence of Trotskyism in the Twentieth Congress of the Communist Party of the Soviet Union (CPSU) in 1956 which denounced Stalin. It will at least touch upon some of the one hundred or so Trotskyite, International Socialist and other groups that emerged in the 1960s.

On Trotskyism, Ted Grant's *History of British Trotskyism*[26] is useful, although it only covers the period between 1924 and 1949. Also, there is some, rather limited, material available of the Socialist Party of Great Britain (SPGB), which was formed out of the 'impossibility' revolt within the Social Democratic Federation in 1904. R. Barltrop's *The Monument* outlined the history of the SPGB without being able to access its records, since he was a lapsed member.[27] However, he had access to his own records and copies of the *Socialist Standard*. Small and sectarian as this organisation was, it experienced a late flourish in the Leeds and Bradford area, as well as in London, in the mid and late 1970s, and its work and activities merit attention in the educational approach it adopted to the creation of a Marxist state based upon the writings of Karl Marx and Karl Kautsky.

The work of some of the numerous other Trotskyite and splinter groups from the CPGB will also be examined in order to assess what other developments were occurring. Those discussed will include the Communist League of Great Britain, with its journals *Combat, Compass* and *Intercom* which appeared in the 1970s; the International Marxist Group (IMG) of Tariq Ali, which published *Black Dwarf* between 1968 and 1970; Marxist Leninist Organisations of Britain, which published *Class Against Class* in the mid 1970s; The Revolutionary Communist Party (RCP), which produced *The Next Step* between 1981 and 1990; the International Marxist groups/Socialist League, which produced *International, Red Weekly* and *Red Mole* in the 1970s and 1980s and *Socialist Action* in the 1980s and 1990s; Revolutionary Marxist Tendency of the Fourth International, which produced *International Marxist Review* in the early 1970s, the Revolutionary Workers' Party, which produced *Red Flag* between 1963 and 1997, and many other Trotskyite organisations.

In total about 70 Trotskyite parties, and hundreds of splinter groups, have been formed in Britain since the Second World War in addition to those that existed before. It is not possible to examine all of these, and for some, often, only the most tenuous of information survives. However, this book aims to examine some of the alternative Trotskyite groupings to the CPGB and to examine their views and positions in the light of developments within British Marxism. Many, such as the Revolutionary Workers' Party, which was influenced by South American Marxists such as Posadas, were dominated by foreign Marxist influences.

The work of the 'educational and propagandist' SPGB will be examined, as will be the ideas and activities of the various Trotskyite groups of the Fourth International, the Workers' Revolutionary Party, the International Socialists (IS) and other groups, such as the Revolutionary Communist group, which split from IS in 1974. They are examined alongside the many splinter groups from the CPB, such as the CPB which split from the CPGB in 1988 taking with it the journals/periodicals *The Morning Star* and *Communist Review*.

Conclusion

Notwithstanding the work of Trotskyite and splinter organisations, it is the CPGB, as the largest Marxist organisation in Britain, that forms the basis of this book. Its problems, and almost constant declining membership since 1945, provide the context in which British Marxism has to be judged. Its alarms at the demands for wider Party discussion in the 1950s, its reaction to Eurocommunism in the 1970s and 1980s, and its failures to counter Thatcherism in the 1980s will be examined alongside the more obvious international problems of the Party highlighted by Hungary in 1956, Czechoslovakia in 1968 and the collapse of Eastern European Marxism in the late 1980s and early 1990s. It will be suggested that there was probably little prospect that the CPGB could have ever become a significant or mass party by the late 1940s. In addition, it is clear that the continuing influence of Stalinism and Moscow's influence blighted the CPGB's prospects of remaining a viable political organisation and that the eventual backlash of Eurocommunism in the 1970s and 1980s tore the party apart. The Eurocommunist members of the Party might wish to emphases the independence from Moscow of their own era but this hardly equates with the reality of Comintern, Stalinist or Moscow influences before the 1970s.

1 The Communist Party of Great Britain during the emergence of the Cold War 1945–56

The CPGB emerged from the Second World War as powerfully organised and as influential as it had ever been or was ever to be and could be said to have almost entered the mainstream of British politics. Operation Barbarossa, the German invasion of the Soviet Union in 1941, led to a profound change in the CPGB line which encouraged the full involvement of its members in the British war effort against Nazi Germany. The CPGB membership, which had been below 3,000 in the early 1930s and had risen to about 17,000 in 1939 swelled to around 56,000 in December 1942 as a result of a wave of Russophile sentiment which swept through British society, following the Red Army's heroic defence of Stalingrad.[1] Yet the political honeymoon of the Party did not long survive the end of the war. The Cold War, which began in the late 1940s, following Winston Churchill's famous speech at Fulton, Missouri, on the iron curtain that was descending across Europe, isolated the CPGB from the mainstream of British political life although, ironically, the Party's new policy statement *The British Road to Socialism* (1951) jettisoned the last vestiges of its revolutionary heritage by abandoning its commitment to Soviet power, and thus its acceptance of full-blown Marxist–Leninist ideas. These developments in policy contrasted with the Trotskyite opponents of the CPGB, such as the Workers' International League (WIL) and the RCP. They were small in number and influence, but rejected Stalinism and still believed in revolutionary activities. Unlike the CPGB, they were prepared to support strike activity throughout the Second World War.

None of the CPGB's attempts to work with the post-war Attlee Labour Governments, to develop a stronger trade union and women's base to the movement and to project a more moderate face to British communism in the 1950s did much to sustain its power and influence in British society. The rapid loss of membership at the time of the Soviet invasion of Hungary also did much to damage a party and a movement which was already in serious decline. For the CPGB, the Hungarian crisis was the worst situation they had hitherto faced in the twentieth century. Concern about the Soviet Union was brought about by Krushchev's severe criticism of Stalin at the Communist Party of the Soviet Union's (CPSU) Twentieth Congress in February 1956. This opened up a debate about democracy within the Party which preceded the invasion of Hungary in October 1956. By that time Party membership, which had been 45,000 in 1945 had fallen to 33,000, and it fell further to about 26,000 by 1957. The frustrations of many Party members at the invasion of Hungary and the lack of internal democratic developments within the Party proved too much for 7,000 members who either left the Party or joined Trotskyite organisations.[2]

This decline was both dramatic and worrying for the Party. In 1945, the CPGB was still more or less at the height of its power. It had two MPs – Willie Gallacher and Phil Piratin – many local councillors and Arthur Horner was secretary of Britain's largest union, the newly created National Union of Mineworkers (NUM). However, in September 1947, faced with a sudden loss of members, the Party stated that:

> The new situation [the economic crisis in Britain] demands that the Party overcome, once and for all, the stagnation in membership which has persisted since the end of the war and which in present circumstances hinders the full mobilisation of the people. To overcome this stagnation and build the Party is now vital for the advance of the entire movement.[3]

By 1956 the Party had no MPs, its membership had fallen further, its municipal support had declined and its influence in the trade union movement had fallen considerably, despite its involvement in numerous industrial disputes, such as the dock strike in 1951. Attempts to improve its membership did not work, and the Party had polled badly in the 1955 general election. Its position had not been helped by the show trials of Communist Czechoslovakia in 1952 and the Soviet army's repression of the general strike movement in eastern Germany in June 1953.

As suggested by the CPGB itself, the hostile political climate of the Cold War was partly to blame for this decline, but there were other factors at work. The Labour Party was acting to remove communists from its ranks, and the trade union movement, encouraged by Vic Feather and other officials, was also seeking to limit the power of communism within trade union ranks. There were also tensions within international communism which saw a greater splintering of Marxist groups and the growth of British Trotskyite organisations. This was fuelled by the Soviet invasion of Hungary in 1956 which gave Trotskyite organisations further grounds for their opposition of Moscow, and led to the loss of CPGB members, some of whom, as already indicated, switched to rival Trotskyite groups.[4] The Party considered the very question of its declining membership in the autumn of 1947. It concluded that:

> [...] To overcome the stagnation and build the Party in now vital for the advance of the entire movement.
>
> The principle [sic] political reasons responsible for the slow growth of the Party since the General Election [1945] includes the campaign of reaction against Communism, a campaign in which the Labour leadership have played a leading part. Another feature was the widespread feeling that with Labour's victory there was now no need for the Communist Party and its activities, that the Labour Government was self sufficient, the Tories were defeated, and orderly progress and social advance would now be the order of the day.[5]

Nevertheless, the CPGB maintained that there were many people frustrated with developments, in particular the failings of the Labour Government, and experiencing a political awakening and that much work could be done by the, hitherto poorly performing, Young Communist League (YCL). The YCL did increase its membership from 2,991 in April 1951 to 3,281 in April 1952, but soon relapsed as its membership declined along with the rest of the Party.

Despite these problems, Party life was vitally important and sustained the core of the declining Party in its first post-war decade. Many Party members retained a faith in the internal life of the Party which looked towards Moscow for its guidance. This was beautifully illustrated by Raphael Samuels in two articles which he circulated, to some criticism, within Party circles.[6] That faith in Stalinism was not seriously challenged until 1956 when the truth about its horrors began to emerge, even though there has been considerable evidence of Stalin's activities in the 1930s.[7]

The Second World War, the General Election of 1945 and the changing attitudes to the Labour Party and the Attlee Labour Governments of 1945–51

The new pacific approach of international communism to the capitalist nations was confirmed by the dissolution of the Comintern (the Communist International) in 1943. This action, and the Soviet involvement in the War effort, encouraged a positive attitude to British Marxism in Britain. However, despite the enormous growth of the CPGB's membership in war-time, a measure of its true importance was indicated when it was not invited to join the Cominform, the new international Marxist organisation set up by nine Communist parties in September 1947.[8] The CPGB had been ignored on the grounds that it was politically insignificant. Despite this international estimation of its limited status, the Party, in its loyalty to Moscow and the Teheran (1943) and Yalta (1945) agreements, recognised the need to improve international relations between the capitalist world and the Soviet Union through organising a movement for international peace towards the end of the Second World War and in the early years of the post-war Cold War. These international agreements by the Soviet Union certainly continued to impinge upon the domestic policies of the CPGB.

During the Second World War, and its immediate aftermath, the CPGB was particularly intent upon improving its relations with the Labour Party through an attempt to affiliate to it and its supportive policies. Indeed, it gave conditional support to most of its legislative programme of the first Attlee Labour Government, and particularly to its policies for nationalisation. However, the Labour Party and the Attlee governments were never prepared to respond to such support as Britain was drawn into a post-war alliance with the United States and to consequent hostility against the Soviet Union.

The attempt of the CPGB to affiliate with the Labour Party had been turned down several times during the 1920s and again in 1936. However, as a result of the new spirit of co-operation in the Second World War, the Central Committee of the CPGB, which became the EC in 1943, decided to reapply for affiliation of the Labour Party. Harry Pollitt, the general secretary of the CPGB sent a letter to J. S. Middleton, secretary of the Labour Party, on 18 December 1942 asking for the

CPGB's affiliation request to be put before the Labour Party conference in June 1943, and hoping that there could be interim meetings between the officials of the CPGB and the Labour Party. The Labour Party's National Executive Committee (NEC) meeting of 27 July 1943 opposed the application.[9] Middleton's reply to the CPGB was that it was not free from the influence of the Comintern and therefore could not be supported in its application. In response, Pollitt suggested that the CPGB's affiliation with the Labour Party would raise no difficulties with the Comintern and that the CPGB was self-financing. There ensued a protracted debate between the CPGB and Labour.[10] Notwithstanding the rebuff, the CPGB mounted a further campaign to gain support to which the Labour Party responded with articles in the *Daily Herald* and a pamphlet entitled *The Communist Party and the War – A Record of Hypocrisy and Treachery to the Workers of Europe*.

The dissolution of the Comintern in May 1943 did little to allay Labour Party criticism of the CPGB. Although the CPGB claimed that nearly 3,400 Labour groups had passed resolutions in support of their application by June 1943, the Labour Party swept its request aside, with 712,000 votes for the CPGB affiliation and 1,951,000 against.[11] Nevertheless, the CPGB maintained the hope of affiliation, although its other political recommendations, most notably the introduction of a new system of proportional representation in parliamentary voting and local conferences of progressive organisations to select candidates in the forthcoming general elections, were rejected at the 1944 Labour Party conference.

Labour leaders drew a distinction between British Communists and the far more powerful CPSU. Whilst international agreements could be made with the one, no alliance was possible with the other. By the same token the Labour Left, including Fenner Brockway and Emrys Hughes (editor of the *Glasgow Forward*), were far more critical of the United States, an 'expanding Imperial power', than of Soviet Russia. They even acknowledged that the USSR might have needed political reassurance at the end of the War. As Aneurin Bevan, the left-wing Labour leader who became Minister of Health and Housing in the first Attlee Labour Government, wrote:

> It is quite natural and inevitable that Russia should influence preponderantly the life of nations immediately on her borders and that she should seek to prevent them from combinations that may be aimed at her. That is the price we have to pay for a bitter recent past.[12]

However, the Labour Left carried little influence within the Labour Party. The majority of Labour MPs were inclined to support the Soviet Union in the war effort but were not prepared to entertain close relations with the CPGB.

Despite this situation, it is clear that the CPGB was concerned about the future post-war situation. On one major issue, of whether the CPGB should support the continuation of a post-war government of national unity or a Labour-led government of unity, there has been some considerable debate.

Neil Redfern has recently suggested that the widely held belief that the CPGB campaigned for a continued coalition or national government of Labour and

Conservatives in the July 1945 general election is a myth which was fostered by Henry Pelling and erroneously accepted by a succession of historians such as James Hinton, Noreen Branson, Kevin Morgan and Willie Thompson.[13] Instead, Redfern argues that developments were more complex than that. He argues that in 1943, the CPGB began to drift towards the idea of continuing with wartime national government in peace time because any peacetime government of unity would be dominated by progressive rather than reactionary forces. It appears that this was enforced by the meeting of Churchill, Stalin and Roosevelt at the Teheran Conference of December 1943, which anticipated a peaceful post-war existence. The CPGB, influenced by this meeting, also began to see the Labour Party not as the third bourgeois party but as 'a vehicle for social advance in the post-war world'. It hoped to work with the Labour Party, even though Labour was continually spurning its overtures. In its equivocal discussions on forming a post-war national government or working in an electoral alliance with Labour, the balance of the CPGB thought was tipped to Labour by the fact that the Commonwealth [Common Wealth] Party won the Skipton parliamentary by-election in January 1944 on a 12 per cent swing against the Conservatives. However, Redfern notes that after the Yalta Conference of February 1945, which saw Stalin, Roosevelt and Churchill meet again to build up a peaceful post-world order, the CPGB changed this policy temporarily. Indeed, 'For a few weeks after the Yalta Conference the CP did argue that a national government would be necessary to carry out these tasks but it is a myth that it campaigned for the war-time coalition to be re-elected.'[14] However, the CPGB had changed its mind once again by the time of the general election of 5 July 1945. Indeed, this final switch of opinion seems to have occurred by mid-April 1945. The EC of the CPGB had issued a statement in favour of a post-war national government in *The Worker* in late March 1945, but had done no campaigning for this policy. The May Day Statement of the Party made no reference to the government of national unity or to the progressive Tories as it drifted to support a Labour Party committed to fighting the 1945 general election as an independent organisation.[15] Because the Labour Party refused to work with the Communist Party in an electoral arrangement, the Communist Party put forward its 21 candidates at the July 1945 general election, although it advocated the support of all Labour candidates in other constituencies.[16]

Essentially, then, Redfern argues that there were several twists and turns in the position of the CPGB on the continuation of a coalition government or support for a Labour-led post-war government of unity. He maintains that these changes were partly conditioned by Soviet incursions into British domestic politics, through the events at Teheran and Yalta, although the rank and file changed these policies to meet their own concerns for socialist unity, rather than national unity, in the 1945 general election. He also makes it quite clear that he accepts that Moscow was instrumental in developing the strategy of a peaceful transition towards socialism, whilst accepting the views of Andrew Thorpe that the Comintern could not force the CPGB 'over sustained periods, to do what it did not itself wish to do'.[17] At the end, Redfern reiterates his support for the views of Andrew Thorpe, and what is now known as the 'realist' school of thought which emphasis the independent action of the CPGB. He also notes the abandonment of insurrectionary tactics in favour of the wartime unity continuing into peaceful post-war co-existence with the parliamentary road to socialism being advocated. Indeed, he writes that:

> Though the process was conditioned to a considerable extent by the external factors of Comintern and Soviet Union, the Communist Party developed its revisionist strategy mainly under its own steam. Its ideological and political outlook had been comparable to that of the Second International (though even the 'social patriots' of 1912 would have baulked at the CP's war-time praxis). The present writer does not believe that Bolshevism was an 'alien import' into British socialism, but there must be considerable doubt that Bolshevism ever really entered into the soul of most British Communists.[18]

This is clearly an authoritative article written with half an eye to the raging debate between the 'realists' and the 'essentialists'. Yet, it sits uneasily between the two views, suggesting that the primary force was Stalin and Moscow, whilst admitting to local variation within the terms that Moscow laid down, even though Bolshevism carried little support in Britain. Also, it does not explain why in April and May 1945, the Party leadership was apparently ignoring the overwhelming support which the Party membership had shown for the idea of a continuing national government in a vote taken in mid-March 1945. There was pressure on Harry Pollitt to abandon the idea of a continuing national government coming from Walter Hannington and William Rust, who did not like the implications of the Yalta accord, but why did he see fit to overturn the vote of the membership and support a Labour Government? Ironically, it seems as though the Party leadership rather than the rank and file might have acted independently of the general thrust of Moscow's policy. Nevertheless, the main argument of Redfern's article seems right, for it establishes that the CPGB entered the 1945 general election supporting the Labour Party rather than a peacetime national government, a view also supported by Professor John Callaghan.[19]

The surviving evidence generally supports Redfern's views of swings in CPGB policy between the opposing ideas of a post-war national government and a Labour-led progressive administration. The Teheran Conference of December 1943 was the endorsement of a post-war national government possibly led by the Labour Party. Thereafter, in 1944, there seems to have been a drift towards the idea of a Labour-led socialist alliance. Indeed, although the CPGB called for a continuation of the coalition government on 2 September 1944, it stated, on 2 October 1944, its support for a progressive alliance led by Labour. This decision seemed to be in tune with the developing situation, for the NEC of the Labour Party agreed to fight the coming general election as an independent party 'based on socialist principles' on 7 October 1944. Yet at the Yalta Conference, the Allied war agreed upon a communiqué which committed them to building up a new world order 'dedicated to peace, security, freedom and the well-being of all mankind'.[20] This once again raised the issue of a post-war unity coalition and led Pollitt and the CPGB to swing once again to the idea of a post-war national government.[21]

The CPGB still believed that an outright Labour victory was unlikely, but that a coalition or national government could continue, led by a Labour majority. The Yalta

Conference had played a part in this decision for if the Soviet Union could live in peace with capitalist powers it seemed logical to press for the continuation of a coalition 'popular front' government. The CPGB had made its position quite clear by calling for 'Labour and progressive unity' and that the wartime government should 'be replaced by a Labour and progressive majority on the basis of which we believe a new National Government should be formed'.[22]

To confirm its approach, the CPGB asked its members to vote on the issue of post-war electoral unity with Labour, the Conservatives and the Liberals – in a coalition, or national, government. The vote was taken at regional meetings on 17 March 1945 and the results were presented to the EC. Of the 8,684 members who voted, 7,850 favoured national unity, 278 were against and 556 abstained; each district voting overwhelmingly in favour, although 425 of the 556 abstentions came from the London district where there was clearly some unease at the policy.[23]

Yet the CPGB fear of continuing Tory dominance was real and in April and May 1945, as Redfern has noted, the Party leadership appeared to drift away from the idea of a national government at a time when the Labour Party declared its political independence at the forthcoming general election. Indeed, in May 1945 the Labour Party re-affirmed its earlier decision not to support a post-war electoral alliance with the Conservative and Liberal parties. Soon afterward, at the end of May, the CPGB decided to support the Labour campaign but put forward CPGB candidates for the general election on 5 July 1945 despite not having secured an arrangement with the Labour Party.[24] In order to avoid splitting the anti-Tory vote, the CPGB in fact reduced the number of its parliamentary candidates from 52 to 22, later to 21, even though the Labour Party had refused an electoral arrangement with the 'progressive forces' which the CPGB thought essential if Labour was to be victorious.[25]

The Party's Political Committee (PC) (a Committee of a small group of leading CPGB officials, theoretically implementing the decisions of the Executive, formerly Central, Committee, which had replaced the old Political Bureau in 1943) reflected this concern in announcing that:

> To end Tory domination in Parliament will not be an easy task. This is why the present policy of Labour leaders refusing to meet the Communist Party leaders to discuss electoral unity, or to try to prevent it being discussed at the Whitsuntide Conference of the Labour Party is not only criminal but is giving the Tories a better chance that they already have. We shall continue our campaign for electoral unity between the Labour Party, the Communist Party and all really progressive parties.[26]

Two months later, Harry Pollitt went even further, stressing that:

> this [the CPGB's] experience in working with such allies during the war – even when an out-of-date Parliament has given the Tory party the dominant position in the National government and a majority in Parliament – has proved to be in the interests of the working class.[27]

Yet it was not to be desired especially now that Labour had decided to go it alone. The CPGB even more determinedly desired a post-war alliance with Labour.

In the end, Communist fears that Labour could not win a parliamentary majority on its own were unfounded. In fact, the Labour Party won 393 seats out of 640 in the 1945 general election, a majority of 146. The CPGB did not share in this landslide victory. Only Willie Gallacher and Phil Piratin were returned, whilst Pollitt was narrowly defeated in West Fife as was John Campbell in Greenock.[28] Twelve deposits were lost but the Party did receive about 100,000 votes and an average of 12.5 per cent of the vote in the constituencies it contested.

Notwithstanding its disappointments, the CPGB pledged its wholehearted support to the new Labour Government in the continuing war against Japan and in carrying out the great social changes and the policy of international co-operation 'for which the people voted with such decision and confidence. It also called for the fullest co-operation' of the whole Labour movement in fighting against the Tories, declaring that 'the Communist Party will do its utmost to develop this unity and to strengthen the organization of the Labour Movement in their active support of the Labour government.'[29]

In this climate, the 1945 CPGB Congress renewed its efforts to gain affiliation to Labour. Pollitt sent a letter to Morgan Phillips, secretary of the Labour Party, on 21 January 1946 asking for the application to be put before the annual conference. The NEC opposed the application, the CPGB mounted a campaign and the *Daily Herald*, the Labour organ, condemned the CPGB's actions. Indeed, the Labour Party's archives reveal the considerable pressure applied to the Labour Party to allow Communist affiliation, the Howdenshire Labour Party indeed calling for 'working-class unity in the country by allowing the Common Wealth, the Independent Labour Party (ILP) and the Communist Parties to affiliate with the National Labour Party'.[30]

Yet there was never a realistic possibility that the Labour Party would allow the CPGB to affiliate, and about one month before the Labour Conference of 1946 the Labour NEC issued a pamphlet written by Harold Laski, Chairman of the Labour Party, entitled *The Secret Battalion*, which launched a devastating attack upon the CPGB's political opportunism and class collaboration policy which, the pamphlet said, sought to compromise the political independence of the Labour Party. It began with the NEC statement:

> It is clear that the temporary Communist talk of working-class unity behind the Labour Party is merely a clumsy camouflage for their real aim of breaking up the Labour Movement so as to increase their own chances of establishing a party dictatorship.
>
> If the Communists really believe in unity, their course is plain – to abolish their own party organisation and to join the overwhelming mass of the British workers as loyal and individual members of the Labour Party.
>
> Their steadfast refusal to take this long overdue and obvious step is the clearest indication of the insincerity of their present campaign for affiliation.[31]

Laski continued to examine perceived differences between authoritarian and democratic socialism, condemned the CPGB policy of penetration, attacked its vacillating position on the Second World War, and scorned its policy of seeking to be admitted to the Labour Party as a party rather than as individuals.[32] Laski further reflected that:

> If it is true that, as Communists in Great Britain claim, that they can accept the constitution and principles of the Labour Party in full loyalty and without hesitation, Socialists see no reason why there should be a separate Communist Party, with, above all, its own electoral organisation. What then seems obvious is that, as a separate party, it should disband itself and urge its members to apply for membership within the Labour Party.[33]

Morgan Phillips, the secretary of the Labour Party, also discouraged talk of Communist affiliation and prepared detailed reports on how to counter Communist influence. Phillips emphasised that whilst the Labour Party stood for democratic socialism and wished to use the full powers of Parliament and local government:

> the aims of the Communist Party are different. They aim at what they call the 'Dictatorship of the Proletariat'. This in practice does not mean the Dictatorship of the Proletariat at all. It means a Dictatorship over the Proletariat, exercised by the Communist Party bureaucracy.[...] If the Communist affiliation was foolishly granted the position would be intolerable. There would be within our Party another highly organised Party working for its own supremacy. Every local Labour Party would become a battleground for democratic socialism versus communism.[34]

In June 1946, the Labour Party's annual conference rejected the motion for affiliation by 468,000 votes to 2,675,000 – a larger majority than in 1943. At the same conference, a resolution was passed preventing any organisation with its own rules and constitution, that was not affiliated to the Labour Party by 1 January 1946, from ever affiliating. This blocked further attempts by the CPGB to affiliate to the Labour Party. Emilé Burns reflected that 'several trade Unions that formerly supported us have now, by considerable majorities, turned against us. Divisional Labour parties which welcomed our aid in elections and were full of goodwill are today bitter opponents.[35] Where was the CPGB to go from here?

As early as 1943, the CPGB was contemplating the end of the Second World War when it set up six major sub-committees, including one on foreign relations and another on organization.[36] The CPGB's *Britain for the People: Proposals for Post-War Policy*, published in May 1944, also demanded that the war-time gains should be maintained in the post-war world and the needs to secure full employment, social security, good wages, a comprehensive health service and a lasting peace based upon a wider-based democracy. To ensure a post-war world with these objectives it was considered necessary to maintain state controls, widening public ownership and the creation of a socialist society.

This document, the final form of which was accepted at the seventeenth Congress of the CPGB held at Shoreditch Town Hall, London in October 1944, was an amazing change of direction for the CPGB, which had argued, in *For Soviet Britain* (1935), that socialism could not be achieved through Parliament. The new policy suggested that this could be done, particularly if the House of Commons was reformed through a system of proportional representation based upon a 'single transferable vote' arrangement. The CPGB had assuredly abandoned its revolutionary objectives just as the dissolution of the Comintern in 1943 had effectively ended the goal of world revolution in 1943. By October 1944 the CPGB was using the terminology of Marxism–Leninism to support reformist policies which were in reality departing from genuine Marxist ideas. The change of stance arose from the meetings between Roosevelt, Stalin and Churchill in Teheran, Moscow, the Crimea (Yalta) and Potsdam, which seemed to prepare the post-war world for peaceful co-existence.

This policy, and its subsequent changes, have already been examined in detail. It is clear that at the time of the Yalta meeting, Pollitt was convinced that national unity should be advocated, and the personal files of MI5 on Pollitt indicate the extent to which 'the Party was not going out for a revolutionary policy'.[37] Labour's decision to contest the 1945 general election independently, and the landslide victory it achieved, changed the agenda.

The CPGB expected to work closely with the Attlee Government and during the first two years of the Attlee Labour Government gave constitutional support to much of its legislative programme. Indeed, Pollitt wrote that 'the spread of Marxist thought is so essential for the carrying through of Labour's General Election programme' and called for another attempt to affiliate to the Labour Party which, as already noted, failed.[38] Robin Page Arnot, the prominent inter-war communist, endorsed this view noting the vital nature of cooperation during the Second World War.[39] The Party continued to support Labour candidates in parliamentary by-elections and, as late as September 1947, was opposed to industrial action in the Yorkshire coalfields. It also focused upon the need for rapidly increasing production to meet the fuel crisis, housing crisis and balance of payments crisis in 1947. Pollitt was so concerned with production at this stage that he encouraged the East European model of the 'great weekend volunteer brigades' to help British industries. In other words, he was convinced of the need for post-war production to rebuild Britain's economy. The CPGB also supported Labour's welfare state programme and the National Hospital Campaigns in 1946.[40] In so doing, the CPGB had taken its political cue from the end of war settlements which had suggested that it was possible for the Communist world to live in peaceful co-existence with the capitalist world.

Nevertheless, the political honeymoon with Labour soon ceased. Churchill's 'Iron Curtain' speech at Fulton, Missouri, in 1946, the increasing dependence of Britain upon American finance and the final rejection of Communist affiliation by Labour fully undermined the confidence of the CPGB in both the Labour Party and the Labour Government. The onset of the Cold War put paid to the hopes of achieving international harmony.

As the Cold War between the communist and capitalist countries progressed, and as the Labour Government became increasingly dependent upon the United States and hostile to communism, Pollitt became increasingly critical of the Labour Party. Indeed, in January 1947, fearing a third world war, Pollitt stressed the need for 'closer co-operation between Britain, the Soviet Union as the main foundations for the United Nations, and for influencing progressive developments in America'.[41]

In 1947, Pollitt still held hopes that the Labour Government might produce a 'free, happy and Socialist Britain' in his book *Looking Ahead*.[42] This was only possible with the 'unity of the Big Three' but reflected that 'Today it is Wall Street and American Big Business which is leading the reactionary drive. But that has only been possible because of the policy of the Labour Government.'[43] Written and produced at the height of Britain's financial and industrial crisis in 1947, the main focus of this book was that Britain should formulate an economic plan which would put industries into the hands of the country and not the capitalists, and would increase the wages at the expense of the rich and secure British independence from American capitalists:

> We are fighting for the independence of Britain, for its independence from Wall Street and from those Tory reactionaries in Britain, who in order to maintain their privileges and personal power, are ready to sell out the interests of this country to foreign trusts.[44]

By mid-1947, however, Pollitt was beginning to rue the poor economic performance of the Labour Government, now faced with an economic crisis resulting from the collapse of coal production in the severe winter of 1946–7 and from a failure of industrial production. In a report to the EC of the CPGB, Pollitt focused upon Herbert Morrison's speech to the House of Commons on 8 July and blamed Britain's economic plight upon British foreign policy and the terms and arrangements of the American Loan which was likely 'to be exhausted early in 1948'.[45] The CPGB also produced a leaflet on *Why the Communist Party says Reject the Marshall Plan*, which stated that:

> If the Marshall Plan is accepted, Britain's difficulties will become greater than ever. The Americans make no promise about buying goods from us in exchange for goods we get from them, What we get under the Marshall Plan is more debt for Britain and therefore harsher terms from Uncle Sam.[46]

By 1948, the CPGB was, therefore, criticising openly, the shortcomings of Attlee's Labour Government. It had 'failed to attack the class distinction which is still the outstanding feature of our educational system. It had failed even to provide for material conditions to allow of an advance in standards within our existing system'.[47] The CPGB also put forward more election candidates, returning 64 for the various elected urban district councils and rural district council seats in 1948.[48] In the autumn of 1948, it put Peter Kerrigan into the Gorbals parliamentary by-election against the Labour candidate, and when he was defeated it was noted that Labour ran a 'scurrilous anti-social and anti-Communist campaign'.[49]

At this moment it seems that Kerrigan, who it was alleged had the backing of John Gollan and R. Palme Dutt, who was the mouthpiece for Moscow, was lobbying at the Liverpool Congress of the CPGB for 'an intensive fight on the industrial field' which it was felt would, despite casualties, create a revolutionary situation. Pollitt was more cautious, wanted a Labour Government returned at the next general election and was opposed to the idea of an extensive field of candidates being put forward. Kerrigan, on the other hand, and according to MI5, was demanding as many candidates as possible and hoping for a strong reactionary Tory Government to bring about the direct participation of the workers in a fight against reactionary forces.[50] It seems that Kerrigan won.

By the 1950 General Election, the CPGB was openly hostile to the Labour Party and maintained that in comparison the CPGB had associated the parliamentary struggle with the mass struggle of the workers and constantly reiterated that its 'historic mission is to lead the workers in the victory over Capitalism, to destroy Capitalism and replace it with the power of the working class'.[51] Its manifesto, first drafted in July 1949, suggested that after four years of Labour Government, 'class divisions are deeper than ever', adding that profits were high and wages were lagging behind the cost of living.[52] It complained that despite nationalisation, four-fifths of British industry remained in capitalist hands. However, the most severe criticism was levelled at Labour's foreign policy. There was an attachment to the general election programme 'For Peace and National Independence' which stated that 'The foreign policy of Mr. Bevin and the Labour Government is the policy of Churchill and Toryism. It is the policy of Churchill's notorious Fulton Speech in 1946, in which he called for an Anglo-American Bloc against Socialist Russia.'[53] Naturally, it condemned the formation of North Atlantic Treaty Organisation (NATO) in 1949 and asserted the right of nations to be independent.

Against a backcloth of an intensifying Cold War and irritated by the perceived failures of the Labour Government, the CPGB decided to put forward 100 candidates at the general election in February 1950, after intense discussion of the possibility of this policy allowing Tory candidates to beat Labour candidates.[54] In the end the policy was a disaster for the Party which lost the two seats gained in 1945 and faced 97 of its candidates losing their deposits. Indeed, the 100 candidates received a mere 91,815 votes compared with the 102,780 received by the CPGB's 21 candidates in 1945. Mick Bennett, of the Yorkshire District Council, was one of many who criticised the policy of the EC.[55] As a result of this fiasco, the CPGB reduced its initial list of 25 candidates down to 10 for the 1951 general election.[56] In the event, all 10 failed to gain 12.5 per cent of the votes cast in their contests and all lost their deposits. Opposition to the Labour Party and the Labour Governments had not worked. Part of the reason for this was the disastrous industrial and trade union policy of the Party.

Despite these setbacks, the CPGB continued its joint policy of selective criticism of the Labour Party whilst extolling its commitment to working to change it into a Party prepared to emphasise scientific socialism. Indeed, at the Twenty-Second Congress of the Party, Pollitt reflected:

> At the last Congress of our Party, I made clear our Communist attitude to the Labour Party. It is not we who are trying to wreck the Labour Party. We stand for the strengthening of the Labour Party; for a Labour Party that democratically embodies all sections of the Labour Movement. It is our belief that the day will come when the ranks of the Labour Party all accept the idea of Scientific Socialism and a single working-class party will be achieved in Britain. But this can only come through the democratic process of conviction, never by force, pressure or compulsion.[57]

The political picture was poor for the CPGB, although from time to time it did secure some political gains. Indeed, the local elections of 1952, which saw the Labour Party win 1,357 borough and districts seats in England, Wales and Scotland saw some considerable success for the CPGB as a result of 'factory gate and outdoor meetings', with 162 contests securing 49,983 votes compared with the 220 candidates who secured 37,443 votes in 1951. The Party won 16 seats and lost 4.[58] However, this was considerably down on the local and municipal successes, already referred to, for 1948, when there were 64 successes. Also, the general election of 1955 brought further disappointments as did the 1955 local election results. There was no disguising the fact that the CPGB was no longer a viable force in British politics. This declining influence was also evident in the falling circulation of the *Daily Worker*, which fell from 120,000 in 1945 to 91,000 in June 1950 and to 79,000 in 1955, before it recovered to 93,000 in December 1956, following a major circulation campaign. Sales in Yorkshire fell from 5,706 in April 1951 to 3,727 in April 1956, and in London, for the same dates, from 37,696 to 25,281.[59] Indeed, District reports reflect upon how bleak the picture seemed.

Party organisation in the early 1950s

The CPGB membership decline provoked an intense debate within the Party. The pressures placed on the *Daily Worker* to make it into 'a mass political paper' were also failing as were many other actions.[60] This meant that the burden of organisation and recruitment fell more heavily on the CPGB's district organisations. The initiatives and problems of these organisations are beautifully revealed by the activities of the Yorkshire District which performed reasonably well in the 1950s. Its 17-page confidential report to the Party in January 1951 revealed the extent of the problem facing the Party. After surveying the industrial state of Yorkshire, and particularly the agitation in mining and railways, it reviewed the performance of the CPGB.[61] The Party had pressed forward with its demands for peace and its opposition to German re-armament, improvement of living standards and the campaign for working-class unity, but had clearly achieved little. There were only 12 communist municipal contests in May 1954, although this was 4 more than in May 1953 and contests in Bradford, Halifax and Huddersfield occurred for the first time since 1950.[62] However, the number of votes remained low. Progress had been made in other directions as well, the number of industrial branches increasing from 18 to 21 between 1953 and 1954, with 5 having more than 20 members in 1954 as opposed to only 2 in such a position in 1953. The new branches were to be found in mining, engineering and clothing. The great success was in mining where there were over 200 miners in 7 units.[63] Yet the report was one of failure rather than success if one sees beyond the myriad details of small gains and losses. There had been 'no real advances in woollen textiles', one of the major industries in Yorkshire, the YCL was practically standing still even though it gained 300 new members in 1954, and the women's groups were under-appreciated by male members and 'not increasing or developing' in the Party.[64] The District was attempting to tackle these problems by publicising the importance of women's organisations, targeting a number of branches for expansion, by employing three extra full-time staff including Joan Bellamy as assistant to the Leeds District secretary, by targeting the miners and by expanding the YCL. However, there were aspirations which, in subsequent years, failed to materialise in any substantial manner. The Yorkshire District experience was not untypical of what was occurring in other districts. The fact is that the Party was declining in the long run, although there were occasional minor increases in support. It is clear that the CPGB's ventures into extending its membership had not worked and that the CPGB's industrial policy did not turn the tide.

The Communist Party, trade unions, industrial policy and factory organisation

There were two major industrial problems facing the CPGB at the time. The first was its concern about the economic relationship with the United States, the subject of Pollitt's book *Looking Ahead*. This led the CPGB to demand more nationalisation and the drive to increase industrial production in Britain as part of an economic plan to fend off the economic controls of Wall Street.[65] The second was the CPGB's worsening relationship with the Trades Union Congress (TUC) and the trade union leadership.

In the immediate post-war years, whilst it was still supporting the Attlee administration, the CPGB had encouraged nationalisation as a way of increasing the efficiency of the economy. However, with Britain's rising financial difficulties, the fuel crisis of the winter of 1947 and the resulting economic crisis of 1947, Britain became dependent upon the American loan. The CPGB felt that this was unfortunate, particularly as the terms of the American credit included the importation of American goods.[66] Indeed, James Klugmann, who was later the official historian of the Party, wrote that:

> ...the subjection of Britain to American imports would mean catastrophe for the British people...The British ruling class, and its spokesmen the Labour Government, like their counterparts in other Western European countries, are selling out to Wall Street the national independence of their country in order to preserve their own class position and privilege.[67]

This problem was further highlighted by Pollitt, who was particularly critical of the economic statement made by Herbert Morrison to the House of Commons on 8 July, concerned about the political collusion that was going on between the Labour Government and the Tories, and particularly concerned about the American Loan to Britain, which he predicted would be exhausted early in 1948.[68] The *Daily Worker* also produced a leaflet *Why the Communist Party says Reject the Marshall Plan*, the great concern being that this would make Britain increasingly dependent upon the United States and because the Americans made no promises of buying British goods in exchange for goods Britain would buy from them.[69]

The second major industrial consideration was the relationship of the CPGB to the trade union movement. The Communist Party extended its influence within the trade union movement in the 1930s despite the opposition of the TUC which was acting in concert with the Labour Party to root out Communist influence. There is no doubt that the CPGB's industrial work continued apace in engineering. Len Powell, a Communist, was, for instance, full-time general secretary of the Engineering and Allied Trades Shop Stewards' National Council. Its monthly organ, *The New Propeller* which became *The Metal Worker*, reached a circulation of 94,000.

Immediately after the War the CPGB felt that it would extend its power and influence within trade unions following Labour's general election victory in 1945, but problems began to occur with the switch over from war to peace production and the end of Essential Work Order in 1946. By the summer of 1946, there were reports in *The Metal Worker* of victimisation and lock-outs and the firm of Shardlow's, in Sheffield, faced a strike of 1,100 workers after the dismissal of Communist convenor Bill Longdon. Ultimately, the stoppage led to his re-instatement. In 1946, the Communist-led Shop-Stewards' National Council conference decided to start a campaign for a 40-hour week in place of the prevailing 47-hour week. By autumn, the Engineering Employers' Federation had agreed to a 44-hour week, with some firms introducing even shorter hours.[70] It is clear that some of the successes in the industrial field were partly the result of Communist pressure, although they have to be placed into the wider context of issues which arose naturally out of trade unionism and it is impossible to measure precise proportions of influence. In addition, the decline in sales of *The Metal Worker* – 23,000 in January 1946, 35,000 in January 1947, 26,000 in January 1948, 20,000 in January 1949 and 16,000 in September 1949 – suggests that the TUC's anti-Communist campaign of the late 1940s was working.[71]

There was a similar situation in the building trades. Frank Jackson, a full-time worker in the Industrial Department of the Communist Party, helped launch the *New Builders' Leader* in 1935. This journal became the focus of a formative pressure group in favour of the ultimately unsuccessful pre- and post-war attempts to create one union in the building industry.[72]

Through *The New Propeller*, the Party also participated in the campaign to get equal pay for women, and it also favoured the trade unions having two members on the National Coal Board set up under the 1946 Coal Industry Act.[73] The CPGB complained of the lack of rank-and-file trade union involvement in the running of the coal industry and feared that the trade union leaders might become cut off from their members.[74]

The CPGB's frustration with the Labour Government led it to criticise the obvious failures in Labour's industrial policy. The Nineteenth Congress of the CPGB, held at Seymour Hall in Marleybone, London, on 22 February 1947, demanded that Labour stop compromising with big business. It argued that there was a severe manpower shortage, that men should be withdrawn from the army and that women should be given equal pay. Indeed, Pollitt urged delegates 'that joint production machinery – national, regional, local and factory – should be set up without delay' to boost industrial production in order to retain Britain's industrial independence.[75] Yet the Twentieth Congress of the CPGB on 1 February 1948 admitted that it had had no success in this direction and by 1949 Rajani Palme Dutt, editor of *Labour Monthly*, was attacking the Labour Party's industrial policy and referring to the nationalised industries as 'capitalist pseudo-nationalisation'.[76]

Increasingly, the problem was that the CPGB was being isolated from the wider labour movement. Morgan Phillips launched a campaign on 21 December 1947 to reduce the Communist influence within the Labour Party and the trade union movement through a circular which condemned the slavish support of the CPGB for the Cominform. It further condemned the back-door methods by which Communists were winning seats on trades councils and trade unions.[77] However, in January 1948 all five Communist members of the EC of the South Wales area NUM were re-elected after a secret ballot. Walter Stevens, a Communist, was also elected general secretary of the Electrical Trade Union (ETU).[78] Two communists were voted on to the London regional council of the National Federation of Building Operatives. Les Ambrose topped the poll to be the Amalgamated Engineering Union (AEU) organiser and Walter Hannington, the pre-war leader of the National Unemployed Workers' Movement and frequent member of the Central Committee of the CPGB was returned to the AEU's executive.[79] Eight communists were also returned to the general executive council of the Transport and General Workers' Union (TGWU), including Bert Papworth of the London bus workers who had led the rank-and-file movement against Ernest Bevin's leadership in the 1930s.[80] Ten members were also elected to the Scottish NUM Executive in 1948.[81] Clive Jenkins, who courted communism in his early days, became the youngest full-time officer of the Association of Supervisory Staffs and Executive Technicians (ASSET) in 1947.[82]

The CPGB felt that Morgan Phillips's attack upon it was provoked by the Labour government's decision to impose wage restraint. Ever since the financial crisis of 1947, the threat to wage rises had been on the government's agenda. On 6 August 1947, Attlee asked both the workers and the TUC not to demand wage increases and on 4 February 1948 the government issued a White Paper (Cmnd 7321) outlining the need for wage restraint.

The possibility of a wage freeze was central to the discussions of the Twentieth Congress of the CPGB in February 1948. In opposition to the projected Government freeze, the Congress called for measures to keep profits down, to increase taxes on the rich, and to modernise industry. Pollitt stressed that 'the Government had put increased production as their principal method of solving the crisis, in order to cover up their anti-working-class policy as a whole'.[83] The CPGB asserted that the workers had fought hard for the nation and could not be expected to respond to the government's request for a wage freeze.[84] Indeed, one of the constants of Party policy in the 1950s was a militant wages policy which was developed to strengthen the Party and bring forward the politicisation of the trade unions in their conflict with the state.[85]

The General Council of the TUC accepted the wage restraint measures of the government on 24 March 1948, although communist trade union leaders such as Abe Moffatt and Arthur Horner stood against them. A motion opposing wage restraint was lost by 5.2 million votes to 2.1 million. As a result, wages rose by 6 per cent over the following year at a time when prices rose by 10 per cent. This reduction in living standards provoked a spate of industrial disputes, both official and unofficial, many of which the Attlee government attributed to Communist agitators. This was not always the case, although the CPGB generally supported such action for which its members were often victimised.

One major dispute occurred in mid-June 1948, when there was an unofficial strike over 'dirty cargo money' on the Regent Canal dock in London. This resulted in the suspension of 11 dockers for 2 weeks and their loss of attendance money for 13 weeks. Initially, in response, 1,100 men, including some from Liverpool, came out in support in a dispute which soon led up to 31,000 dockers striking. A tribunal cut the 13 weeks penalty to 2 weeks, but the strike continued to the end of the month. The government proclaimed a state of emergency in June 1948 and brought troops into the docks but eventually, on 29 June 1948, a mass meeting at London Victoria Docks led to 6,000 dockers returning to work on the recommendation of the strike committee.[86]

The strike was attacked in the press as being part of a 'Communist plot' to disrupt the nation even though the strike committee of 40 contained 19 Labour Party members and only 5 communists. The trade union movement was similarly critical, with Arthur Deakin, general secretary of the TGWU, which had members on strike, opposing the Communist-inspired dispute. The *Daily Worker*'s industrial correspondent reacted to the 'Communist plot' allegation on 3 July 1948, stating that three of the Communist activists had been in dockland and had served their time in dockland trade unionism. They had not joined the union to cause trouble as the press and Attlee implied.

At the 1948 TUC conference, the president, Florence Hancock, attacked the CPGB for 'fomenting unofficial strikes' and 'undermining' the authority of union officials. A Congress resolution called for 'determination to defeat and expose those elements'. This inspired a TUC-led anti-communist campaign which issued the 'Warning to Trade Unionists' on 27 October 1948 and urged the unions to take energetic steps to 'stop communist activity'.[87] On 29 October, the *Daily Worker* claimed that the latest 'heresy hunt' was motivated by the desire to remove Communist opposition to wage restraint. The TUC replied with the pamphlet *Defend Democracy*, which attacked Communist disruption. Also, in March 1949, the TUC produced another pamphlet entitled *The Tactics of Disruption* in which it argued that the Communists never regarded unions as a means for the 'protection of workers or to improve their standard of living', a statement which was quickly denied by the CPGB.[88]

The opposition to Communist influence within the trade union movement seems to have been greatly influenced by Arthur Deakin, Ernest Bevin's successor as general secretary of the TGWU. At this time, 9 of his union's 34-member General Executive Council were communists as were 3 of his 8-member Finance and General Purposes Committee. Worried by the influence of communists, Deakin sent a letter to Vincent Tewson, general secretary of the TUC, on 26 October 1948 complaining of the CPGB's 'continued interference' in the working of trade unions. Received on 27 October, it cannot have been pure coincidence that the TUC began its campaign against Communist interference in trade union matters just two days later.[89] The TGWU, with 1,300,000 members, carried considerable influence within the TUC.

Several trade unions, including the Fire Brigades' Union, the ETU, the Tobacco Workers and Foundry Workers, resisted moves to ban communists from holding office, though most followed the TUC line. Indeed, the TGWU, at its biennial conference, voted by more than 2:1 against allowing communists to hold office in the union – a ruling which lasted from 1950 until 1968. In September 1950, Deakin also encouraged the government to pass legislation banning the Communist Party.[90] The TUC Conference of 1949 also endorsed anti-Communist action by 6,746,000 to 760,000 votes.[91]

Indeed, the TUC took widespread action against communists, most obviously in London. In 1950 the TUC 'deregulated Stepney, Hackney and Wood Green local Trades Councils' for challenging its decision to take action against communists and 'The TUC informed the London Trades Council that if it does not get clear evidence of its loyalty it will not be re-registered in 1951.'[92] The Trades Council campaigned against the TUC's threat.

The situation was exacerbated by the Communist support for dissident dockers who, in 1951, were complaining of the Docks Delegate Conference's acceptance of a two shillings wage increase and the continuation of compulsory overtime. Arthur Deakin, of the TGWU, was criticised for accepting a wage offer which was well below that demanded by many of his members in London, Liverpool and other dock areas.[93] Tensions between the TGWU and the dockers continued over the next few years and were most obviously evident in the unofficial dock strikes of 1954 which affected Birkenhead, Liverpool, Manchester and Hull, and lead to the departure of about 10,000 TGWU members to the National Amalgamation of Stevedores and Dockers. Deakin suggested that this was a Communist conspiracy, although Michael Foot wrote in *Tribune* that Deakin 'did not know what the strike was about and had little intent to find out'.[94]

The story of the communists and the trade unions in the late 1940s and early 1950s was thus one of resistance in the face of adversity. The CPGB had made inroads into the trade union movement but found itself blocked by the TUC policy of rooting out communism in the late 1940s. Its influence was being neutralised at the same time as it was being blamed for every bout of unofficial strike action.[95] Indeed, between 1945 and 1955, the trade union membership of the CPGB had fallen from 13,600 in engineering down to 4,721 and in transport from 4,350 to 1,800.[96]

The CPGB continued to campaign with the port workers, the bus drivers, the Smithfield porters and other working groups in the 1940s and 1950s but was losing rather than gaining, trade union support. Indeed, faced with intense TUC opposition in the late 1940s, the CPGB changed the emphasis of its industrial policy and began to focus much more upon factory organisation.

This work has been the subject of a recent pioneering study by John McIlroy.[97] He argues that the CPGB decided in 1945 to move from workplace to local representation, and thus from small factory groups and slightly larger and better organised factory branches to factory committees, which were less concerned with organising small groups of militant shop stewards and more concerned with organising all the employees in an organisation with an eye to pressing forward with broader political campaigns as well as industrial issues. This move might be seen as getting into the mainstream of trade unionism by downplaying communism and rank-and-file movements, a process which ran against the grain of the Party's history. Clearly, this did not work as the declining influence of Communist membership of trade unions has revealed. Moves to reverse this 'opportunist' mistake thus began in 1947, when

Harry Pollitt stated that 'in our anxiety to improve our organisation for fighting elections, we did so in many cases at the expense of factory organisation'.[98] Thereafter, according to McIlroy, there was increasing pressure for factory branches to be revived. Substantial ground in this direction was made in the 1950s, although it appears that the war-time position was never recovered and that only about 11 per cent of Party members, perhaps less than 4,000 members in the mid-1950s, were members of factory branches and groups.[99] Nevertheless, Communist organisation in factories led to the burgeoning of factory papers and the re-establishing of trade unionism in the workplace, anathema to the more gentle image of communists offered by the electoral-minded factory committees who were trying to win broad support for the Communist Party rather than to fight for improved conditions for workers. This did not lead to rising recruitment into the Party nor to rising political support for the CPGB in parliamentary and local elections and the mass support the Party was gaining in the Second World War was never recovered. Nevertheless, with rising industrial conflict and a thaw in the Cold War, the prospects of the CPGB achieving success in the workplace seemed bright, despite the healthy scepticism that many working men held for Stalinism and the uneven pattern of organisation throughout Britain. However, the Soviet invasion of Hungary was just around the corner.

McIlroy's assessment seems remarkably accurate. The CPGB had always emphasised its factory – as opposed to trade union – organisation during the inter-war years, but had abandoned the factory branch in 1945 for the political gains to be garnered from factory committees. Pollitt and others had complained of the mistake that had been made, and at an Extended meeting of the EC of the CPGB in February 1949 a resolution on 'The Communist Party and the Factories' was passed encouraging the re-development of the factory branch.[100] During the ensuing nine months, over 1,500 factory gate meetings were organised and many local factory groups were formed into full branches focusing upon economic issues:

> The principal activity of the branches and groups has been on the economic issues. Some good activity has been conducted on national issues such as engineers. But some factory organisations have done little on the national wage questions and have tended to concentrate upon their own shop issues. A number of our branches and groups, including some of the smaller ones, are exercising a measure of leadership amongst the workers and in their organisations on the economic issues.[101]

Indeed, in March 1949, a report to an Extended Meeting of the EC included a report from Bob McIlhone about a factory branch he had helped to form in Glasgow which rapidly increased from 10 to 26 members, which means that the 'Party's Municipal Campaign has increased enormously, and indeed has been improved almost out of all recognition due to the help of the factory comrades'.[102]

The London District of the CPGB was also similarly enthusiastic of the revived factory branch movement. It observed that it had gained 1,500 new members in 1949 and 600 in the 1950 general election but that its membership remained static because of defections; there were 12,906 members in May 1949 and 12,903 in

June 1950, of whom 14 per cent were in engineering and 8 per cent in building in 1950. It felt that its failure to develop was because it was unable to nurture a 'mass movement' and felt that the issue could be addressed by getting 'Communist political work developed inside and outside 500 listed factories through which we can reach half a million industrial workers and their wives. Some results are beginning to come, and there is a changed political attitude...'[103]

Notwithstanding these developments, the fact is that the factory branch movement, which attempted to focus upon the workplace and cut across trade union boundaries, faced serious difficulties. It was, for instance, focused in a small number of industries; in Scotland of the 71 branches, 24 were in general engineering, 9 in mining, 7 in shipyards, 7 in rails and 6 in steel.[104] This narrowness of industrial range was evident throughout other regions within Britain. Yet, even where factory organisations existed, there were other problems. Most obviously, the CPGB complained of a lack of political education and activity: 'This was evident during the general election of 1950 but it is now being seen in relation to our efforts to build a broad peace movement based on the factories and the organised workers.'[105] Indeed, the CPGB felt that it was this 'political weakness which is holding back not only the advance of the Party itself but also the struggle of the workers for their wage demands'. Convinced that many comrades failed to appreciate the importance of factory work, the Party suggested an eight-point plan which focused upon greater publicity, the strengthening of political work and the republication of *The Communist Party and the Factories*. Such hope in 1950 did not last and the decline of CPGB membership over the next 30 or 40 years saw the gradual demise of the factory branch movement. Even before 1956, the movement appeared to be static and official figures, as McIlroy suggests, are confusing. There were 1,165 factory groups, with 16 having over 100 members in March 1944, but only 119 branches with regularly meetings and 400 groups 'at a lower stage' in 1949. By May 1950, there were 189 branches and 308 groups. In 1954, it was announced that there were 476 factory branches, allegedly the highest number in the Party's history – although many of these were probably groups rather than full-blown branches as such. What is clear is, that the factory branch and factory organisation movement had recovered in the 1950s from the change of policy in 1945 but not to the level of their height during the Second World War.[106]

Increasingly, the CPGB found itself isolated by the late 1940s and early 1950s. The policy of encouraging industrial production to establish Britain's economic independence from the United States lacked economic reality and Communist Party influence upon the trade union movement was being challenged by the TUC. The factory branch movement was barely holding its own. The failure of the CPGB to carry much influence in this direction led to some frustration within its ranks. Indeed, Mollie Guiar launched a determined attack upon the failure of CPGB policies noting that the Party had made not one decisive statement in favour of any strike since 1945 and criticising the way in which the political letter of February 1949 and the extended EC meeting of the same month had played down the importance of nationalisation in order to increase industrial efficiency.[107] In some respects these criticisms were justified. The fact is that the CPGB was often torn between claiming influence and denying that its actions were 'Communist plots'. Perhaps it was coming to accept that a party struggling to hang on to its 35,000–40,000 members could do little more than contribute to, rather than shape, events. Whatever the views of the Labour Government and the right-wing press, it is clear that CPGB's industrial and trade union policies were relatively marginal in determining events.

This picture of limited influence continued into the 1950s. The CPGB kept batting away for a £1 increase in the wages of the members of the Transport and General Workers in the 1950s, stressed the central importance of the workers' fight for peace in the 1950s when the Korean War was looming, and pressed the case for increased wages for engineers in 1952, but all with limited impact. It continued to press forward with the peace movement in 1953 and, at a London meeting on 11 January 1953, Pollitt noted the increasing cooperation between trade unions and local labour parties in connection with the CPGB demand for international peace. There were also moves afoot to build up Party organisation in the countryside, where there were only about 170 communist activists amongst half a millions farm workers, only 150,000 of whom were in the National Union of Agricultural Workers.[108]

Indeed, the lack of trade union support forced the CPGB to push forward with a new recruiting campaign. In the wake of a 24-hour strike in shipbuilding and engineering industries, called by the Confederation of Shipbuilding and Engineering Unions for 2 December 1953, and the wage demands in the building, rail and transport industries in the autumn and winter of 1953, the PC of the CPGB began to re-assess the possibility of building up its trade union organisation again.[109] The two-page document that emerged suggested that there were now greater possibilities of recruiting non-unionists into unions, that inter-union rivalries should be avoided, and that communism could play an important role in 'building 100 per cent trade unionism and powerful shop organisation'.[110] Little came of these suggestions although the CPGB had other furrows to plough.

Women and communism

There was a surge of activity by women's organisations in the early 1950s, focused mainly upon the standard of living of women, wages, concerns for the future of children, the peace and the anti-German re-armament movement. The CPGB sought to direct this movement but found, that despite its enormous efforts, the women's peace movement simply endorsed Communist programmes rather than provided a fertile field for increasing Communist support. Nevertheless, the CPGB organised its First National Conference of Communist Women in 1951, attracting 74 delegates from the districts and 26 consultative delegates. Of these, 36 were housewives, 39 trade unionists from 17 trade unions, and 'every delegate with the exception of four was a member of a Co-operative Society or Guild'.[111] The Conference did not anticipate that the CPGB's 'correct explanations' would gain support quickly, but felt that once women became more incensed about their standard of living, wage levels, rising nursery charges, and the need for peace in the face of the Korean War, they would attach themselves to the cause. In this the CPGB had helped, it claimed, to achieve 100 per cent trade union organisation in a hosiery factory in Mansfield and participated in the formation of peace groups. The winning of support was considered to be slow but it was felt that changes would occur when 'living experience is added to correct explanations'. However, in addition, it was felt that:

> above all, the Conference was an additional proof that today many thousands of women are joining the movement in defence of peace and that hundreds of thousands more are prepared not openly to talk peace but to act for peace.

It was hoped that this National Conference would act as the basis for a powerful mass peace movement and bring *The British Road to Socialism* (which is mentioned on p. 35) to the 'widest circle of women'.[112]

Some work in the direction of organising women had already been done prior to the First Women's Conference. The London District Committee Report of the CPGB in 1951 contains a substantial discussion on the demand for peace from women's groups in 1950:

> The outstanding feature has been the way in which women have taken a leading part in every aspect of the fight for peace. The women were particularly ready to sign the atom bomb peace petition, and some of the 'champion collectors' were women, and they carried on many forms of agitation. These include a deputation from 250 women to the House of Commons calling for the banning of the atom bomb and two deputations to the House of Commons called by the I.W.D., one on the atom bomb and one on German rearmament. The London Women's Peace Council 'had carried through a number of activities and there was wide protest movement against the arrest of 11 women in connection with the Trafalgar Square peace demonstration'.[113]

They were also involved in campaigns against increased charges for, and proposals to close nurseries, and against increased charges for school meals. Women were not greatly involved in factory work, but there were some developments and improvements in Bermondsey and nearly 200 women attended the London Women's Conference in January 1951. By June 1951, there were 58 Women's groups in London and 75 boroughs with a Women's Committee. The sale of *Women's Today* had also increased from 2,600 to 4,000.

This activity emerged from the enormous reaction amongst women's groups, of many political persuasions, to the outbreak of the Korean War but seems to have encompassed other issues as well, including the low wages of women, the rising cost of nursery charges, living standards, the future of 'our children' and, ultimately by 1954, the concern about German re-armament. The Communist Party took part in this mass protest movement, although the movement's impetus was fleeting, focused mainly on the years between 1952 and 1954, and its presence was incidental rather than formative.

On International Women's Day, 9 March 1952, the National Assembly of Women held its first Assembly, attended by 1,400 delegates, in which its declaration, read by Miss Charlotte Marsh, a veteran suffragette, finished with the high aims of 'FOR LIFE NOT DEATH. FOR PEACE – NOT WAR. FOR THE FUTURE OF

OUR CHILDREN', and demanded the recognition of the International Charter for Women 'as mothers, workers and citizens' and to secure a 'better standard of life' and a 'happy future for the children'.[114] It received a welter of supporting comments from bodies and individuals such as the Gorbals Tenants Association, a 15-year-old schoolgirl and Mrs Billie Horne, of the Communist Housewives of Luton, who complained of the rising cost of children's clothing. Yet others complained of the workload of teachers who were teaching with classes of 50 or more children.

This was a rather cosmopolitan movement with non-Communists such as Margaret Airey as National Organiser and Mrs Monica Felton (chairman of the Third Assembly), although the CPGB also took a deep interest in the broad-ranging women's movement of the early 1950s. Indeed, Felton made it clear that the Assembly brought together a variety of experiences: 'We come from different political parties. We are women of different religious views. We come from Co-op, Guilds, from the Labour Parties, from churches, from associations of many different kinds...' The Assembly harnessed this support to demonstrate for peace on the anniversary of the Korean War on 25 June 1952, when more than a 100 relatives of 35 towns marched through London to the House of Commons.

The Second Assembly of the movement was held on 8 March 1953, at two venues in London and Glasgow and 2,142 delegates took the pledge 'The Declaration For A Better World', which began by stating that:

> We demand a world free from the fear of want and war; a world where there are enough free schools, nurseries, recreation centres and hospitals; a world where comfortable homes and the best food and clothes are within the reach of all; a world where every child who leaves school is guaranteed a training, a job and a life of security.[115]

As with the First Assembly, the message was one of seeking a better life for 'our children' and of continuing to press for peace, and the cosmopolitan nature of the movement was evident. At the London meeting there were 1,713 delegates present of whom 8 were from national organisations, 19 from trades councils 119 from trade unions, 51 from factories, 81 from peace groups, 41 from co-op guilds and organisations, 37 from political parties, 302 from Assembly groups and 945 from 'Groups of twelve women'.

Within 24 hours of the Second Assembly, delegates were entering government offices in Whitehall. The movement prospered and doubled its membership by the time the Third National Assembly of Women was held on 7 March 1954 in London (1,076 delegates), Manchester (926) and Glasgow (378). With 2,380 delegates, and each delegate representing at least 12 women, it would appear that the active membership of the movement was around 30,000 all fighting for equal pay, peace and a more certain future for children.[116] By that time the movement had a magazine, *Our Women*, the front page of which had Monica Felton's statement that 'We fight that the great resources of our nation shall be spent on the things we need for life instead of on the means of destruction.'

The CPGB was certainly interested with and involved in the National Assembly of Women, particularly in its hay day of the early 1950s, but it was only part of a broad-based and relatively temporary movement which obviously blended with the interests of the CPGB, and it was not until the 1960s and 1970s, with *Link*, that the women's movement in the CPGB began to really develop. Nevertheless, there was a reasonable Communist input into its activities and in August and September 1952, the Assembly sent 12 women as individuals to the Soviet Union in response to the invite of the Soviet Women's Anti-Fascist Committee, which later reported in *Our Women* on the role of women in Soviet society 'as mothers, as workers, as citizens' and concluded that 'the Soviet Union does not want war'. The group included Mrs Elwyn Jones, a member of the Writers for Peace and Mrs Antionette Pirie an Oxford academic and member of Scientists for Peace.

Organisation Commission and changes

Even though the CPGB membership was declining from its peak in the Second World War, there were still about 40,000 members in the immediate post-war years. The rapid increase in membership in the 1930s had created difficulties for the Party to ensure that its members were properly represented on the Central/Executive Committee. The issue of representation surfaced in the 1940s but, as will become evident later, resurfaced in the mid-1950s when E. P. Thompson and John Saville challenged the representative nature of the Party in *The Reasoner* debate when inner party democracy was seen as being vital to the continued attractiveness and well-being of the Party but only within the constraints imposed by democratic centralism which was dominated by the leadership of the CPGB.

The volatility of membership figures encouraged the Party to examine the possibility of new organisational arrangements in the 1940s. An Organisation Commission was set up at the Seventeenth Congress of the Party in October 1944 and reported to the EC on 17 December 1944, suggesting that all members of a branch should be resident in the branch area. Committees were to be elected by people working in factories. The new structure kept the branch as the focus of organisation, as it had been since 1936, but no longer allowed people working but not living in the area to be members. The plans were confirmed at the Eighteenth Congress in November 1945 but there remained problems in the collection of dues which led to the formation of a commission to modify the functions of the various bodies in the Party.[117]

This Organisation Commission reported to the EC on 10 September 1946. Peter Kerrigan, its chairman, and the 5 EC members and 6 party members, recommended that the leadership should give more guidance and that industrial leadership should be increasingly organised through district industrial committees which would keep a list of those prominently placed in trade unions and co-ordinate the work of factory committees. Developments needed to be made in new areas and Party cadres were encouraged to circulate around new branches and it was felt that there should be 'more checking on decisions and self-criticism'.[118]

Yet, despite the recommendations, since 1944, it had proved difficult to collect membership dues, and in 1947, the EC decided that factory committees should be set up wherever possible, without the stringent requirements that members both live and work within the area.[119] The powerful London District acted quickly and set up 17 new factory branches with 677 members in a few months.[120] The new move was endorsed by a change of rules at the Twentieth Congress in February 1948 under which branches consisted of 'members living, in some cases working, within a defined area'. There had been a return to the old system.

The Twentieth Congress also introduced changes in the methods of electing the Party's EC in order to improve Party democracy. Between 1929 and 1943, the Central Committee had been elected by a panel system under which a commission, consisting mainly of listed appointees from the districts, were appointed to go through the nominations made by the branches and districts. Delegates could propose additions to the list and then it was voted upon by Congress. In 1943, the panel system was abandoned. The Seventeenth Congress, in 1944, decided that the new EC would be elected by a ballot of all those nominated, without a recommended list. This arrangement was used at both the Seventeenth and Eighteenth congresses. However, there was some dissatisfaction with the new system since it was felt that it favoured the high-profile activists at the expense of the hard-working, less well-known, Party members. Therefore, after the 1945 Congress, the EC of 30, co-opted 6 other representatives. Another commission was then set up and endorsed the revival of a recommended list although delegates would be able to nominate others. This arrangement was finally approved by the Nineteenth Congress in 1947.

The success of these amendments, some of which were undone as quickly as they were done, is far from certain. On 8 March 1948, the Party had 38,833 members compared to the 37,579 it had in June 1947, and it was hoped that the figure would increase to 43,500 by 1949.[121] Within 3 months 4,240 members were recruited by the new members campaign. However, losses of existing members meant that it was difficult to get membership figures above 40,000.[122] Indeed, the London District Committee reported in June 1950 that 'our overall position is that of barely holding our ground. While 1,500 members were made in 1949 and 600 in the General Election (1950), our total membership remains what it was a year ago'.[123] The situation with the YCL was a little better. Its membership was 2,991 in April 1951 and a year later it had increased to 3,281. Three months later it had risen to 3,474 and the sales of its paper *Challenge* had risen to 11,218.[124] In general, then, the national membership of the CPGB continued to decline in the early 1950s from about 38,000 in 1950 to 27,000 in 1957, although about 7,000 of the loss occurred after the Soviet invasion of Hungary in 1956. The problems of Party organisation obviously led to some membership decline but the situation was also exacerbated by the development of the Cold War and the foreign policy of the party. The emergence of a new policy document in 1951 did little to halt the decline.

The British Road to Socialism

The CPGB's new policy and direction emerged in *The British Road to Socialism*, a document which was discussed with Stalin and which signalled a fundamental change in the direction of the CPGB. It was probably the Popular Front strategy of the Seventh Congress of the Comintern in 1935, and its re-emergence in the peoples war of 1941–5, that drove the CPGB in the parliamentary direction. However, there were more immediate considerations leading the way. Throughout the Second World War, Pollitt was convinced that there would be a continuation of an arrangement with capitalism in the post-war world. Stalin appeared to be moving in that direction and it seemed sensible for the CPGB to follow. However, Pollitt believed that conflict could never be ruled out. The Comintern had been disbanded in 1943 along with the revolutionary concepts that had brought it into being. Pollitt now posited the idea of a nation's working class advancing ever more determinedly towards a greater say in the nation's affairs, participating in parliamentary democracy through their own democratic organisations.

The new strategy brought about a dramatic change of line. In 1935, the Party had advocated that a socialist society could never be achieved through parliamentary legislation and that the only alternative was to abolish Parliament and to replace it with a system of workers' councils and soviets. By May 1944, the idea that Parliaments should be discarded had been abandoned. The CPGB now aimed to democratise the Parliament and the existing political system. The Proposed 'British Road to Socialism' advocated a change to proportional representation in the form of a single transferable vote, a measure which Willie Gallacher and the Communist MPs, advocated in the House of Commons on 18 February 1944. The Party turned its attention to its new programme at the Seventeenth Congress held at Shoreditch Town Hall in October 1944. It envisaged the idea that the post-war domestic policies could not be separated from international policy and that there would be some element of continued class collaboration after the War. Such views had previously been put forward by Earl Browder, general secretary of the Communist Party of the United States, and seemed to be accepted by the CPGB. Indeed, it was not until August 1945 that Browder's ideas were seriously challenged because they went too far in suggesting the winding up of the Communist Party of the United States.[125]

Any attempt to block the new political line was opposed by Pollitt and when Walter Hannington – the leader of the unemployed in the inter-war years – objected, Pollitt described his objections as 'the policy of 1928 – Class Against Class'.[126] Discussions continued in the Party's weekly *World News and Views* and at the Eighteenth Party Congress in November 1945. There were further complaints that the Party was not democratically run, but Pollitt refuted this and suggested that the CPGB was the 'most democratically run political organization in the world'. Also, he would not budge from the Yalta standpoint regarding the sphere of influence of the Three Great Powers, which meant that he accepted the Attlee position and the possibility of peaceful existence in the post-war world.

The CPGB was invariably concerned about its declining membership at this stage and this was the motive for discussions on The British Road to Socialism. The Party's decline has been explained in many different ways but sectarianism and narrowness of perception were factors which Pollitt highlighted. According to him: 'The Party wants to be a narrow Party, it wants to be a Party of exclusive Marxists'.[127] His attack seems to have been directed against Willie Rust, a party functionary who constantly opposed Pollitt, in whom there were few redeeming features.[128] It is clear that

Pollitt's initial support for the Attlee Government was countered by Rust's opposition to such moves but the Party's leading functionaries – J. R. Campbell, Peter Kerrigan, Willie Gallacher and John Gollan – generally favoured Pollitt rather than Rust.

The new line developed over the next two years and was advocated by Kitty Cornforth, amongst others.[129] In August 1947, Pollitt published a lengthy pamphlet entitled *Looking Ahead*, chapter six of which was 'The British Road to Socialism'. This stated that:

> Marxists have never maintained that the Road to Socialism in any country is neatly mapped out and time-tabled, that each country will pass to Socialism in the same way and at the same speed, with similar forms of state organization.... Communists have never said that the Russian Revolution in October 1917, is a model which has exactly to be copied. Indeed, the whole work of Marx, Engels, Lenin and Stalin... has been to explain to the people how to recognise the deep laws of development of society, and to show how the working class and the people can decide on correct slogans and correct programmes based on a study of the economic and social forces at a given time. Communists have always said, on the other hand, that the study of the Russian Revolution and of all previous revolutions... is pregnant with meaning and lessons for the working class. But this does not mean that these lessons must be learnt by heart, or initiated mechanically, or applied at different times and under different conditions.
>
> The progress of democratic and Socialist forces throughout the world has opened out the new possibilities of transition to Socialism by other paths than those followed by the Russian Revolution.[130]

Pollitt's views on a peaceful transition to Socialism/Marxism were soon to be affected by the Cold War, but in 1951 his underlying commitment to a peaceful and parliamentary transition to Socialism/Marxism emerged in the CPGB's new long-term programme, *The British Road to Socialism*.[131] This ground-breaking document claimed to offer a conception of democracy that had emerged from the 'people's war' and that gave Pollitt's agenda for Britain a distinctively parliamentary slant. The main break with earlier Marxist thought lay in the claim that it is now possible for the working class to win control over the capitalist state in Britain by constitutional means, and then to transform the capitalist state into one that met the needs of the working class. In other words, the idea of the parliamentary *cul-de-sac* was abandoned and the parliamentary road to socialism took the place of the proletarian dictatorship as advocated by Marx, Engels and Lenin.

The immediate reason for the production of this document seems to have been Pollitt's visit to Stalin to discuss the British political situation in the summer of 1950. Stalin suggested the need for a long-term perspective after discussing the disastrous general election results of 1950. Pollitt presented his report of the meeting to a meeting of the EC on 8 July 1950. So began the Party's final moves towards *The British Road to Socialism*.

The EC issued *The British Road to Socialism* in January 1951 for discussion. Predictably, it criticised the Labour Governments for only nationalising about 20 per cent of the

British economy and over its commitment to American foreign policy. It also advocated socialistic nationalisation of all industries which, it argued, could only be achieved by the move from capitalistic democracy to a people's democracy. This involved 'transforming Parliament, the product of Britain's historic struggle for democracy, into the democratic instrument of the will of the vast majority of the people'. The working class, along with some sections of the middle class, it was felt, would be more than sufficient to return a majority representing the interests of the British people to Parliament and would be able to remove the rich and establish a people's government. This government would introduce a planned economy based upon socialist principles and democratic electoral reform. Proportional representation was to be introduced and the voting age would be reduced to 18. Finally, the House of Commons would be made the sole national authority and the House of Lords would be abolished.

In an attempt to counter widespread misconceptions, the CPGB emphasised that there was no need to fear aggression from socialist states, that bloody revolution was not inevitable and that there was no desire to abolish Parliament. The intended new programme was issued as a 3d pamphlet and sold about 200,000 copies. *The Communist Review* also published many articles on the new policy in 1951, indicating its relevance to the British labour tradition and the needs of the changing international situation.[132]

Finally, in the spring of 1951, the policy was finally adopted at the Twenty-Second Congress of the CPGB. Although it was partly redrafted in 1957, to include the term 'socialist government' in place of 'people's government', and further redrafted on later occasions, this document remained the programme of the Party until it was replaced in the late 1980s and early 1990s by the *Manifesto for New Times*, with its more 'pick and mix' type of approach for 'Marxist' activists. In addition, *The British Road* provoked a number of subsidiary discussions, most obviously the formation of the 'Commission on the Party and the Middle Classes' in 1954.[133] This was part of the 'Fight for a Broad Alliance' in which it was suggested that many of the professional middle class were from working-class families whose interests would be best served by the CPGB.[134]

The CPGB and Trotskyite opposition

In the late 1940s, CPGB influence and membership was further undermined by the first post-war split in the international communist movement and the Stalinist show trials in Eastern Europe. During the summer of 1948, the CPGB gave its support to the Soviet criticism of Tito's regime in Yugoslavia's expulsion from Cominform. It also publicly supported Stalin's show trials. This earned the criticism of the British Labour and Conservative parties. It also fostered deep hostility from the deeply divided Trotskyite movement in Britain, the RCP.

The Trotskyite organisation, named after Leon Trotsky who rejected Stalin's and the CPGB's willingness to compromise and advocated perpetual revolution, first emerged in Britain in the 1930s in bodies such as the Balham Group, Marxist Group, the Marxist League and the Militant Group. They supported the Russian revolution and the Soviet state as it had existed under the leadership of Lenin and Trotsky, and opposed the subsequent 'Stalinist degeneration' of both the Soviet Union and the CPGB in their support for a tyrannical and privileged aristocracy which they saw as effectively restoring capitalism.[135]

The British Trotskyites formally identified with Trotsky's Fourth International, formed in 1938, to fight for a democratic internal regime within the CPSU and to develop revolutionary tactics and strategy. Most British Trotskyite organisations formed themselves into either the (United) Revolutionary Socialist League (RSL), with about 150 members, or the WIL, with about 250 members. They merged in January–February 1944 to form the RCP, led by leaders such as Gerry Healy and Jock Haston (formerly of WIL). The RCP was the origin of three of the main Trotskyite organisations that subsequently emerged in Britain between the 1950 and the 1960s – the Socialist Labour League (SLL), the IS/Socialist Workers' Party (SWP) and Militant Tendency (MT), dominated by Gerry Healy, Tony Cliff and Ted Grant, respectively.[136]

The formation of the Attlee Labour Government in 1945, and its commitment to social reform, led to one of many splits within Trotskyism. Some members of the RCP, including a minority led by Healy, questioned the continuation of all separate socialist, Marxist and Trotskyite organisations now that the Labour Party was in government. He and his group proposed that all RCP members should enter the Labour Party, and they published their views through an organ called *Militant* rather than *Socialist Appeal*, the official RCP organ.

The RCP was deeply divided over the issue of entry into the Labour Party but did not finally split until 1947 when the minority, known as The Group and led by Healy, pushed for entrism. Healy's assumption was that the working class had become radicalised and that this would see the rise of the number of militants within the Labour Party. With the RCP membership stuck at about 300–350 members, Healy felt that entrism had to be tried. However, the majority, led by Haston, opposed entrism.

With the agreement of the two sections of the RCP, the International Secretariat of the Fourth International (ISFI) divided the British section into two when the Second World Congress of the Fourth International was held in April 1948; Healy's section pursued entrism and published their views through their newspaper *Socialist Outlook* whilst the Jock Haston and Ted Grant, remained opposed to entrism. Nevertheless, in the summer of 1949 the declining membership of the RCP and the failure of the 'left turn' to emerge within the Labour Party rank-and-file forced the remaining groups of the old RCP to support entrism. This was agreed to by the RCP and also by the International. But there were other tensions developing within the RCP.

Tony Cliff, who had come to Britain as Ygael Gluckstein and later became the leader of the Socialist Review Group – the forerunner of the SWP-broadcast the International Secretariat of the Fourth International's theory of the degeneracy of the Soviet workers' state in his typed statement 'Russia: A Marxist Analysis'. This argued that Stalinist dictatorship in the Soviet Union had degenerated and neutralised the progressive achievements of the October revolution (although Cliff later modified his views in the 1960s and suggested that the Soviet Union was a form of state capitalism rather than a bureaucratically deformed workers' state). This was a view which neither Haston nor Grant subscribed to.[137] Attitudes about the impending Third World War and how to characterise Tito's Yugoslavian Communist regime also created tensions. Was the Soviet Union to be supported against the West despite Stalinism and was Tito really a Stalinist, despite his conflict with the USSR, and anti-Trotskyite?

Faced with such tensions, the RCP was wound down and replaced by an informal alliance, usually referred to as 'The Club'. The new democratic organisation was approved at The Club's 1950 Congress and endorsed by the Third World Congress of the Fourth International in 1951. However, this occurred at a time when the Fourth International was itself riven by conflict for, in February 1951, Michel Pablo, the International secretary, began to develop the idea that the unstable capitalist world could be brought to an end by the precipitating of a war and war-revolution in which Communist parties would be forced to respond in a revolutionary way to mass pressure. He thus advocated entrism into the Communist parties of the world to influence their policies. The Fourth World Congress of the Fourth International, held in 1954, adopted Pablo's document on 'The Rise and Decline of Stalinism' which moved to support communist states, such as China and Yugoslovia, who were in conflict with the Soviet Union, whether or not they were bureaucratic in form. The result was a number of splits which led to the 'establishment of three "Fourth Internationals" plus a "Revolutionary Marxist Tendency of the Fourth International" which, however, maintains that the FI does not exist...'[138]

The Club, in the divided world of international Trotskyism, soon disintegrated with the Haston group defecting to reformism whilst other leaders of the former majority were expelled and some members drifted out of politics altogether. Tony Cliff's supporters regrouped around the duplicated paper *Socialist Review*, which was published from the end of 1950 and focused upon a study of the state capitalism of Eastern European regimes. Indeed, the new Socialist Review Group, of 33 members, held its founding conference at Whitsun in 1950, and rejected entrism and The Club's policy of support for the 'deformed workers' state of North Korea in its war against South Korea.[139] But it was Healy's group which became ascendant. Healy, and The Club/The Group, continued to work through its newspaper *Socialist Outlook*, which moderated its tone, and appealed to the movements within the Labour Party, going so far as to work with *Tribune*.

As already indicated, the British Section of The Club, was formed at the Third World Congress of the Fourth International 1951 and a resolution was passed which maintained that the Third World War was imminent that it would be a combined effort of imperialist powers 'directed by Washington against the revolution in all its forms' but that all the conditions for a socialist success existed 'except for the existence of a revolutionary leadership', although conflicts between some national Communist parties and the Soviet Union suggested that a new leadership was emerging.[140] The potential for Marxism to defeat imperialism was thus considered to be emerging.

The main British representatives at this 1951 Congress were John Lawrence, editor of *Socialist Outlook*, and Gerry Healy but both had left the Fourth International before it held its Fourth Congress in 1954. Lawrence and Healy, at that time, were running *Socialist Outlook* but in November 1953 both became influenced by James P. Cannon and the American Trotskyite Socialist Worker Party who published *The Militant*, which attacked Pablo, the secretary of the Fourth International. Cannon set up a Committee of the Fourth International and Healy did the same in Britain, being expelled from the Fourth International as a result of his actions. Lawrence, Healy and their supporters quickly took up the position of becoming left Labour and became more friendly in their approach to the CPGB, in the hope of winning support and influencing policy, and Lawrence eventually split from The Group/The Club and joined the CPGB. In effect The Group/The Club was going nowhere until the international developments of 1956, but then developed to become the SLL in 1959.

The CPGB kept a watchful eye throughout these complex machinations within Trotksyism. It was always suspicious of Titoists and Trotskyites entering the Party and reported that it also 'expelled from our ranks the agents of British Intelligence, as well as provocateurs'.[141] However, it was in 1956 that the Party had to be most vigilant.

After the Twentieth Congress of the Soviet Union, in early 1956, which saw Krushchev's attack upon Stalin, both the Lawrence and Healy groups tried to take advantage of the situation:

> Gerry Healy has been extremely active re-arranging old questions, making contact wherever possible inside the CPGB and urging Party members to raise question of a recall Congress immediately, and maintaining his influence in the 'Tribune' where he writes anti-Party articles. He was critical of the reformist document *The British Road to Socialism* and was encouraging his supporters to remain within the Party.[142]

The interest of 'The Group' increased when there were discussions about inner party democracy within the CPGB led by E. P. Thompson and John Saville who published *The Reasoner*. Betty Reid was in charge of an inquiry on the matter when the Soviet invasion of Hungary occurred in 1956. More opportunities emerged for 'The Group' when Peter Fryer was sent to Budapest to report for the CPGB's *Daily Worker* but found his reports rejected by them. On his return to Britain his reports were published in the Fleet Street press, where he depicted the Hungarian revolution as a socialist working-class revolution directed against bureaucratic monolithism. He was subsequently expelled from the CPGB and found his way into The Club/The Group which eventually became the SLL in 1959. Healy took up on Fryer's theme with The Club and argued that 'all members of the Communist Party and the YCL should immediately demand a special congress to repudiate the leadership line in Hungary. Stay in the Communist Party and fight it out.'[143] Healy's appeal achieved little and, as is indicated in Chapter 2, the CPGB closed ranks and quashed much dissident opposition in its Commission on Inner Party Democracy and at its Twenty-Fifth (Special) Congress in 1957.

By the mid-1950s there were also two other Trotskyite organisations reflecting upon the events of 1956. There was the relatively weak and small British Section of the Fourth International left over after the departure of The Group and the McShane

Group, the Social Workers' Federation, associated with Harry McShane who had left the CPGB in 1953. The first of these attacked the reformist policies of the Soviet Union and denounced Healy's tactics of entrism whilst the second – which had support in Glasgow, London, Liverpool, Birmingham and Manchester and had a stake in the ETU and the AEU – wished to work within both the Labour Party and the CPGB much as Healy had wanted to.

These organisations were, in 1956, attempting to gain support both inside and outside CPGB in order to become involved in the discussions of the Twentieth Congress of the CPSU. Interestingly, the PC of the CPGB received a report from the magazine *The Fourth International*, published by the revivified British section of the Fourth International, the RSL, that had decided to reform a section in Britain sympathetic to the Fourth International. This body was led by S. Bornstein, an old pre-war Trotskyite, and had its headquarters at 21 Sidney Street, London, E.1. What was published was a report, presented to the Seventeenth Plenum of the International Executive Committee of the Fourth International, written by Ernest Germain (Mandel) and released in May 1956, suggesting that in small Communist parties the RSL would seek to support those who wanted the continuation of a revolutionary Communist party. The CPGB stressed that the RCP was not connected to the Healy group which was launching its own journal *Labour Review*, nor with the McShane organisation. To the CPGB it was clear that this meant that there would now be two organisations – those of Healy and McShane working secretly within the Labour Party and the CPGB and a third organisation, with a magazine, the *Labour Review*, working openly to do so.[144]

A report to the Trotskyite Fourth International suggested that there had been a split within the CPSU, that this had led Stalin, rather than Beria and others, to be blamed for bureaucratic dictatorship and promised that there would be changes as the 'cult of the individual' was rejected. What interested the CPGB most was the suggestion that the attack upon Stalin had unleashed a crisis within both large and small Stalinist parties and sects and that the mass Communist parties should be won over by a 'Broad Left Revolutionary Current' and that small Communist parties would be influenced by the 'support of sane elements among the rank and file who oppose the reformist–liquidationist manoeuvres'.[145]

It was also at this time that the movement of academic socialists developed in the universities and, from the spring of 1957, the *Universities and Left Review* (ULR) was published. Although this will be examined in more detail in Chapter 2, it is clear that the events in Hungary were the cause of an academic outburst against the CPGB. According to Dutt, in his information sheet for the EC of the CPGB on 10 May 1958:

> The attitude of the leaders [of the ULR] to the Party is obvious. In the months after Hungary they went through the usual emotional revulsion against the Party, common among intellectuals. Since then they have paid no attention to it, regarding it as negligible. They are more worried about Trotskyism, when they want at all cost....[146]

Healyite and Trotskyite ideas certainly played a part in the events of 1956, and the CPGB certainly kept a watchful eye on them, but all they did was to galvanise the movement to close the ranks of the CPGB at a period of stress and force it to re-affirm its support for the Soviet Union. Trotskyism was a factor in the thinking of the CPGB in the mid-1950s but was never the force or concern that it became for the CPGB in the 1960s with the widening of Trotskyite influence in the universities.

The CPGB, India, the Commonwealth and Foreign Policy

The CPGB was critical of Britain's support for the foreign policy of the United States, which involved the Cold War and the creation of NATO in 1949. On 17 December 1949, the PC of the CPGB fiercely attacked the foreign policy of the Labour Government in a press statement which suggested that 'the Government is now confronted with American demands that Britain should pay for the maintenance of U.S. forces and equipment in Britain'.[147] It was therefore naturally opposed to Britain's involvement in supporting the Americans in the Korean War (1950-3), the proliferation of atomic weapons and German re-armament. Indeed, after an initial attempt to work with the Labour Party and the Labour Government, the CPGB came to accept that it had failed to influence the post-war evolution of British foreign policy. Indeed, the Draft of the General Election Programme for the CPGB, drawn up by George Matthews the assistant secretary of the CPGB in July 1949, stated that 'The foreign policy of Mr. Bevin and the Labour government is the policy of Churchill and Toryism. It is the policy of Churchill's notorious Fulton Speech in 1946, in which he called for an Anglo-American Bloc against Russia.'[148] Indeed, a few months later the Party released a press statement noting that the new Atlantic Pact had led to 'American demands that Britain should pay for the maintenance of U.S. forces and equipment in Britain', and other onerous demands.[149] Labour's policy was one which attached it to the United States and against the Soviet Union.

Fearing war, by the late 1940s, the CPGB had set up a National Peace Council and in January 1949 was seeking to extend its work and influence, although it ruled out the formation of a National Committee for the Co-ordination of the Peace Movement.[150] It also helped to direct the activities of movement which saw the formation of the National Assembly of Women, which reached its zenith between 1951 and 1954.

All the districts of the CPGB were involved in the peace campaign. The London District organised 800 people who lobbied the House of Commons in July 1951 to oppose the Korean War and 35 MPs were present. A National Peace Conference was attended by 350 delegates and 20,000 people attended the Trafalgar Square Peace Conference. In January 1951, there was a Trafalgar Square meeting, addressed by Harry Pollitt and John Mahon, against German rearmament. There were numerous other meetings and leaflet distributions and a petition against the Korean War gathered more than 330,000 signatures.

By the same token, the loyalty to Stalin ensured that Soviet transgressions were often overlooked. The *Daily Worker* gave wholehearted support to the show trail communists in Hungary, Czechoslovakia and Bulgaria in the late 1940s and the break with Tito and Yugoslavia in 1948. There was also little criticism of the Red Army's bloody repression of the general strike movement which spread through East Germany in June 1953. However, the 1952 trials of communists in Czechoslovakia did create real tension since John Gollan, who became general secretary of the CPGB in 1956, had been a friend of Rudolf Slansky, the Czech general secretary. This did not stop James Klugmann writing in his 'Lessons of the Prague Trial' that the development in Czechoslovakia had shown the dangers of Trotskyism and bourgeois nationalism.[151]

The Empire, and particularly India, also figured prominently in the thinking of the CPGB. This was due to a number of factors. In the first case, Marxist writers attacked Imperialism because of its exploitation and emphasised the people's right to self-determination as a matter of course. Second, Rajani Palme Dutt, who was half Indian, had constantly written on the issue of independence for India and the need for self-determination, during the inter-war years and the Second World War. Indeed, as Indian independence approached, the CPGB and Dutt produced *India Newsletter*, the first copy of which appeared on 20 June 1946, which aimed to explain 'India to the Labour Movement and developing in the country an understanding of the tremendous political events now taking place'.[152] It demanded an immediate declaration for Indian independence, the withdrawal of troops from India and the establishment of an interim free Provisional Government 'based on Indian unity to fight the famine' in the removal of 'Princely autocracy'. These themes were constantly reiterated and Dutt emphasised these needs in his article 'Stand by the Indian People' in August 1946, in which he also doubted that the Attlee Government's Cabinet Mission would give them independence.[153]

Dutt and the CPGB were greatly influenced in this demand by the Second Congress of the Communist Party of India (CPI), held in 1943, which sought complete independence for India from the British Empire, close ties with 'genuinely democratic nations and especially the Soviet Union', the abolition of the landlords, the formation of a Union of national people's democratic national republics based on the principle of national self-determination, the ending of feudal principalities, the nationalisation of key industries, the confiscation of British and foreign assets and the improvement in the position of the working classes.[154] Indeed, Dutt's pamphlet *Freedom for India*, as well as *Indian Newsletter*, emphasised the right of the different nationalities in India to self-determination in their homeland, which, of course, raised the issue of voluntary federation or union, of 'Freedom for India' and 'Freedom for Pakistan'.

International and national Marxist thinking and a touch of personal interest had combined to ensure that the CPGB would be critical of the British Empire at a time in the post-war years when change was about to occur. Indeed, events were moving quickly. Clement Attlee's post-war Labour Government sent a delegation of Cabinet Ministers – Stafford Cripps, Frederick W. Pethwick-Lawrence and A. V. Alexander – to India in February 1946 to conduct intricate negotiations with the Indian Congress and the Muslim leaders. They found no consensus and were forced to produce a complex three-tier system of government which ruled out the idea of creating the state of Pakistan for the Muslims. As a result, an interim government was formed, under Pandit Nehru, in September 1946. But the rising level of violence between the Hindus and the Muslims threatened its continued existence and led to the Mountbatten Plan for the partition of India in May/June 1947, which anticipated a vote that might result in the formation of the Dominion of Pakistan, which would be largely formed out of the partition of the Punjab, Bengal and the Dominion of India. This plan was reluctantly accepted by Pandit Nehru and the Indian Congress in June 1947, although it still strove for full independence for a united India. However, continued violence provoked the Viceroy of India, Lord Mountbatten, to bring forward the withdrawal of British troops from India to 15 August 1947 – the day on which the Indian Congress finally agreed that India and Pakistan would formally become independent states and full members of the Commonwealth. The occasion was marred by widespread bloodshed and it is estimated that up to half a million people lost their lives in violence during the period when Muslims and Hindus moved from their minority to their majority areas.

Dutt and the CPGB EC introduced a draft resolution for the EC of the CPGB criticising the Mountbatten Plan for India, indicating that a 'statement was to be circulated to the press and fuller details given in next month's *Labour Monthly*, on 14 June 1947. However, the *India Newsletter* printed the CPGB statement soon afterwards, on 17 June.[155] This argued that the Mountbatten Plan provided no final solution to India's problems and indicated that the CPGB maintained its support 'for the full independence of a united India' to be achieved through the self-determination of the many different nationalities in India. Nevertheless, the CPGB declared itself willing to work with the new Dominion governments of India but – like the Communist Party in India, the All-India Trades Union Congress (AITUC), the All-India Peasant Association and the Indian Congress – would continue to seek the unity of India. It also seriously doubted the economic viability of the partition, suggesting that Pakistan would have the main agricultural resources of the old India whilst the Hindu section, in the new India, would have most of the industrial resources.

The CPI was at this very moment, from 10 to 20 June, holding a special congress which declared its opposition to the Mountbatten Plan because it did not give India real independence and might force the impoverished Pakistan to become attached to Anglo-American finance to survive.[156] By and large, then, the CPGB was following closely the events in India, and agreeing with the actions of the CPI.

On 15 August 1947, Indian Independence Day, the CPGB produced an Independence Issue of the *India Newsletter*. It reported upon the continuing riots and disturbances in Lahore and Calcutta and noted that Jinnah, the new Governor-General of Pakistan, had arrived in his new capital of Karachi and that thousands of Muslims had migrated to the Sind and other areas in Pakistan. Subsequent issues reported on the continuing riots and problems with the new constitution of India. Increasingly, the CPGB became more critical of the new Indian state and reported that 'The Mountbatten Award has given India a false independence' and suggested that the Indian bourgeoisie was collaborating with capitalist and imperialist forces and beginning to suppress the working classes.[157]

The EC report for the Twentieth Congress of the CPGB Party Congress, on 10 April 1948, complained of the arrest of Indian working-class leaders, including Comrade Mirajkar, President of the AI [All India] TUC and Comrade Dange, the actions against the Communist Party in several provinces, the banning of newspapers and the wave of repression by the Government of India and Provincial Governments against the Indian working class.[158] It very quickly came to accept the view that the Indian bourgeoisie, Gandhi, Nehru and others had sold out to Anglo-American capitalism and that the only real hope for India was for the CPI to organise the working class as a tool for revolutionary change and for the CPI to give the lead to peasant revolts: there had been 2,057 peasant risings and outbreaks in the United Provinces of India in the first half of 1949.[159]

Communist activity throughout the British Empire/Commonwealth did little to widen the popularity of the CPGB. The Party faced public hostility after attacking the British Government's action in dealing with the Malayan guerrilla war crisis of the early 1950s and there was significant Party criticism of the way in which the government dealt with independence movements in Kenya, Guyana and Cyprus in the early 1950s. The CPGB's constant demand for colonial independence carried little weight with a British public which believed that the CPGB was still subject to the authority of the Soviet Union. Such hostility to the CPGB's position was fuelled further by the anti-Soviet revolt in Berlin in June 1953.

The PC of the CPGB reflected on the problem of foreign policy on 2 February 1956 in a statement written by William Gallacher entitled 'The Problem of Leadership':

> In 1945 there was a terrific surge of feeling against the old order. This expressed itself in the return of a great Labour majority with a mandate to lead the country along the way towards Socialism. The Tories were despondent. It looked bad for them and for their class. But by 1946 Bevin made it clear that the Labour Government was continuing the foreign policy of its predecessor, the policy enunciated by Churchill at Missouri. From that time on there was a steady deterioration in the Labour movement. The Labour Government was tied to the Americans, and had at the command of the latter, to engage in a great rearmament programme. This with the dollar payments insisted upon by the Americans, brought on the economic crisis of 1947 on top of the general crisis of capitalism. Unable, through the desertion of socialist policy, to solve the crisis in the interests of the workers, the way was left open for the revival of Toryism.
>
> This has now led to a situation where the capitalist class, with a Tory Government in power, is making an all-out offensive against the working class, in a desperate effort to find a solution at the expense of the workers. [This then goes on to explain the deepening of crisis in Empire and attacks the bureaucratic leadership of the Labour Party.]
>
> [...]This bureaucratic leadership has succeeded to a considerable extent, by bans and proscriptions, to isolate the Party from the general labour movement.[160]

To end this isolation, Gallacher advocated that the CPGB should press away at the trade unions and press forward with the slogan 'Save Labour for Socialism'.

The EC Report connected with the EC Resolution on 13 July 1956, which deals with the impact of Krushchev's attack upon Stalin, contained a reference to the imperialist policy of the Party in its discussion of changes in *The British Road to Socialism*:

> Third, in the light of the enormous advances of the colonial liberation movement since the end of the war, the character of British imperialist policy towards colonial peoples, and the need to develop the joint struggle of the British and colonial peoples, we can and should expand the section of the programme which deals with these issues.
> Very many questions in relation to the fight for national independence are now emerging, partially as a result of the Socialist System and its ability to help former colonial peoples and maintain their independence from imperialism. Our progress will need to reflect these changes.[161]

The Cold War isolated the CPGB and threw it into conflict with the post-war Labour and Conservative governments. Not surprisingly the CPGB was supportive of a Peace Campaign and favoured the end of the Cold War. The events of 1956 ensured that such hopes proved fruitless.[162]

The Twentieth Congress of the Communist Party of the Soviet Union, inner party democracy, *The Reasoner* debate and the Soviet invasion of Hungary

During the inter-war years there were always some significant defections by leading members of the Party as well as the rank and file in frustration at the policies and actions of the CPGB. One of the most prominent post-war defectors was Harry McShane, a prominent member of the Party from 1922, who left the Party at the end of July 1953. The defection was widely reported and McShane's criticism of the Party was published in the press. His main criticism of the Party was that, after Earl Browder's decision to liquidate the Communist Party of the United States in 1945 the CPGB started on the same route with bureaucratic developments: 'The factory organizations were closed down and an appeal was made for national unity.'[163] He felt that the Labour Party's general election victory of 1945 had taken the CPGB leadership by surprise, that it had had to adjust its position in regard to this victory and that the leadership had tightened its grip on the Party and made it almost impossible to challenge their control. This last factor had created the climate which encouraged him to depart once conflict between the Party leadership and some of the leading members of the CPGB in Glasgow began. He was later to form his own Trotskyite group. It was this type of local conflict and the domination by the leadership, to the exclusion of significant criticism, that provided the backcloth to *The Reasoner* debate and the tremendously damaging defections of 1956.

The British Road to Socialism, despite selling more than 200,000 copies between 1951 and 1956, had not revived the Party fortunes. At the 1956 Party Congress, Pollitt kept alive the hope that the Party would be more than a 'ginger group' but he resigned in May 1956 in favour of John Gollan. The Stalinist ideas he had supported all his life had been challenged by Krushchev at the Twentieth Congress of the CPSU in February 1956; Krushchev's secret speech was released for public consumption in the West by the US State Department in early June 1956 and was published in Britain by the *Observer* soon afterwards.[164] According to Harry Evans, a journalist in whom Pollitt often confided, this attack was the final straw: 'For Harry thought it despicable to kick the corpse of Stalin' and 'Harry found that he was too old to go in to reverse and denigrate the man who he had admired above all others for more than a quarter of a century.'[165] Pollitt was at the Twentieth Congress of the CPSU but was not present at the secret session on 25 February 1956 when Nikita Krushchev provided the damning indictment of Stalin's tyranny. Pollitt reflected that 'I was being conducted around a French-letter factory. At my age, I suppose it was a compliment.'[166] Nevertheless, he was soon aware of the discussion surrounding the 'cult of personality' which Krushchev had attacked and this led to some discussion within the Party even if the precise speech was not yet released. Indeed, the execution of Laurenti Beria, the acolyte and security chief of Stalin shortly after Stalin's death in March 1953 suggested that change was afoot. Also, in 1955, Krushchev and Bulganin had journeyed to Belgrade and repudiated publicly all the Cominform charges against Tito, the Cominform being wound up a year later. Changes were afoot in international communism, although it was some time before their impact came to be accepted by the CPGB.

At first, Pollitt was reluctant to report the details of Krushchev's criticism of Stalin in the *Daily Worker* and, when a letter debate developed on the matter, J. R. Campbell, the editor, refused to publish any more letters on the matter on 12 March 1956. On 17 March, Laslo Rajk, chief victim of the 1949 purge trial in Hungary, was officially rehabilitated, although the CPGB made little of this development at its Twenty-Fourth Congress in March 1956. However, new, younger members, were beginning to voice their concerns about Party democracy, and would not be deflected by Pollitt's constant assertion that the CPGB should not be afraid to proclaim that it had exercised democratic rights. Harry Evans noted that the younger members of the Party sneered at Pollitt's work and it is clear that his pugnacious response – 'if you have got a headache you should take an aspirin' did little to endear him to them.[167] Soon after the Congress, Pollitt offered his resignation as general secretary on 9 May, ostensibly on grounds of ill-health, but remained an active member of the Party until his death on 27 June 1960.[168]

Nevertheless, the EC of the Party drafted out a long resolution on 12–13 May 1956 to prepare the Party members for the change and in order to clarify the situation. It reported that 'within the framework of colossal Soviet advances' grave abuses had developed between 1934 and 1953 and were 'connected with the cult of the individual and lack of collective leadership'.[169] It stressed that the Party had been belittled by this, that socialist law had been broken, but was gratified that these abuses, that were alien to socialism, had been 'laid bare by the present leaders of the CPSU'. It admitted some errors in the defence of the Soviet Union. In a statement that suggested a response to criticism in the Party it was maintained that:

> We recognise, and stated at our 23rd Congress in 1954, that it is incorrect to try in any way to impose on our Party in Britain the attitudes take up on scientific and cultural matters by our Soviet comrades, though we shall continue to make

them known and recognise them as an important contribution to the development of Marxist thought.

We have always been a responsible and independent British political Party developing our own policy and activities in the light of our knowledge and estimate of the situation.

At the same time, we stand , and stand, for fraternal solidarity between all Communist parties.[170]

In response to the actions of the leadership of the CPSU, it suggested that there was wide discussion going on in the Party to move along *The British Road to Socialism*, and some pride that 'Ours was the first Communist Party outside the socialist countries to put forward a programme of peaceful transition to socialism through the establishment of a broad popular alliance, election of a People's Government, transformation of Parliament and the State.'[171] It therefore set itself the task of maintaining and extending democratic liberties and of increasing the membership of the Party to 50,000 members and to raise the membership of the YCL to 5,000.

The irony of this statement is that the EC meeting of 14–15 May 1956 was already taking disciplinary actions against Edward Thompson and John Saville who were going beyond the restrictive bonds of democratic centralism to open up discussions within the Party.[172] Indeed, 'The Executive Committee took note of the publication and circulation of a duplicated journal addressed to Party members by Comrade Edward Thompson and John Saville of..., and asked the Yorkshire District Secretariat to discuss the questions with these comrades and to report back to the Executive Committee in September.'[173] The early rumblings of *The Reasoner* debate were beginning.

In June, the CPGB gained some clarification of the developments in the Soviet Union when Harry Pollitt, John Gollan and Bert Ramelson met Stalin and the subsequent events saw discussion about the need to update *The British Road to Socialism* and a discussion of the CPSU 30 June paper 'On Overcoming the Cult of the Individual and its Consequences', by the EC of the CPGB on 13 July.[174] The EC of the CPGB indeed, began to emphasise that 'Socialism Britain was different from the Soviet Road' and took pride in the fact that 'we were amongst the first Communist Parties to show considerably the new possibilities of advancing to socialism in the specific conditions of our country', alongside a range of other policies connected with the demand for peace and the challenge to imperialism. In a draft report to discuss changes to *The British Road to Socialism*, including the idea that the Labour Party would be won over to scientific socialism by conviction rather than force and a re-affirmation of the principle of democratic centralism with its emphasis upon the election of all leading party committee, it stressed on the acceptance of the decision of the majority and the acceptance of the decisions of the higher Party organisation by the lower Party organisations.

It was the operation of democratic centralism that was the basis of the subsequent debate concerning *The Reasoner*. At this point, however, the draft report to the EC of the CPGB was attempting to debunk the notion that democratic centralism was only necessary in war-time situations or when communism was operating in a semi-legal or illegal position and that Stalinism proved that it did not work. Its argument was that there were faults but that in the Soviet Union democratic centralism had not been given a chance to work since Stalin emphasised centralism at the expense of democracy.

The slowness and reluctance of the CPGB leadership to respond to the criticism of Stalin and the more critical stance of international communism created tensions within the Party at this time and produced several organised opposition groups. One of the most important was that which gathered around Edward P. Thompson and John Saville and *The Reasoner*, in July 1956.

Thompson, a lecturer in Extra-Mural Education at Leeds at this stage, had been in conflict with the Party Leadership, in numerous letters throughout 1956, because of its reluctance to allow a work school on Marxism to freely examine the history of the British working class alongside those of France during the Revolution.[175] The whole purpose of Thompson's letters was to attack the old style of CPGB operation where democratic centralism – freedom of discussion, unity of action – meant the endorsement of the views of the CPGB leadership and stifled opposition. Thompson praised Khrushchev's 'different roads to socialism' approach and asked 'Why is the *Daily Worker* the bleakest and the least inspired paper in Labour History?'[176] He was particularly critical of the Party leadership, stressing that 'I think the leadership of our Party is opportunist and lacking in socialist principle: de-classed, remote from the working class, and even from the rank-and-file of the Party; contemptuous of theory.'[177] Thompson was attempting to provoke the Party leadership, admitting to Klugmann that 'I have written letters to you containing deliberately provocative statements but have received neither reply or comment upon them.'[178] That was not entirely true for just prior to this letter Klugmann had written to Thompson that 'You seem to be rather cross with King Street [the headquarters of the CPGB], and take it for granted that all Communist officials are a bit dim, dull, dusty and doctrinaire.'[179] Thompson was indeed rather cross with King Street and, in a letter to Bert Ramelson, of the Yorkshire District Committee and the EC, complained of a lack of self-criticism within the Party, reflecting that 'All I can say is, thank God there is no chance of the EC ever having power in Britain; it would destroy in a month every liberty of thought, concern and expression, which it has taken the British people over 300 odd years to win.'[180] It was just after this letter that Thompson's article submitted to *World News and Views*, 'Winter Wheat in Omsk', was reduced from 1,700 words to 1,000 words in a process which he regarded as censorship.[181] Indeed it was so since the article was passed on to the PC which discussed it on 7 June 1956 and objected to Thompson's statement that:

> Comrade John Saville, in a recent letter, referred to the weakening tradition of controversy in the Party in recent years. This is true. How often has the routine of the unanimous vote, the common front against the class enemy, the search 'for the correct formulation', inhibited the development of sharp controversy.
>
> Year after year the Monolith, from its cave inside *For a Lasting Peace, For a People's Democracy*, has droned on in a dogmatic monotone, without individual variation, without moral inflexion, without native dialect.
>
> 'We do not see' (wrote Milton), 'what while we still affect by all means a rigid external formality, we may soon fall... into a gross conforming stupidity, a stark and dead congealment of wood and hay and stubble, forced and frozen together.'[182]

Thompson asked that the Party adopt argument, debate and polemic in order to bring about a rebirth of controversy in place of dogma and opportunism; to take up the tradition of Lilburne, Winstanley, Cobbett, Oastler, Ernest Jones and the Chartists, and to remember that 'the propaganda of Morris and of the early ILP was imbued with a passionate moral protest against capitalism. Tom Mann illustrated his thundering speeches with passages from the Sermon on the Mount'. His point was that such a view was not moral guff. However, neither the editor of *World News and Views* nor the CPGB leadership warmed to the article and conflict proved inevitable.

Saville and Thompson began their broader campaign against the blocking of discussion within the Party by issuing their own journal, *The Reasoner*, in July 1956. It was to be 'A Journal of Discussion' and was headed by a quote from Marx: 'To leave error unrefuted is to encourage intellectual immorality.' The first editorial declared that there was deep disagreement over the meaning of 'Marxism'. The purpose of the journal was to 'perform a practical service in loosening up the constricted forms within which discussion between Communists has taken place in recent years'. It wished to get rid of the Party's procedures which, it felt, had limited sharp criticism and had prevented the development of new ideas and the development of theory.[183]

The first issue of *The Reasoner* also contained an article by Ken Alexander which suggested that democratic centralism, the basis of the CPGB's organisation, should be replaced by the 'concept of democratic control and initiative'. It attacked the development of the CPGB as a bureaucratic centralist organisation that, it claimed, paid little more than lip-service to consultation throughout the Party.

The Party responded by suggesting that the rules of democratic centralism was encapsulated in the Party's constitution and its slogan was 'freedom of discussion, unity of action', although it took no immediate action against the dissidents. In response, both Thompson and Saville suggested that there were no such rules. However, they were called to attend an EC meeting on 8–9 September, when they were told to cease publishing *The Reasoner*, the second copy of which had been published on 7 September. The EC reported that both comrades refused to 'not to produce any further issues of *The Reasoner*'.[184] In appealing to Thompson and Saville the EC pointed to the admittance of the abuses of the past and the decision to appoint a commission to appoint Inner Party Democracy.[185] However, both Saville and Thompson decided that 'As soon as we left we both decided the right course would be to resign and carry on the journal.'[186] After that they intended to cease publication, return to the Party and fight within it for change.

In August 1956, at the very time *The Reasoner* debate was occurring, the PC of the CPGB was considering the 'Report on Working Class Unity', produced by Monty Johnstone, which called for unity of action between the Labour Party and the CPGB and declared that the:

> Party is willing to enter into discussion with any section of the Labour, trade union, co-operative and progressive movement to work out a common programme and the ways and means of developing struggle to defeat the Tory offensive and compel the Government to resign.[187]

However, this was merely a reiteration of the message that had gone on for many years, there was nothing new in this demand spurred on by the changed international situation of communism and, above all, there was not the slightest chance that the Labour Party would respond positively. The CPGB was not responding quickly enough for Party dissidents and the situation worsened when armed rebellions against Stalinist rule in Hungary began at the end of October 1956. This saw the suppression of the rebellion by Soviet military forces at the beginning of November and the whole atmosphere against change in the Party hardened.

The third issue of *The Reasoner* appeared on 4 November 1956 and, in an article on 'The Smoke of Budapest', which began with the statement that 'STALINISM has sown the wind, and now the whirlwind centres on Hungary', Thompson demanded that the CPGB leadership publicly condemn the Soviet action. The editorial made much the same point, comparing the Soviet invasion with the recent cynical imperialism of Britain in Egypt and concluding that the working people and students of Budapest 'were demonstrating against an oppressive machine which gave them no adequate democratic channels for expressing the popular will'. For this demand, and their statement that the Party declare its solidarity for the Polish people similarly threatened with Soviet invasion, Thompson and Saville were suspended from the Party for three months. But they then concluded that the Party was unreformable and resigned on 14 November 1956.[188] In a letter to Howard Hill (a member of the EC of the Party), dated 9 November 1956, Thompson had already admitted 'this Hungary is the last straw' and said that he could not see how he could 'stay within the party beyond the coming weekend' if the EC did not change its position. He hoped that a Yorkshire group of dissident Communists would keep together for 'scores of people are leaving already; if the Party cannot be changed from the inside it will have to be changed from the outside'.[189]

The Reasoner debate was further discussed by the EC on 10 and 11 November 1956 when it was noted that the third issue of *The Reasoner* had been published.[190] By this stage the Party was deeply worried by both *The Reasoner* debate and the situation in Hungary, although Party records suggest that two-thirds of branches supported the EC over the events.[191] The West Yorkshire District, firmly under the control of Bert Ramelson, condemned the publication of *The Reasoner*, and many others did the same in the collection of resolutions, presented by the EC on 15 December 1956.[192] Nevertheless, the Writers' Group, in a letter with 13 signatures attached, attacked the EC's handling of the dispute : 'EC prepared to resist uprooting of the last vestiges of Stalinism – prefers journalistic discussion or discipline – against full discussion and free publication.'[193] Not surprisingly, since Thompson lived in Halifax, the Halifax branch 'wholeheartedly supported' the publication of *The Reasoner*.[194] Indeed, five members of the Halifax Branch of the CPGB resigned from the Party immediately after Thompson.[195]

There is an interesting postscript to this debate in the fact that at the beginning of 1957 the PC discussed a report on 'Some Thought About Intellectuals', probably written by John Gollan, which stated 'I think middle-class intellectuals who join the Communist Party and continue to live the lives of middle-class intellectuals are bound to create certain problems both for the Party and themselves, ...' There then followed a diatribe on how intellectuals were often out of touch with reality and putting themselves at the head of a petty bourgeoisie attempt to take over the Party.[196]

This was one way of saying that the Party would not change and the events in Hungary endorsed this stand.[197]

The Hungarian rising occurred against the background of the general strike developing in Poland during the summer of 1956. Soviet intervention in Poland was only narrowly averted in October 1956 but when Hungary rebelled against Stalinist rule in favour of 'communism with a human face' and a 'degree of national sovereignty', the Soviet army was sent in to crush the revolution. Soviet troops were called in on the night of 23 October only to be withdrawn on 30 October as sections defected to the revolution. These were replaced by troops from Siberia who believed that they had been sent to Berlin to fight German fascism and, whose second invasion on 4 November crushed the Hungarian rising at a cost of over 20,000 casualties.

The *Daily Worker* agreed that the Hungarian rebellion had a popular basis but ignored the reports of one of its own reporters of the deep-seated rank-and-file nature of the revolt and argued, instead, that it was inspired by the United States. John Gollan, who had replaced Pollitt as general secretary, reflected that 'there is the greatest danger that reaction can obtain victory in Hungary'.[198] The Party was clearly closing ranks behind the Soviet Union.

A special EC meeting on 3 November 1956 supported the Soviet intervention. Gollan referred to the 'cult of the individual' but argued that the Hungarian revolution was the product of reactionary forces and pre-war Hungarian fascism. George Matthews, the assistant general secretary of the Party, argued that there was little dissent against the Soviet intervention within the Party. Yet Howard Hill opposed the use of the Red Army in Hungary and felt that 'its threatened use in Poland [is] a violation of Socialist principles', claiming that the majority of the members present at the meeting were also opposed to the Political Committee's support for the Soviet Union.[199] Brian Behan also expressed the personal view that the Soviet troops should not have been sent in and should withdraw quickly.[200] Peter Kerrigan, Industrial Organiser of the Party at the time, also supported the dissident line. Nevertheless, the hand-written notes on the meeting favoured Gollan's view that the majority of the meeting supported the Soviet Union and was concerned at the way in which the Twentieth Congress of the CPSU had been handled. Arnold Kettle, Phil Piratin, Idris Cox, and many others, did not object to the use of Soviet troops, although some members felt that their use in Hungary was a blunder.[201] As Idris Cox suggested, 'What is at stake is the whole future of Socialism in this country' and James Klugmann paid tribute to Party for giving one 'of the finest demonstrations of loyalty... that has ever taken place'.[202]

Brian Behan, who was later active in the SLL, was less enamoured of this stance when he wrote of it many years later. At the EC Meeting of 3 November he moved a resolution demanding the withdrawal of Soviet troops. The vote was defeated by 33:1 and 'so we missed yet another opportunity and broke the hearts of devoted comrades'.[203]

Despite the differences of opinion in this meeting, the draft resolution that emerged from the meeting kept both sides happy, endorsing the Soviet invasion but also claiming that the newly formed Nagy Government of Hungary had been responsible for 'mistakes and wrong practices utterly contrary to Socialist and

Communist principles'. The Party declared that it was uncertain whether or not the Hungarian Government should have called in the Soviet troops but felt that 'the Soviet Union was absolutely correct to respond to the call when it was made'. However, it should be remembered that the short-lived Nagy Government of 29 October–4 November had never called in the Soviet troops and, instead, on 2 November it had renounced the Warsaw Pact treaty and appealed to the United Nations for support against Soviet intervention. Krushchev had sent in the Soviet Army following the failure of the Nagy Government to bring an end to the uprising by peaceful means.[204] Such details were ignored by, or unknown to, the Party's EC which diverted attention to the British Conservative Government's recent invasion to secure the Suez Canal.[205]

The PC of the Party was also determined to keep the CPGB behind the Soviet Union and one member, probably Ramelson, stated that 'those open to conviction have in the main tended to stiffen up. But some will go out. But also some v[ery] good have been sh[a]ken to the core'.[206] M. Bennett also suggested, rather accurately as it turned out, that there was 70 per cent rather than 90 per cent support for the EC's position. At a meeting on 15 November, J. R. Campbell felt that the Party should not pin too much faith on the Janos Kadar Government that had by then taken power in Hungary.[207] Not surprisingly, Gollan lamented that 'It is certainly no easy job to be in the leadership of the Communist Party during these days'.[208]

The Hungarian tragedy, along with *The Reasoner* debate, led to the loss of about 7,000 members between 1956 and 1957, including academics, such as Saville and Thompson, and trade unionists, such as John Horner, general secretary of the Fire Brigades' Union, and Alex Moffat, of the Scottish National Union of Mineworkers executive. Although Moffat later returned, he wrote to Gollan indicating that he was 'no longer convinced that a party of our type is a necessary condition to achieve socialism here' and that 'I have had doubts over the past six months and Hungary was the culmination'.[209] In addition, more than a third of the staff of the *Daily Worker* resigned because of the Party line on the Hungarian revolution.

There was clearly widespread disillusionment within the CPGB. The University of Sheffield branch voted 7:3 against the EC's statement and there had been numerous other protests in the seventy or so meetings recorded on the matter.[210] A letter from the Manchester University graduate branch of the CPGB also included a resolution passed on 5 November 1956 which suggested that 'In placing sole reliance on Moscow's report...the CPGB is opening itself to complete and irredeemable isolation' and called for the reversal of the Party line.[211] There was also a spate of resolutions from many branches and many members left their local branches in protest. Indeed, A. A. Willis, secretary of the East and West Riding area of the ETU, resigned from the Bradford branch of the CPGB along with a dozen others, since:

> I could no longer accept the Communist road to Socialism, or the operation of Socialism under Communist administration. I have come to the conclusion that Communism is not the dictatorship of the proletariat but the dictatorship of a well-organized and well-disciplined minority imposing its will upon the majority.[212]

The defensive reaction of the Party led to the invoking of democratic centralism and attempts to repair the damage. Inner Party discussions soon revealed that the EC held a clear majority of support for its stand on Hungary. In 188 branch meetings where votes were held, 2,095 members voted the EC position, with 745 against and 301 abstainers. Area aggregate meetings returned votes of 1,029 for, 295 against and 80 abstentions. This overwhelming support for the Party was also reflected in the actions of the promised Commission on Inner Party Democracy which took no evidence and focused upon general principles rather than the reality of the situation – although it accepted, and distributed, 109 communications; 59 from Party organisations, 45 from individuals. Betty Reid of the Central Organisation Department acted as secretary and John Mahon, a member of the London District and of the PC, was chairman. Malcolm MacEwan, who has been appointed whilst Features Editor of the *Daily Worker*, from which he had then resigned, later wrote that Mahon 'did not see his role as leading an investigation: he saw it as securing the defeat of the "revisionists" who were critics of democratic centralism'.[213]

Christopher Hill and Peter Cadogan, two other dissidents on the commission, were also critical of the way in which the Party had previously been induced to follow the Cominform line by criticising Tito and Yugoslavia, and the way in which the British Communist press had been controlled since the Twentieth Congress of the CPSU. With Malcolm MacEwan, they challenged the CPGB's tight control of the ten members who were committed to democratic centralism and the two 'neutral' members, Kevin Halpin, factory branch secretary of the CPGB, and Joe Cheek, a London teacher and Branch Membership Organiser in the Party.[214] Outnumbered, however, the three dissidents wrote a minority report which challenged the majority report's belief in democratic centralism. The minority report, written mainly by MacEwan, accused the Commission of not discharging the duty which it had been set and believed that it was foolish to compel members to fight for policies in which they had no confidence. They complained that the Commission, which sat between 11 September 1956 and 6 December 1956, had not had long enough to discuss the issues properly, that the Commission's majority report insisted 'on the rigid application of theory of centralism that would continue to stifle the growth of democracy within the Party', complained of the 'panel' or recommended list system for selecting Party representatives which amounted to selection rather than election, and complained that the emphasis upon strong central leadership in the Party was inimical to the development of 'strong Party branches'.[215]

Nevertheless, as was expected, 'The Report to the Executive Committee of the Communist Party on Inner Party Democracy' endorsed the majority report but stated that:

> We consider that our Party should now correct what we believe to have been a serious error – too general an emphasis on centralism and an insufficient emphasis on democracy. The tendency to consider a strong centralised leadership as sufficient has resulted in not enough being done to bring the membership into the discussion of Party problems and in failure to take sufficient practical measures to build strong Party branches.[216]

Although the political fall-out of the Hungarian revolution, *The Reasoner* debate and the Commission on Inner Party Democracy shaped the future thinking and actions of the Party, and will figure in the next chapter, it is clear that the Party was not going to respond to the challenge of change. This was evident at the 'Special' Twenty-Fifth Congress of the CPGB held on Easter 1957, when the dissidents were defeated. Gollan reiterated the claims that the Hungarian reactionaries were responsible for the Hungarian revolution, condemned the 'cult of personality' and condemned the dissidents. Congress, in turn, endorsed the majority report of the commission by a vote in favour of over 20:1. There was to be no change of direction as a result of Hungary.

Conclusion

The history of the CPGB between the Second World War and 1956 was one of a steady decline in membership and influence. The CPGB sought to stave of the continuing decline of its membership and to extend Party influence through the Labour Party, trade unions, women's movement, the YCL and the introduction of *The British Road to Socialism*. But faced with Labour's success in the 1945 general election, the emergence of the Cold War and the challenge from Trotskyite organisations, it was unable to reverse its decline. In truth it was too closely wedded to the Soviet Union and when it was given the chance to become less rigid in its policies, following the attack upon Stalin at the Twentieth Congress of the CPSU in 1956, it missed the opportunity to become more democratic and less bureaucratic in the events surrounding *The Reasoner* debate. The Hungarian revolution merely emphasised that the CPGB was unthinkingly wedded to the Soviet Union by its almost absolute trust in the decisions made by Moscow. Local deviation counted for little in this context.

2 The emergence of the Broad Left 1957–70

Despite losing members as a result of the events of 1956, and failing to link up with the Bevanites in the Labour Party, the CPGB did reverse the decline, albeit temporarily, in the early 1960s. This occurred as it moved towards attempting to create an alliance of the Broad Left. However, from 1964 onwards the CPGB lost members constantly until it expired in 1991. Indeed, for most of the 1960s it was faced by two serious challenges which it never fully came to terms with. First, it had to deal with its industrial and trade union policy which was debased by the serious charges of ballot rigging in the early 1960s and by the constant failure to develop factory groups. Second, it was also faced with a serious challenge from the numerous Trotskyite organisations which proliferated amongst the students of the newly expanded university sector in the 1960s, who looked increasingly to China, South America, or the international community for ideas, direction and leadership rather than the Soviet Union. These Trotskyite groups were hijacking a new generation of socialist/Marxist-inclined students and this led the CPGB to contemplate the need for an even less sectarian approach to its political work. This found expression in a development of the CPGB's Broad Left approach in political and economic work and even, despite the politics of the time, in its determined attempt to win the support of Labour supporters of the new Labour governments of 1964–70. However, the CPGB was never able to win the size of Broad Left support it craved and its problems were made intractable by the Soviet invasion of Czechoslovakia in 1968 which occurred at the height of student protest in Britain and throughout the world.

The expansion and division of Marxism in the late 1950s and early 1960s

The CPGB membership declined considerably in the wake of the Soviet invasion of Hungary, at least 7,000 members leaving in the autumn of 1956. As a result, the CPGB adopted a two-point approach to galvanising its position, first through its Commission on Inner Party Democracy and, second, through its attempts to broaden its alliance with the Left. The first strategy has already been examined and clearly demonstrated that the Party was tightening ranks rather than reforming. The Party also strengthened its links with Moscow, for John Gollan arranged for considerable sums of money, up to £100,000 a year on some occasions, to be obtained from Russia, usually via the Soviet Embassy, over the next 21 years, to finance the *Daily Worker* (*Morning Star* from 1966). John Gollan, Reuban Falber, the Party's assistant secretary, and David Ainley, a Party official, seemed to have been the only Party members to have known about this until it became public knowledge in 1991.[1] Consequently, the Moscow link was endorsed, although secretly, and the Party continued to stifle criticism of Soviet action by restricting the opportunities for democratic debate. Nevertheless, the falling membership of the Party forced it to attempt to broaden its appeal and links with other left-wing groups, which became a feature of its policies in the late 1950s and the 1960s. The 'Broad Left' approach was developing from the late 1950s and throughout the 1960s, before it was fully implemented in 1968.

Having once rejected the Campaign for Nuclear Disarmament (CND) as an unnecessary distraction, the Party suddenly decided to support this campaign from 1960 and also began to work with the Peace movements. Efforts were also made to establish other alliances, and this was helped by Krushchev's condemnation of Stalin in 1956. In this new climate, membership rose from 27,500 in 1961 to more than 34,000 in 1964. YCL membership also rose from just under 3,000 to nearly 4,700 between 1957 and 1963. By the early 1960s, the CPGB was beginning to enjoy greater popularity, although this eventually proved to be something of an 'Indian summer'.

A similar pattern of rising membership was evident in many of CPGB's districts. The Yorkshire District, for instance, normally had had 2,200 and 2,300 members in the early 1950s although it aimed to have 3,000 members by 1955, along with 300 members in the League of Youth, sales of 6,000 for the *Daily Worker* and 750 for *Challenge* (organ of the YCL).[2] However, its membership in 1955 was only 2,161 and that of the YCL a mere 170. In 1958, following the impact of the events of 1956, Yorkshire District membership was 1,765 and there were only 127 members in the YCL.[3] By that stage it was admitting that loss of trade union membership, in the AEU for instance, and the threat of Trotskyism were serious problems although it comforted itself that its sales of the *Daily Worker* were 75 at Grimethorpe, a pit village near Barnsley. However, in both 1959 and 1960 it was reporting some increase in membership and by 1962, it was back to about 2,200 members, a rise of more than 380 members in one year. By 1968 it had reached 2,602 members – about as high as the Yorkshire membership had ever reached in the 1950s. However, this success was secured as a result of enormous effort and was soon to decline in the wake of the Soviet invasion of Czechoslovakia. Thereafter, the Yorkshire District asked the question 'Why do we lose so many of our comrades?'. Its answer was 'Primarily because of our failure to integrate them into the Party.'[4] The other vital and obvious issues of policies and 1960s politics were ignored.

The Yorkshire District did, however, reflect the national attempt to broaden the Party. The Twelfth Congress of the York[shire] District [1968?] stated quite clearly that:

> We want the Labour Government to survive and win victories for the people. We will support any progressive measures or steps it takes. Any criticisms we will make will be to strengthen the Government and its standing with the people. The greatest service the Labour Movement can make to the Labour Government

is to exert sufficient influence to [compel the Labour government] to forsake the policies rooted in capitalist ideology.[5]

The official line was prevailing. At the same time, it was confidently predicting an expansion of support and influence, especially amongst the trade union movement where its support had declined in the 1960s. It reflected that:

In Yorkshire as in the whole of the country the Party's prestige was rising again and well on the way to being re-established to what it was before the impermissible ballot rigging and other crimes against the membership committed by Haxell & Co.[6]

Indeed, in Yorkshire there seem to have been successes amongst various unions such as Associated Society of Locomotive Engineers and Firemen (ASLEF), the National Union of Railwaymen (NUR) and National and Local Government Officers Association (NALGO).

Nevertheless, the CPGB had changed little, and the leaders of 1956–7 were still in charge. John Gollan remained general secretary, George Matthews continued to edit the *Daily Worker*, Peter Kerrigan was still in charge of the Party's industrial affairs, Rajani Palme Dutt still influenced national and international thinking through *Labour Monthly* and James Klugmann, effectively the Party archivist, edited the new theoretical journal *Marxism Today*. The Party also continued to practice the bureaucratic centralism of the past and continued to claim to be the sole defence of the working class: 'It moves together *with*, although it *leads*, the working class and the mass of the people.'[7]

Continuity and propaganda brought little significant improvement in the Party's membership and the immediate objective of winning 100,000 members, later reduced to 50,000, remained a pipe-dream, although membership levels, already mentioned, did recover to 34,000 by 1964. The Party fought election campaigns to raise its profile, sought to widen its trade union base and conducted educational work, publishing the translated Soviet work *Fundamentals of Marxism–Leninism*. The CPGB had limited success. It was unable to win a seat in the 1959 general election and appeared to have lost ground in its trade union activities.

Despite its evolving 'Broad Left' approach the CPGB was an increasingly isolated body, largely because it did not link up with many of the Labour groups such as the Bevanites in the 1950s, did not ally itself to those opposing the attempt of Hugh Gaitskell to remove Clause Four from the Labour Party constitution and because of its opposition to Labour in elections. In spite of the brief rise in membership in the early 1960s, its support was febrile. It did win some trade union support and Will Paynter became secretary of the NUM in 1959 but such influence became increasingly difficult to maintain.

It took about ten years for the CPGB to finalise its 'Broad Left' approach, which occurred at the Party's Congress in 1968. The CPGB had aimed to work with the Labour Left as far as possible. However, its record was not good. In 1964, despite stating that it would attempt to work with Labour, it contested all 32 divisions in the first Great London Council (GLC) elections and continued to contest municipal elections in opposition to Labour candidates. It did badly in the GLC elections and by the mid-1960s it had only 20 local councillors compared with over 200 in 1945. Yet, at the 1965 Congress, John Gollan, the general secretary of the Party, indicated that the CPGB was willing to work with non-communist forces, although the CPGB put forward 57 candidates against Labour in the 1966 general election. As a result, relations with the Labour Party, the Labour governments of the 1960s and the trade unions were relatively poor. Indeed the events surrounding the CPGB activities within the ETU undermined the 'Broad Left' work of the CPGB at the beginning of the 1960s.

The ETU affair of 1961, the Seamen's Strike of 1966 and CPGB Industrial Policy and factory branches

The CPGB had continued to win trade union support throughout the 1950s and 1960s, although its support did temporarily ebb away after the Soviet invasion of 1956, along with a decline in the numbers and activity of factory branches. It did win some trade union support and, as already noted, William Paynter became secretary of the NUM in 1959. Nevertheless, the Party never became involved in the attempt to staunch the decline of the coal industry in the 1960s, a decade which saw the number of miners fall from 600,000 to 280,000. The CPGB also controlled the Executive of the ETU in the late 1950s and early 1960s. However, the ballot-rigging fraud surrounding the election of a general secretary in 1959, which led to a court case and to CPGB condemnation of the ETU officials, ultimately seriously damaged the CPGB's industrial policy.

The ETU had been dominated by the Communist Party for some years but when Les Cannon resigned from the Party over Hungary, he was removed from his post at the ETU training college. At that moment, anti-communists in the union began to support John Byrne, the Glasgow District secretary, and they secured the election of his supporters, such as Frank Chapple. Their campaign led to an attack upon the Communist leadership, and particularly against Frank Foulkes, the president, and Frank Leslie Haxell, the general secretary. When Haxell defeated Byrne for the general secretary post in December 1959, by 19,611 to 18,577 votes, there were allegations of ballot-rigging and the misuse of postal votes and the arrival of extra ballot papers. Indeed, the court case revealed that whilst there were normally about 20 per cent of postal votes in the union elections, many area branches in London, such as Peckham with 153 out of 190, had a much higher proportion of postal votes.[8] There appeared to be one major question to be answered: How could a union with 240,000 members, only 2,000 of whom were communists, have returned Haxell? Haxell, of course, denied the implication of ballot-rigging to the court:

> I have never at any time knowingly supplied or caused to be supplied, ballot [papers] to a Branch Secretary in excess of the number he is entitled, nor have I at any time, supplied or caused to be supplied ballot papers to any person than a Branch Secretary.[9]

He also tended to emphasise that his support reflected his achievements as a trade union leader rather than as a communist.

The lawsuit initiated by Byrne and his supporters, which began in May 1961, was a substantial examination of the activities of 15 Communist members of the ETU. It included statements from CPGB and ETU members, such as John Norman Frazer and Leslie Haxell, which reflected upon how the CPGB organised advisory committees to enable it to control the ETU, which the CPGB denied, and many other charges of CPGB manipulation of union affairs. In particular, allegations were presented to the effect that the returns of some branches, which had voted on 14 and 15 December, were postmarked as 17 and 18 December and had been receipted at Head Office on 21 December, had been tampered with and new vote sheets had been posted. In one investigation of 13 branches, it appeared that Haxell had been favoured, for of one group of 13 branches who voted, the results of only the 7 branches, who voted by a majority for Haxell, were allowed to stand whilst the vote of 6 branches, who voted by a majority for Byrne, were disallowed.[10] The implication was that there may have been tampering with the posted forms by the 'biased' acceptance or rejection of ballot forms, actions in which Justice Winn felt that some of the defendants were implicated: 'The defendant Frazer is, in my judgement, no less likely than Mr. Haxell to have posted some of the envelopes.'[11]

After 38 days of court discussion, Justice Winn made a 35,000-word judgement in which he concluded that Haxell, and four other Communist members of the ETU, had 'conspired together to prevent by fraudulent and unlawful devices the election of the plaintiff Byrne in place of the defendant, Haxell'.[12] The Communist union officials were thus found guilty of conspiracy to prevent Byrne's election by disqualifying the vote of branches that supported Byrne and by stuffing ballot paper in others.[13] Justice Winn's judgement stated that:

> As an abstract proposition it appears that any Political Party, or other organised groups of persons sharing a common way of thinking might gain or exert control of such a body as a Trade Union, comprising a sufficient number of its supporters to be influential in other of two principal ways. It might appoint from amongst those supporters to whom, when summoned from time to time orders could be given; or it might entrust to one or a few of such supporters a degree of independent discretion in deciding how best themselves to organise the activity of other supporters in order to achieve the objects of the Party. In my judgement in 1959 the Communist Party of the United Kingdom controlled the E.T.U. by the latter method through the allegiance of Mr. Haxell and other Communists in the Union whom he directed.[14]

The presumption was that Haxell, since he was a communist, was bound to accept the orders of the CPGB, something which the CPGB always denied strongly. The court thus decided that Byrne should replace Haxell as secretary of the TUC. There was an appeal against Justice Winn's judgement on 31 July 1961, largely on the grounds that there had been no direct evidence to support Justice Winn's judgement that corruption had occurred and that he had rather assumed that members of the

CPGB would follow its instructions and misuse their powers in order to control the union. This was eventually rejected.

In the meantime, the TUC demanded that Foulkes, the president of the ETU, should re-submit himself for election. When he refused, the union was expelled from the TUC. But the communists on the ETU were soon routed; Byrne, Cannon and Chapple secured control of the union and sought, and gained, readmission to the TUC.

Throughout these events the Party supported the Communist defendants but after the verdict, it sought to distance itself from such corrupt leadership. Peter Kerrigan reported to the CPGB's 1963 Congress that:

> We have declared that the ballot rigging in the Electrical Trade Union was a complete violation of the principles on which Communists have worked for over forty years, and took place without our Party leadership being aware of it...
>
> The conduct of the election at the Head Office of the ETU gravely compromised our Party and all those progressive forces in the trade union movement who, for a number of years, defended the ETU against attacks of the Reactionaries. Our Party has taken steps to ensure that Communist Party members will never be again involved in such an affair.[15]

Nevertheless, the saga continued on 13 July 1964 when J. T. Byrne distributed to all branches of the ETU a list of Executive Council decisions of 12 July which suggested:

> That it is established to the satisfaction of the Executive Council that there has been outside interference by the Communist Party in the internal affairs of the Electrical Trades Union calculated to determine a substantial part of the agenda of the Rules Revision Conference.[16]

The EC of the ETU thus invalidated some of the rule changes and agreed upon those who were eligible to vote on the new clause to Rule 9, Clause 3, f that 'the member is not a member of the Communist Party'.

The fact is that, according to its own records, the CPGB had been attempting to mobilise support within the ETU to influence the rule changes going on within the ETU. However, it argued that it:

> seeks to influence the unions in a democratic way, convincing trade union members of the need for a progressive policy, so that they will carry that policy through delegate conference. In short we work to change the unions by changing the outlook of the union members, and by seeking election, alongside other progressives, to ensure that union policy is carried out as the members wish. In short we wish to change the unions by persuasion in the direction of militant struggle, whose ultimate aim is the capture of power by the workers and the achievement of socialism. That is the policy, which against all opposition we will continue to press forward.[17]

John Gollan, general secretary of the CPGB, also made it clear to the press that the ETU executive had never communicated with him regarding the charge of communist interference in the internal affairs of the ETU and objected to the 'Ban the Reds' campaign now being conducted by the new ETU EC and the *Daily Express*.[18] Despite the protestations of Gollan and the CPGB, the anti-communist measures were carried through and there was an exodus of ETU officials from the Party; the CPGB papers include a list of 15 ETU officials who had left the Party. It admitted that there might be others.[19]

The ETU affair brought home to the Party the reality that its trade union base was precarious even in unions where its members had a significant presence. From that time onwards, it began to recognise that it would have to share power with other progressive forces, a fact which was accepted at the Twenty-Eighth Congress of the Party in 1963. The Broad Left strategy was developing. This became even more evident in the Seamen's strike of 1966 which further undermined the influence of the CPGB and threw it into conflict with the Harold Wilson Labour governments of 1964–70.

The CPGB exerted some influence within the dockers' unions and amongst port workers in the 1940s and 1950s. Throughout the 1950s and 1960s they had also built up further support amongst the dockers and port workers. In 1966 the CPGB also took up the case of the seamen whose demands had already been achieved by many groups of workers throughout the country.

The dispute was anticipated on 2 May 1966 when a conference of the National Union of Seamen (NUS) endorsed strike action to achieve their demands for a 40-hour week while at sea and a £14 minimum wage. On 11 May, the NUS rejected the ship owners' counter offer plus the idea of an inquiry. Faced with a threatened strike Harold Wilson's Labour Government had to react. 'Harold said firmly that we had no choice: it was make or break for P[rices] and I[ncomes]', Barbara Castle noted on 12 May and the Cabinet had agreed.[20] On 13 May Hogarth and ten members of the NUS saw Harold Wilson and other representatives of the Labour Government but rejected the idea of an inquiry and, on 15 May, Wilson stressed to the NUS leaders that the government could not permit a wage increase which was outside the Prices and Incomes limits. From that moment the Labour Government was effectively endorsing the position of the employers against the NUS.

The strike began on the 16 May, quickly paralysed the docks and put pressure upon the pound. Wilson therefore declared a State of Emergency and announced the formation of a Court of Inquiry under Lord Pearson. He then talked to the nation on television and declared the strike to be against the interests of the state.

As the crisis deepened Wilson saw the seamen and the ship owners on 26 May and, on the 27 May, Ray Gunter, Minister of Labour, formally announced the formation of the Court of Inquiry. The seamen did not cooperate with the Court of Inquiry but issued an ultimatum on 30 May that it would block all shipping if its demands were not met. On 7 June it carried out that threat. On 8 June, the NUS rejected the Pearson Report (Court of Inquiry) which maintained that the differences between the seamen and the owners should be halved and that this arrangement would give seamen 4 per cent on the base standard and that this would allow them to earn up to £34 per week. The NUS replied by suggesting that such pay levels were based upon some improbable overtime earnings.

There then began a wave of meetings. The Finance and General Purposes Committee of the TUC met the NUS on 9 June and the ship owners met and accepted the Pearson report as a basis for negotiation on 10 June. On 14 June the TUC representatives met Wilson to offer him compromise terms, which Wilson rejected. Wilson then met Hogarth and nine other members of the NUS EC on 15 June in an attempt to use Pearson as a basis for settlement but were unable to get the NUS to negotiate.[21] At this point Hogarth is reported as saying that 'This is a fight with the Government not with the ship owners.'[22] However, faced with an increasing balance of payments crisis, Wilson made his 'Red Bogey' speech in the House of Commons on 20 June in which he stated:

> It is difficult for us to appreciate the pressures which are put on men I knew to be realistic and reasonable, not only in their executive capacity, but in highly organised strike committees in the individual ports, by this tightly knit group of politically motivated men, whom as the last General Election showed, utterly failed to secure acceptance of their views by the British electorate, but who are now determined to exercise back-stage pressures, forcing great hardship on the members of the union and their families, and endangering the security of the industry and the economic welfare of the nation.[23]

He added that:

> I believe they [the seamen] are losing public sympathy by the fact that some of them at least are showing blatantly that they are more concerned with harming the nation than getting justice (some Labour protests). I have seen on television leading members of the Seamen's Union saying this.

He continued:

> I am absolutely convinced, as he [Ray Gunter] is, that when the 48 members of the Executive left Downing Street on Friday afternoon, most of then knew what the score was, and that it would be better for industry and the seamen, to call off the strike. My doubt is – and this is not just a question of individual extremists – about how far they are their own masters in taking decisions of this sort.

When asked about outside pressures he stated:

> I do not say what I said without being very clear in my mind what was going on. It was not based on rumour or second-hand account. I am quite certain it would be better not to go further this afternoon. But when individual members of the Executive know what is happening, and when members of the union know what is happening, I think they will reconsider the matter in the light of what we have proposed.

It is clear that Wilson was attacking communist agitators without actually openly saying so. Equally it is clear that some of his fellow Cabinet ministers and his friends 'thought he had taken leave of his senses'.[24] 'The 'Red Bogey' issues were the final accusation in a dispute where 400 ship owners and the government were in a desperate struggle with the NUS.

The leaders of the NUS struck back against the 'Red Bogey' accusations. Joe Kenny, the Executive member of the NUS for Liverpool, stated that all the Executive members were probably Labour Party members or supporters. In addition, the seamen's leaders, and particularly Mr Hogarth, asked Mr Wilson to offer proof of the charges he was making in 'painting us with a Red Brush'. They also pointed out that the Pearson Interim Report had been used to give government blessing to the ship owners case and the government's own income policy.

Despite the limited extent of direct CPGB influence, it is clear that the CPGB gave support to the NUS from the start of the dispute in mid-May, noting their heroism during the Second World War, and adding: 'As for the Communist Party, it expresses its fullest solidarity with the seamen and confidently calls upon all its members to do all in their power to ensure full support for the seamen.'[25] The PC statement also added that 'Every trade unionist and the general public should note the open alliance of the shipowners, the press and the Labour Government against the seamen now on strike' and re-emphasised the right of seamen to the 40-hour week which many trade unionists had already achieved.[26]

On 23 May, James (Jimmy) Reid, Scottish secretary of the Party, reminded Party members that whilst the seamen were in the front line 'It is every worker's fight.'[27] Reid felt that the support of the strike was necessary especially since the previous Budget had raised the cost of living for the working classes and he discounted the government argument that well-paid workers were being selfish at the expense of their poorer brothers on the grounds that there was no mechanism to transmit the higher wages of some workers to the lower-income bracket.

After Wilson's House of Commons speech John Gollan, the general secretary of the CPGB, also suggested that 'Mr. Wilson's statement is an insult to the seamen and shames the Labour Party.' Bert Ramelson, the Yorkshire member of the CPGB EC and a barrister who had fought with the International Brigade in Spain and in the Second World War, noted that there was only one member of the EC of the NUS, a Mr Wilson, who was a communist.[28] John Gollan later added that 'The Communist Party had declared its position openly and clearly. It supports the seaman's struggle and their just demands... Tens of thousands of Labour Party [supporters] have done the same.'[29]

George Woodcock, the general secretary of the TUC, also noted that Wilson had not consulted the TUC before making his statement and added that 'the fact that the Communist Party had shown an interest in the strike is to me something to spend a lot of time not bothering about'.[30] The seamen also produced their own defence of their demands in a 30-page pamphlet written by Charles Hodgson and John Prescott, later Deputy Prime Minister in the three Blair Labour governments.

The week after Wilson's statement, he named names in the House of Commons but immediately after his second statement the dispute ended. Wilson felt this had led to a reaction against the outside pressure of the CPGB but in fact the strike was about to finish. Indeed, the strike was settled on 1 July and the government preserved its incomes policy, although this sparked a renewed attack on the incomes policy by the CPGB.

Needless to say other Marxist organisations, and particularly the Trotskyite groups focused upon the dispute, although their involvement was little more than lip-service. The Revolutionary Workers' Party (RWP), British Section of the Fourth International, was run by J. Posadas and published its views through its journal the *Red Flag*. Its main concern was to condemn the role of the TUC, the government's desire to 'gain a "victory" for the incomes policy' and the desire to turn the seamen's strike into organising a general strike.[31] The RWP saw the imminent collapse of world capitalism. It also criticised the CPGB for its lukewarm support of the strike and its 'pacifist co-existence' with capitalism, as evidenced in *The British Road to Socialism*, and suggested that there was a need for workers' power organised through trade unions. In the months before the seamen's strike *Red Flag* had been advocating the alliance of unofficial factory committees.

It was at the very moment of the Seamen's Strike that the CPGB turned its attention to stimulating, once again, its flagging factory branches which seem to have declined since their resurrection in the early 1950s probably as a result of the reaction to the events of 1956. At the National Factory Conference in Dundee, held on the 11–12 June 1966, 236 delegates from 62 factory branches and 12 delegates represented the EC of the CPGB, the Party and the *Morning Star* with John Gollan in the Chair in a meeting which was described as 'one of the most important conference the Party has held for years'.[32] The report of the conference added that:

> The Government attack on the seamen in the interest of the incomes policy, is a clear indication of the lengths to which it is prepared to go, and shows the need for decisive counteraction. The Government's continued support for the US war in Vietnam is arousing widespread anger and concern.

The conference further agreed that the factory branches would be decisive in generating mass action issues such as anti-trade union legislation, advocating war not peace and objecting to British support for the US action in Vietnam. It also encouraged the formation of 50 new factory branches and the strengthening of old ones, and stressed that it should not be seen as the undermining of local branches. At that time there were claims that there were 222 factory branches with 2,779 members, that is, approximately 8.5 per cent of the membership of the Party. By 1967 there were claims that there were 234 factory branches but only 213 were said to actually exist and 34 of these were not actually functioning. This meant that there were only 179 functioning factory branches. Many of these were deemed not to be functioning as effective political campaigning units.

The PC of the CPGB, meeting in February 1968, reflected upon this problem, noting the EC's statement of 1962 that:

> All our experience points to the fact that unless the whole Party is convinced of the initial importance of building up our membership and organisation in the factories, pits, depots and jobs, we will not succeed in noting the change the

situation demands, and winning the organised worker in the Trade Union, Coops, and Labour organisations for the line of our Party. We therefore put on the first objective of all our activities building our Party membership in the factories, increasing sales of the *Daily Worker* on the job, strengthening and improving all existing factory organisations, and creating new ones out of greatly increased activity.[33]

The PC also emphasised that there were few factory branches that did 'all-round activity'. Indeed, in 1968, matters were worsening and the number of factory branches had fallen to 155, the membership had declined to 2,576, and there may have been as many as 34 non-functioning branches. A note and detailed listing of factory branches, possibly for 1 January 1968, gives a detailed analysis of a problem and refers to the 'appalling state of the organisation; which saw members scattered around the transport industry, and other areas, in ones and twos.[34] There were 23 members in an effective and functioning factory branch at Rolls Royce in east Kilbride and one similarly effective and functioning in transport in a branch of 75 at Shardlows in Sheffield, where members were active in the trade unions and amongst shop stewards. But there were many that were not so well organised, such as the four or five who were not effectively organised at Hull docks and the six on Leeds buses and the three on Sheffield buses who had the most occasional of activity. In this climate of disorganisation the CPGB claim that the factory branch was 'giving the worker daily leadership' looks exaggerated.[35]

Communism and the Labour Government 1964–70: an attempt at political and economic action

The Seamen's Strike did provoke the Party into a more aggressive reaction against the new Labour Government's incomes policy. The 'lobby organising committee' which had existed among rank-and-file organisations, principally in London, during the 1960s held a meeting with the shop stewards' co-ordinating committee on Clydeside in September 1966 and decided to campaign through mass meetings and deputations. This was certainly a revival in the activity of the CPGB whose political profile had declined since the 1950s.

The Communist Party had, indeed, achieved little in parliamentary politics in the 1950s and 1960s. In the late 1950s the Party favoured the defeat of the Tory Government and the return of a Labour Government pledged to peace and social advance. But this did not work and the Party failed to win a parliamentary seat in 1959, and never won a parliamentary seat in any subsequent general election. At the 1965 Congress John Holman (President of the Congress) indicated that the CPGB was willing to work with non-Communist forces, although the Party stood 57 candidates against Labour at the 1966 general election – all of whom were defeated.

This failure in parliamentary politics was also to be seen in municipal politics where there was failure and humiliation. Lawrence Daly, a promising party activist in Scotland based in Ballingray, Fife, a member of the Scottish District Committee and secretary of a miners' trade union branch, announced his departure from the CPGB in March 1957. He then formed the Fife Socialist League as a new political party, argued that the CPGB was subservient to the CPSU and criticised the CPGB's failure to reform itself in the light of Krushchev's revelations about Stalin and the Hungarian rising. His organisation beat Communists in local union elections and won seats against sitting Communist councillors.[36]

In 1964, despite stating that it would work with Labour, it contested all 32 divisions in the first GLC elections and continued to contest the municipal elections in opposition. It performed badly. Elsewhere, municipal and local successes were equally slight. In Yorkshire there was a determined attempt to get electoral representation in the early 1960s. Sam Cairns and Bill Carr became councillors for Moorends on Thorne Rural Council, near Doncaster, in 1961 and both contested again in May 1964, although it is unclear whether or not they were returned. Bill Carr had also won 1,638 votes in the previous and recent West Riding County Council elections 'But the desertion of the usual Tory and Independent voters of "their own" candidates in favour of the Labour candidate, Councillor Kenny, there is no doubt that we would have had the first Communist Councillor on the West Riding County Council.'[37] The two councillors had campaigned for a vast expansion of social services and objected to the 'weak-kneed' policy of Labour on Thorne Rural Council, as well as for more houses at cheaper rents, better road and public transport, better facilities for the old, health centres and nursery schools. Such success was, however, small scale, often isolated and regionalised, with parts of the West Riding and Wales seeing local success.

Such success was, however, small scale, often regional, with only parts of Yorkshire and Wales, in the Rhondda Valley, achieving any significant success. Indeed, in the mid-1960s the Party had only about 20 local councillors compared with over 200 and more it had had in 1945.

Nevertheless, the events surrounding the Seamen's Strike in 1966 seemed, temporarily at least, to revive both the Party's industrial muscle and its political activity. The lobby organising committee and the shop stewards' co-ordinating committee on Clydeside formed, in 1967, the Liaison Committee for the Defence of Trade Unions (LCDTU) whose main task was to organise a major campaign against the wage freeze being imposed by the Labour Government. Thus the grass roots of the Party noted that 'the strike of municipal busmen due to start on August 12th is the clearest indication that the incomes policy is state interference with collective agreement'.[38]

The Party felt that any attempt at wage restraint would lead to a fall in workers' living standards. Although the Donovan Commission examining industrial relations did not want state wage restraint it wanted some voluntary restraint and therefore came in for a hostile reception from the CPGB, which conducted considerable agitation against government policies. In the Lancashire and Cheshire District of the CPGB it was noted that 'the fight against the Wage Freeze, Redundancy, legislation on Trade Unions against American Methods of Industry, etc., as well as support for Peace in Vietnam have all figured in the industrial action and activity of Trade Union, the Shop Steward and Rank and File movement'.[39]

Yet there was still a feeling that the Party still needed to be better organised in its industrial activities. The EC was concerned to improve its factory organisation and Kerrigan talked of the creation of 24 new factory branches.[40] The PC also raised the issue of factory branch life and produced a draft report in October 1968 to encourage greater participation, the broadening of the struggle and the raising of the profile of *The British Road to Socialism* since the 'overall situation in our factory branches is unsatisfactory' and 'the majority don't meet regularly, don't have a factory Branch Committee, don't have a place of work or a clear perception of their work'.[41]

Nevertheless, the Party did reasonably well out of the revolt against the wage freeze in the late 1960s and campaigned against Barbara Castle's White Paper *In Place of Strife* when it was published in 1969, since it proposed wage controls. However, ultimately the industrial policy of the Party was little more successful than its electoral policy. The Party now attempted to broaden its approach in order to gain a greater degree of support. However, it was faced with an enormous challenge from Trotskyite and dissenting communist organisations, even though it gained some kudos and influence from its opposition to the Vietnam War.

The Trotskyite challenge and the student revolt

From the late 1950s and throughout the 1960s the CPGB attempted to widen its appeal amongst left groups and within the expanding university student population. This was the beginning of the Broad Left approach which dominated the 1970s and with the student population rising rapidly – from 70,000 students of the pre-War years to 144,000 by 1954 and 300,000, 11 per cent of the age group, by the summer of 1968 – the opportunities for the CPGB to extend its influence and membership seemed good.[42] In particular, the student revolt protests in 1968, and over issues such as the Vietnam War, should, and would, have increased support for the CPGB had it not been for the proliferation of numerous small Trotskyite organisations.[43]

Rajani Palme Dutt, the CPGB writer and intellectual, had kept a watching brief on the developing Trotskyite organisations of the 1950s and 1960s. His first main concern in the late 1950s was, as suggested in the previous chapter, the emergence of the *Universities and Left Review*, which started in the spring of 1957, although it emerged from the Communist Club which resigned *en bloc* from the CPGB in November 1956, and which was in danger of being infiltrated by Trotskyites. Dutt reflected that it had published only three issues so far, although it had held a number of meetings in London and in the provinces. Apparently 'Organisationally it was a shambles', edited by four editors who were, or had been, at Oxford, and Dutt doubted that it would last the year. There was a club and there were other activities but the 'whole organisation is shadowy'. He likened the organisation to the Left Book Club activities of the 1930s, 'overwhelmingly middle class' but 'strongly rebellious and progressive', attracting 'the student-art type' and reminiscent of those who met at 'Trafalgar Square at the start of the Aldermaston March'.[44] Estimates of supporters of this organisation varied between 150 and 500 but included Doris Lessing, the writer, Kenneth Tynan, the playwright, Lindsay Anderson, the film maker, Christopher Logue, the poet, John Berger and many other well-known public figures. Dutt reflected that this was not a gathering of ex-CPGB members, and 'the usual lunatic fringe of intellectuals are naturally present' but that many were people who had not been in politics. After 'Hungary they went through the usual emotional revulsion against the Party, common among intellectuals'. But since then they had lost interest in Hungary and were worried about infiltration by Trotskyites. In summary, then, Dutt saw this organisation as part of the re-politicisation of the middle classes and intellectual youth of Britain.

More serious was the attack which Peter Fryer, an ex-member of the CPGB. Fryer launched his attack in his weekly paper, *The Newsletter*, which was associated with the Group and with the SLL from 1959. Fryer circulated a sheet advertising *The Newsletter* in April 1957 noting that the first issue would be from 10 May 1957. It was stated that:

> The Newsletter will not be a journal of opinion. It will not be a forum. It will not provide a platform for any one group or organization.
>
> Its main concern will be NEWS – and primarily news which the Daily Worker and the capitalist Press alike, for their various reasons, distort or mutilate or suppress altogether.[45]

It was going to deal with the continuing crises of community parties in Britain and the United States, the rapid growth of socialist forum movement, bringing together communists and ex-communists, the re-Stalinisation in Russia and eastern Europe, the fate of the victims of Stalinism and the rise of the 'mass movement' in Britain. Its main concern was to comb for news and to provide accurate news and not tamper with 'disagreeable facts'. Its editorial board of ten, which included five members of the CPGB and five lifetime Trotskyites, included Michael Banda, active in the Social Forum Movement, Brian Behan, a well-known militant in the building industry and brother of the playwright Brendan Behan, Tom Kemp, a lecturer at Hull University, Cliff Slaughter, lecturer at Leeds University and Peter Kerrigan, a Liverpool port worker and previously a prominent figure in the CPGB. In other words, *The Newsletter* was part of that protest of ex-Communists who had left the CPGB over Hungary. Brian Behan had in fact been a member of the EC of the CPGB in 1956 and had forced a vote opposing the Soviet invasion of Hungary which he lost by 33 votes to 1.[46]

The political fallout from the events of 1956 had fallen in many directions. Some of the Party members had left politics altogether, whilst others had joined the Labour Party. Others, such as Fryer, gravitated towards Trotskyism. Indeed, one major route to Trotskyism was through The Group, which became the SLL in February 1959. Fryer, and his *The Newsletter*, soon moved in that direction. But, as seen in the 1940s and early 1950s, Trotskyism was little more than a warring set of sects at this time. Gerry Healy's SLL was founded in February 1959 and held its first annual conference in May 1959. It was essentially a union of pre-war Trotskyites, recruits from the Labour Party and ex-CPGB members who had moved towards Trotskyism after Hungary. This brew of protestors was never going to work easily. Indeed, Peter Cadogan, an ex-member of the CPGB and a member of its Commission on Inner Party Democracy, was expelled from the SLL in February 1959 and, a week later Fryer left the SLL claiming that Healy 'had made it clear that he will not tolerate free discussion any more than John Gollan will; and his methods of silencing dissenters are odious'.[47] Fryer later returned to the SLL but eventually resigned in the autumn of 1959. The SLL also published the *Labour Review*, a quarterly journal founded in January 1957, but its original editors, John Daniels and Robert Shaw, both left the journal's editorial board in early 1959.

Walter Kendall, writing in Independent Labour Party's paper *The Socialist Leader*, 9 January 1960, asked the leadership to reply to the charges that they were 'acting in a manner undistinguishable from Stalin' and to reject Fryer's charge that 'The outstanding feature of the present regime of the S.L.L. ... is the rule of a clique.' Kendall also accused Healy of abandoning his previous policy, and that of the SLL, of working inside the Labour Party because of the counteraction of the Labour Party. Indeed, Healy did so in the early 1960s in order to 'build a revolutionary party', though with an organisation of less than 1,000 members.[48]

Regardless of these problems the SLL held its first conference at St Pancras Town Hall, where it created a five-point programme: work sharing instead of sackings to counter unemployment, nationalisation of basic industries without compensation, defence of shop stewards, defeat of the Tories, and ending of nuclear-bomb manufacture. The irony of these policies is that the SLL was, nevertheless, opposed to measures that would bring peace and attempting to create a trade unions and workers' movement outside the existing trade union movement.

The fact is that the SLL was deeply divided by 28–29 January 1961 when the SLL produced a 28-page report in which it attacked the leaders of the SWP (the old International Socialists soon to become the IS again) because of its militancy in industrial matters, urging it to look to its political work. Indeed, Walter Kendall, highlighting its general swipes at all other organisations, noted its own internal conflicts and divisions and stressed that:

> Everything the S.L.L. has touched it seems to destroy. The much-vaunted National Assembly of Labour, uncalled this year, is a wrecked and shattered shell. The contacts in the docks have almost vanished to a man. In the Labour Party the whole ground gained by the S.L.L. has been lost. In the E.T.U. the tiny S.L.L. faction which began by organising the Catholic Byrne against Communist Haxell has now turned full circle and by some strange logic now defends Haxell, legally declared improperly elected against its former ally Byrne.
>
> The colonial journals which linked up even temporarily with the 'Newsletter' Group, the *West Indian Clarion*, the *Somali Voice*, the *Arab News*, the *M.N.A. Journal*, are now all in ruins. [...]
>
> In short, after Hungary, with a great influence of talented new members, with a magnificent vista of opportunity clear ahead, the S.L.L, instead of carrying the movement forward, destroyed the cadres it had taken two decades to create. Police spies indeed, they could not have done better.[49]

The fact is that the SLL was becoming bankrupt as a meaningful Trotskyite organisation and events were overtaking it. Indeed, Alan Johnson, noting the political amnesia which has sometimes affected the memories of some participants and the

Stalinism of Healy's approach, reflects that:

> For years comrades such as Cyril Smith, Jack Gale and Tom Kemp have been the whipping boys of Healy at C[entral] C[ommittee] meetings. Every CC member knows this to be true. These comrades have been reduced to tears many times in front of CC meetings when attacked as anti-party over contributions they have made.[50]

The SLL did try to revamp *The Newsletter* in 1964, using young people in their twenties as the basis of the editorial board. It was also reported that Jean Kerrigan, the daughter of Peter Kerrigan the Industrial Organiser of the CPGB, joined the SLL in 1964. In a press statement, on 7 August 1964, she put the record straight on the statement made in the *Daily Worker* of the same day. She indicated that she had challenged Bert Ramelson, a prominent Yorkshire member of the CPGB Executive, to answer her criticisms, which he could not, and explained that her reason for leaving the Party was because of 'The failure of the Party to face up to its Stalinist past as revealed in these discussions in my opinion inevitably has led to an abandonment of Communist politics and of Marxist theory by the Party.'[51] She felt that the principles of Marx and Lenin were best reflected in the programme of the SLL.

Nevertheless, such well-publicised success was rare for the SLL. It later captured the leadership of the Young Socialist section of the Labour Party but its leading figures were expelled in 1965, after publicly criticising Harold Wilson in the midst of the 1964 general election campaign. The SLL then set up its own misleadingly titled Young Socialists. Its adult membership was only a few hundred in 1967 and 1968 but it claimed 30,000 members in the Young Socialists. The organisation had widespread support at universities such as Bristol, Exeter and Sheffield and its anti-Stalinist policies drove it to support the Chinese Cultural Revolution of the mid-1960s, to criticise Castro and to support Black Power. Nevertheless, its real power was very limited and other developments amongst Marxist and socialist groups in the 1960s were overtaking it. Indeed the IS became one of its main challengers.

The IS (first formed in 1950) became the SWP in the 1960s and was led by Tony Cliff. On January 1964 it produced *International Socialist Journal*, which intended to publish theoretical and descriptive articles based upon the experiences of the working classes, and was sponsored by the socialist left in France, Britain, Italy and Belgium. Its editorial board reflected this international composition, and included Ernest Mandel of Belgium. The British representatives on the editorial board were Ken Coates, Jim Mortimer, Ralph Miliband and Frank Allaun.[52] The IS believed that the post-war Soviet Union was no longer a bureaucratically deformed workers' state but a form of state capitalism. In addition, the IS rejected both international blocks in their slogans 'Neither Washington nor Moscow' and campaigned and struggled in the defence of trade-union rights. Because of its broad-based policies it attracted many young left-wing students and lecturers in universities. Among the IS leaders were John Palmer, William Fancy, Raymond Challinor, Paul Foot, Nicholas Hood, Peter Sedgewick and Alistair Macintyre. The membership was a mere 360 in 1967 but had risen to between 600 and 800 in 1968. The growth was assisted by the fact that, after the exclusion of the SLL members from the Labour Party Young Socialists (LPYS) the IS inherited the leadership of the LPYS. The IS claimed to be operating 35 clubs in its own right but was intent upon working through the Labour Party, which had not proscribed it, and was later claiming 58 clubs. Its policy of working through the Labour Party was, however, reversed in 1969 when the Labour Government sent troops to Northern Ireland; the IS later withdrew from the Labour Party and organised independently again as the SWP.

There was also the MT, organised around the *Militant* newspaper (launched on October 1964) and led by Ted Grant, who had led those in the RCP (formed in 1944) who had resisted the move into the Labour Party in the late 1940s. As a result, his supporters had lost ground and the MT was rather obscure in the mid-1960s, though it gathered considerable support at the University of Sussex and its members began to enter the Labour Party. After the withdrawal of IS from involvement in the Labour Party, MT became the dominant grouping within the LPYS, and grasped the opportunity for enhanced recruitment this presented.

In 1964 the Trotskyite Fourth International urged MT to fuse with a fourth body, the International Group (IG). The IG was based at Nottingham, led by Tony Topham, Ken Coates and Alan Rooney and produced a journal called *The Week*. The Fourth International held the MT responsible for the failure to do so and in 1967 the MT was replaced as the British Section of the Fourth International by the IG, which altered its name to the IMG and attracted figures such as Tariq Ali, a leading Marxist student activist. Ali, born in 1944 and a Pakistani, went to Oxford University. Yet he did not see himself as a political theorist, nor as an intellectual but as an 'agitator, a pamphleteer'. His prominence in the political issues of the day did, however, raise the profile of the IMG.

Most obviously, Tariq Ali and the IMG were associated with the birth of *Black Dwarf*. The original *Black Dwarf* had been established in 1838 by Thomas Wooler. A Sheffield printer working in Fleet Street, Wooler had led dissent in the 1820s and 1830s, urged the West Indian slaves to rebel against plantation owners, attacked big business monopolies and supported unlimited immigration. He preferred passive resistance but defended the right of people to obtain their freedom by any means possible. When *Black Dwarf* was re-established in 1968 it was claimed that:

> *The Black Dwarf* will be different from other Socialist papers. Our principal aim is not so much to instruct and educate, but to *learn* from working-class experience, opinions and knowledge, and report our findings. We believe in the class struggle here and now, and we want the working class to control this country and every other. [...]
>
> Are we Syndicalists, Trotskyite, Maoists, Labourites or New Lefts? We see sectarianism as irrelevant to our job. All socialists must take part in the persistent struggle for the day-to-day interests of the working class, helping them ward off attacks on their living standards. At the same time, we must be constantly reminded – and reminding others – that there can be no fundamental improvement in their position until the power of capital is removed, our principal objective.[53]

Other Trotskyite groups emerged and conflicting views further undermined Marxist and socialist unity. The small London-based SPGB, formed in 1903 and publishing its ideas through the *Socialist Standard* revived its criticism of the Labour Party. Most obviously there was the RWP, formed in 1963, which produced *Red Flag* from 1963 until 1997. It was a Trotskyite organisation dominated by the writings of J. Posadas, the South American revolutionary, who sought workers and peasant governments based upon Soviets and communes in every country and the fight against imperialism. It particularly rejected the CPGB's emphasis upon winning 'key posts' in trade unions in favour of workers' control.

Within its own Trotskyite ranks, the RWP caused significant dissent. It attacked Healy and many other Trotskyite leaders for their failures since the Second World Congress of the Fourth International was held in 1948.[54] In international affairs it favoured the Chinese bureaucracy over the Soviet bureaucracy since it had participated in bringing about revolution and change in China, and felt that the workers should prepare for power as the Labour Party refused to lead.[55] However, Posadas, his few hundred supporters and the *Red Flag*, were primarily concerned with international communism, about Trotskyism in Brazil and Cuba, the deepening Sino-Soviet dispute, and the fate of Che Guevara. When dealing with Britain it was mainly concerned to attack Healy and the SLL, the SWP and rival Trotskyite groups.[56] In Britain, however, it mounted a united front campaign of factory committees, trade unions and Labour Party branches to oppose the 'squeeze' being imposed upon British industrial production and against the trend of unemployment which had reached 340,000 and was rising: 'The working class must now overcome the weakness of its own organisations, purge them of their conciliatory leaderships, and take once more the offensive against capitalism.'[57] By 1967, it was detecting a slide into a Third World War and was urging factory committees to seize the offensive, to impose workers control and to occupy factories.[58]

Divisions between the Soviet Union and the Chinese Communists on the approach to Communism further undermined the unity of the CPGB, and Marxism, in Britain on a larger scale than the RWP threatened. Chinese communism, with its emphasis upon the involvement of the whole community in the process of agricultural and industrial production, rather than the Soviet emphasis upon the role of the expert and heavy industrial development, had produced conflict with the Soviet Union from the time of the 'Great Leap Forward' in 1958. The rift had persisted into the 1960s despite Mao Tse Tung's loss of power, and was galvanised by the tendency of different Communist parties to support one or the other. This was evident in the Soviet Union's clash with Albania in 1961, which led different Marxist groups to identify with one side or the other. The split became even more evident in late 1963 when the Chinese accused Krushchev and the Soviets of revisionism. It became more intense when the Chinese Cultural Revolution began in 1966, refining and developing the policies of 1958.

The CPGB remained loyally Soviet throughout, a situation galvanised further by the Cuban missile crisis of 1962. It also supported the Soviet Union in its erection of the Berlin Wall in August 1961. The *Daily Worker* commented that it was the war-mongering activities of the United States 'playing with fire at the most explosive point in Europe which have made it necessary for the Government of the GDR, at the request of the Warsaw Treaty Powers, to take new steps to control the West Berlin border'.[59] The EC of the CPGB acknowledged the split between Moscow and Peking in January 1963 and published a statement entitled *Restore the Unity of the International Communist Movement*. This theme was continued in *Marxism Today* when Palme Dutt and James Klugmann made further appeals for unity.[60] With some reservations, the Party supported the Soviet Union when it came to the crunch.

There was a small Maoist movement within the CPGB, led by Michael McCreery, from New Zealand, which gained the support of a couple of London branches and a few individuals. In 1963 McCreery formed the Committee to Defeat Revisionism for Communist Unity, which produced the monthly paper *Vanguard* for a short time. He also published several pamphlets, the most famous being *Destroy the Old to Build the New* in which he attacked *The British Road to Socialism* and the notion that the working class could win control over the capitalist state in Britain by constitutional means. He suggested that the armed forces would take over control of the capitalist state in Britain in order to prevent it being taken over by Marxists and socialists, adding:

> How is this threat to be countered? By mobilising the 'political and industrial strength' of the people. But political parties and trade unions cannot stand against an army. There is no escaping the need at some stage of the revolution, for *armed strength* to back the political and industrial strength of the people. Only the *people in arms* can counter a putsch of the army. To ignore that fact is to ensure the defeat of the revolution. But it is ignored in *The British Road to Socialism*.[61]

The split between the soviets and the Maoists was of limited significance in Britain. The Party supported the Soviets and partly redrafted *The British Road to Socialism* in 1957–8, 1968 and 1977.[62] Only a few of the Trotskyite societies, such as the SLL, other than McCreery's organisation, found their way to supporting Chinese communism.

Much more important to the development of the CPGB was the capturing of the expanding and radical student market of the 1960s. The Trotskyite organisations mentioned, and others, challenged the CPGB for control of the expanding and radical student body and were therefore watched closely by the CPGB which always found it difficult to win significant support in this sector. Considered sectarian and ultra-leftist by the CPGB, the Trotskite organisations were mentioned in duplicated listing which was circulated in March 1964 under the title *The Attack upon the Party from the so-called 'Extreme Left'*, and an article connected with it was written by Betty Reid and published in *Marxism Today*.[63] This was produced at a time when the CPGB had just purged itself of its pro-Chinese factions and was just about to begin its witch-hunt against the Trotskyites. It was maintained at the time that 'Anyone who opposed the "peaceful road to socialism" myth, whether he was a militant trade unionist or a Young Socialist is already a Trotskyite so far as the Communist Party leaders are concerned.'[64] The list was updated in 1968 when Betty Reid produced a catalogue of 88 socialist parties, groups, newspapers and journals of the ultra-left, with brief outlines of their history and fragmentation.[65]

The New Left and the CPGB

By that time the New Left, which had emerged after the events of Hungary, was also becoming a challenge to the CPGB. Its leaders, in particular E. P. Thompson, were seeing it as a vestige of hope emerging from the traumatic events of 1956 and evidence that there were some who were hoping to democratise Communist states and Communist parties.[66] Broadly based, this movement aimed to work with the Labour Party and other organisations to more effectively represent the interests of the British Left. The CPGB sought to take some advantage from this development.

James Klugmann, who updated the Betty Reid's Trotskyite organisations list in 1968, suggested to the CPGB that there were some organisations that should be encouraged. In particular, he favoured those groups who gathered around *New Left Review* and the New Left May Day Manifesto Group, which published the first draft of the May Day Manifesto on 1 May 1967. This was edited by Raymond Williams as the *May Day Manifesto 1968* and published by Penguin in May 1968. Cyril Smith, a later Liberal figure, reviewed and criticised it in the SLL's *The Newsletter*, suggesting that the May Day Manifesto was characterised by 'wordiness' and 'brand-new clichés' in the rediscovery of poverty in Britain which they felt would be dealt with by the bankrupt idea of a Labour Government taking society further along the road to progress.[67] But then SLL members were being expelled from the Labour Party and there was increasing doubt about the wisdom of operating through the Labour Party.

The Manifesto Group included in its ranks leading Marxists and socialist intellectuals such as Raymond Williams, Edward Thompson and Stuart Hall. The views of these leaders were represented, by one report, in the following manner:

> Very many people are now ready to combine into a purposeful extra-Parliamentary opposition, a socialist movement that's not limited to elections and industrial conflict, in which all groups can participate openly and sincerely in effective work about 'extra-Parliamentary opposition' to emphasise the features of different local groups on partial issues (rent, education, racialism, housing, etc.).[68]

To many of the leaders, then, the May Day Group was to be an alliance of socialist groups that would take up a broad range of social issues.

Agreement ended there, for within the May Day Group there were deep divisions between those who wished to form a new socialist party and those who wished to remain linked to the Labour Party. Williams and Thompson wished the group to maintain its connection with the Labour Party while others, most obviously Tony Cliff and the IS faction, who were present, wanted to create a new socialist party.

The CPGB, still wishing to operate within the Labour Party to extend its influence, followed the events of the May Day Manifesto Conference in April 1968, with great interest. It noted the absence of the main leaders and criticised Tony Cliff, who made a 'wild and damaging speech', and his IS supporters who wanted to form a new independent socialist party. However, it supported the ideas of Stephen Yeo, a Labour Party candidate for Haringay in 1966 and an academic historian, who demanded a 'loosely structured organization' and opposed very strongly 'a great declaration of the need for a new movement'. In the end, the conference agreed, by 65 votes to 35, to condemn the Labour Party as a capitalist party, and decided upon a systematic approach to implementing the 'May Day Manifesto, 1968' and to the holding of a National Convention in the autumn of 1968.

The IS had won and was moving towards the creation of a new party which saw the emergence, indeed, re-emergence, of the SWP. Nevertheless, on 26 and 27 April 1969 Raymond Williams organised and chaired the National Convention of the Left at Camden Town Hall which brought together several hundred representatives of left-wing organisations to discuss a variety of issues such as the events in Czechoslovakia in 1968 and the Labour Government's policy *In Place of Strife*. Raymond Williams' circular in March, inviting left-wing organisations to the Convention, stated that 'It will provide an opportunity for organisation to meet on an open and equal footing to discuss common problems and common strategy, while retaining all their existing freedom of thought and action.'[69]

1968: the year of the student revolts

Despite these diversions, student protest also reached a peak in the summer of 1968 with the French students' protest in Paris, led partly by the internationalist German student Daniel Cohn-Bandit. Indeed, up to 500,000 protesting students marched through Paris in 1968. In Berlin, three days before Easter a young thug shot, and almost killed, Rudi Dutschke and within hours students in every major city in Germany were on the streets. In New York, students at Columbia University struck in early May against a proposed new building on public land adjoining Harlem and secret defence contracts between the University and the Pentagon. A 1,000 police removed students from 5 liberated buildings, arresting 720 and injuring a further 132. There was a meeting of the most famous international socialists in London in June, where The Internationale was sung.[70] There were disturbances in Italy and the students in Prague rallied to Mr Dubcek in an attempt to rouse workers against 'this pampered, petit bourgeois elite'. There was, indeed, student protest both sides of the Iron Curtain.

The *Sunday Telegraph* conducted a survey amongst students at two universities, Cambridge and Sussex. It indicated that 67 per cent of the students at Sussex University and 50 per cent at Cambridge believed that protest and demonstrations served a useful purpose. On other issues it produced a survey of student opinion and noted that four issues commanded absolute majority support at both universities.

There was also significant support for a widening of student grants, student representation in academic affairs and for opposition to the Labour Government's

Table 1 Students support on four issues (%)

	Cambridge	Sussex
South Africa and apartheid	69	85
Smith regime in Rhodesia	60	72
Nuclear weapons	58	80
US involvement in Vietnam	54	78

Source: *Sunday Telegraph*, 30 June 1968, from a survey taken by the *Daily Telegraph Magazine*.

home and foreign policies. The year 1968 was a major year of worldwide students' protest. However, the Marxist and Socialist organisations in Britain did not build up the base of support they might have expected given the extent of protest throughout 1968 and the extent of feeling and protest over the Vietnam War. Indeed, Peter Cadogan's The Committee of 100, formed in 1957 out of the Direct Action Committee against the nuclear bomb which participated in the first Aldermaston March of 1958, expired in September 1968.

The CPGB's student support was won through its promotion of the popular unrest against racism and Vietnam. The CPGB also linked up with CND in its demand for nuclear disarmament. It particularly linked up with CND in opposing the Wilson Government's commissioning of nuclear submarines in 1969. These issues gained the CPGB support in the expanding British universities where, like France and the USA, there had been student unrest. Indeed, this policy paid handsome dividends in 1971 when the Communist Digby Jack was elected president of the National Union of Students.

Yet despite the CPGB's determined efforts to attract student support, and in its commitment to working through the Labour Party, Party membership did not increase. It acquired some student support, though probably less than the combined efforts of its opposing student-based socialist societies. As far as the CPGB was concerned it struggled to win the student vote, losing out to Trotskyite organisations, and found its limited success undermined, if not destroyed, by the Soviet invasion of Czechoslovakia in August 1968.

Czechoslovakia

In 1967, the Party endorsed the view that all communist and socialist countries should be allowed to develop socialism in their own way. This meant that socialist nations should not invade other socialist nations. The Soviet invasion of Czechoslovakia in 1968 challenged this approach.

In January 1968, Anton Novotny was dismissed as the President by the Czech Communist Party leadership, an action which was followed by the liberalisation of the 'Prague Spring'. The *Morning Star* supported these developments and favourably compared them with *The British Road to Socialism*, welcoming the 'positive steps taken to tackle the wrongs of the past and strengthen socialist democracy'.[71]

Throughout the spring and summer of 1968, Eastern Europe was at the forefront of discussions within the Party and a draft statement was made on Czechoslovakia which noted that 'Respect for the autonomy of each Communist Party is the only real base on which to build working-class internationalism.'[72] By 8 August, the Party was emphasising the point and hoping that the talks, in Bratislava, on 3 August between the Soviets and Alexandra Dubcek, general secretary of the Czechoslovakian Communist Party, and Svoboda, a leading Czech Communist, would be successful.[73] This proved deceptive and the Soviets decided to invade.

Before and during the invasion there were numerous CPGB expressions of concern at the Soviet threats and invasion. Deanne Lubelski, secretary of Middlesbrough branch, referred to the branch support for the Czechs, as did several others. On the other hand, the Bexley branch condemned the PC for its open anti-Sovietism, a position adopted by Sid French of the Surrey District Committee.[74]

In condemning the Soviet invasion on 24 August 1968 the EC of the CPGB was in line with British public opinion. The PC of the Party discussed the situation on 29 August 1968 and referred to the moving speech made by Dubcek, noting that 'Both he [Dubcek] and President Svoboda stated that there is no going back to pre-January days.'[75] In September, a draft statement by the PC, which outlined the developments, angrily rejected the statement of the Central Committee of the CPSU that the majority of the Presidium of the Czechoslovak Communist Party and government had asked the Soviets for immediate help:

> It is now clear that this statement is not true, that there was no majority, neither in the Presidium nor in the Government which appealed for entry of the troops. We must register the strongest objection to your attempt to mislead us in this way. Mutual trust between Brother Parties must be based on honest and principled behaviour.[76]

Later in the month, the EC made a statement 'deploring the intervention of the Warsaw Pact troops into Czechoslovakia'.[77] It wished for a quick settlement to the dispute and welcomed the Moscow meeting between the Soviet and Czech leaders as a basis for settlement. In the meantime: 'In our view the quickest possible withdrawal of troops is needed so that the Czechoslovakia working people, the Communist Party and the Government, can act with complete sovereignty, to develop their Socialist system in accordance with their own decisions.'[78] The mutual co-operation of socialist states had become the principal driving force of CPGB actions and there was some frustration that the Soviet Union had contravened an agreement of non-intervention signed by the Communist states in 1967.

The YCL Executive issued its own condemnation of Soviet action on 3 October, criticising both illegal imprisonment of Czech leaders and the presence of 600,000 Soviet troops in Czechoslovakia.[79] The London District Congress, held on 16–17 November, also deplored the invasion of the Warsaw Pact troops which it referred to as a 'tragic mistake' whilst rejecting the 'anti-Soviet policies of the capitalist press' and the 'aggressive policies of NATO' which were the 'main danger to peace in Europe'.[80]

Trotskyite organisations were less forgiving. The Czech-Soviet Crisis, the subsequent suicide of a Prague student who burned himself to death and the other events surrounding the invasion produced an interesting Resolution of the International Secretariat of the Fourth International, on 24 January 1969, which condemned all sides in the events. It condemned the suicide of the student who did not, it felt represent the will of the Czech people; it condemned capitalist scheming and also:

> The absence of Soviets, of proletarian democracy, of the independent functioning of trade unions, of political and revolutionary life in the Workers States, allows a climate to be created which disconcerts; a climate of deception, of confusion, of lack of satisfaction, of restraint of struggles of the masses in the Workers' States.[81]

80 *Emergence of the Broad Left 1957–70*

In other words, frustrations were built up against the Soviet Union because of its lack of application of true Marxist–Leninism.

Despite its condemnation of the Soviet action, the Soviet invasion of Czechoslovakia damaged the CPGB and its membership continued to decline from 33,000 in 1967 to 27,000 by 1971. It fluctuated around that level in the 1970s as the industrial relations of Edward Heath's Conservative Government created dissent and until the rise of Eurocommunism in the late 1970s convulsed the Party in internal conflict.

Women

Unlike the 1950s, when the CPGB was drawn into women's protests against the Korean War and protests against rents and other related issues, it is clear that the women's movement was not vital to the CPGB, perhaps largely because the Women's Liberation movement (WLM) was in its infancy. At its 1961 Congress, the Party supported the rather bland and general resolution that 'Congress believes that in the coming period our work must help women to enter into wider and more united action on the day-to-day issues, and play a full and rightful part in the political, social, economic and cultural life of our country.'[82] This was seen as part of the challenge to capitalism, which imposed restrictions upon women. The 1965 Congress had progressed only a little into accepting that women's equality required 'fully coordinated social services for families'. Such demands were all very general and pushed by no forceful feminist movement, unlike the situation in the 1970s. In effect, the CPGB's attitude towards women's issues had not progressed beyond what was achieved in the early 1950s.

Conclusion

The membership of the CPGB was just over 27,000 in 1957 and about the same in 1971. However, this masks the dramatic changes in fortunes the Party had faced which saw it increase its support in the early 1960s before losing ground in the late 1960s. At the beginning of the 1960s, it was exercising some influence within the trade union movement, and was recovering from the Hungarian affair. Effectively, it recovered the support lost as a result of Hungary. However, from the mid-1960s onwards it found itself strongly opposed by the Wilson Labour Government over strikes and, whilst achieving some success within student ranks, found that it lost much of the student protest in the expanding university sector to the numerous, but small, Trotskyite organisations. Losing support, slowly at first, its membership fell by about 6,500 between 1967 and 1971. In 1968, the year of student protest, there were numerous opportunities for expansion but the CPGB, once again, found its hopes dashed by the Soviet invasion. No matter how much it condemned Soviet action in Czechoslovakia it was associated with these events. As a result the Broad Left policy, which it had fully adopted in 1968 was patently halted in its tracts and it was not until the 1970s, the 'Red Seventies', that it attempted to apply this broader strategy with full vigour. By that time, however, other international developments were afoot which were to throw the Party into terminal decline.

3 The Red Seventies

Industrial conflict and the emergence of Eurocommunism 1971–9

For the Communist Party the 1970s marked its concern to reverse the downward trend in its membership through forming a broad democratic left alliance. The concept of a tightly unified and narrowly focused British Communist Party had gone forever. Party membership had fallen in the late 1950s and the late 1960s, as a result of the Soviet invasions of Hungary and Czechoslovakia, and regaining this loss became a primary objective of the CPGB. To this end, the Party became associated with three main campaigns which, in the end, brought it nowhere near its primary objective. The first was its opposition to the anti-trade union policies of the Heath Conservative Government and the almost equally reactionary policies of succeeding Labour Governments. The second was to participate in the re-emergence of a vibrant feminist movement, often referred to as either 'second-wave feminism' or the WLM, in the hope of increasing the representation of women within the Party. The third was to re-examine Party policies and structures – *The British Road to Socialism* and the application of democratic centralism – in the desire to offer policies, more right-wing policies, which might attract wider support. This last campaign led to serious internecine conflict between two fairly right-wing movements within the Party largely as a result of the emergence of a new communism, Eurocommunism, which challenged the old Party which had been governed by its association with Moscow. British Marxism, and particularly the CPGB, did modestly well in dealing with the first two of these issues, winning wide support for its policies, but disintegrated when faced with British support for the Eurocommunist ideas first advocated by Santiago Carrillo and F. Claudin in the mid-1970s.

The fortunes of the CPGB were deeply affected by these developments. Its membership was steady at about 29,000 in the early 1970s, and in fact reached 29,943 in 1973 when opposition to the Heath Government was at its greatest. However, it fell dramatically from to 21,145 in 1978 and there were only about 22,000 in 1979, largely as a result of the conflict surrounding the challenge of Eurocommunism and the defection of some members who objected to the challenge to Moscow's authority.[1] Indeed, George Matthews, one-time editor of the *Morning Star* and Head of Press and Publicity for the CPGB, admitted in an interview with *The Times* in July 1978, timed to coincide with the television series on the Party entitled *Decisions*, that only 22,000 cards had been issued at that point in 1978. Full membership counts were taken every two years and the previous count, in the summer of 1977, indicated that there were

25,293 members compared with the 28,519 in 1975. In other words there was a continuing decline in membership of between 5 and 10 per cent per year.[2] Indeed, even more seriously, some of the Party's leading trade unionists, such as Jimmy Reid, left in the late 1970s. This loss of membership, which Matthews optimistically claimed was 'A temporary situation...' actually anticipated the even more rapid decline in the 1980s which eventually saw the CPGB expire with a mere 4,742 members in 1991. It was part of a general malaise in left-wing politics which had reduced the support for the Tribune Group on the Labour Left, although it would also appear that the CPGB was not just losing members but losing some of them also to its two main Trotskyite opponents, the SWP and the IMG who were claiming 4,500 and 1,372 members, respectively, in the late 1970s. Thus the CPGB began a process of rapid decline in the 1970s which foreshadowed its eventual collapse as the main representative of British Marxism in Britain. Eurocommunism produced a fragmentation in British Marxism which was at least as deep seated as that which occurred in the 1960s although such division was now occurring in a climate of less radical politics and declining student interest. In the 1970s, the writing was on the wall for the CPGB if not entirely so for Marxism more generally.

Industrial politics of the 1970s

At the beginning of the 1970s the CPGB appeared to be arresting the decline in its membership and, indeed, recapturing some of its previous popularity. The main reason was that the Party became deeply involved in supporting the workers in their industrial struggles against the newly formed Conservative Government.

Edward Heath's Conservative Government was returned in the general election of June 1970 and immediately resolved to put some legal teeth into British industrial relations. The outline of its news approach appeared in a consultative document in October 1970 and the Industrial Relations Bill became law in 1971. This established the National Industrial Relations Court (NIRC), which was to have jurisdiction over most industrial disputes, could advise the secretary for Employment to impose a 'cooling-off' period in industrial disputes and require a ballot in cases where strike action would be a serious threat to the economy. The Court could also impose fines of from £5,000 to £100,000, according to membership, on unions that undertook 'unfair industrial practices', and thus the closed shop became an issue of some importance. The right of individuals to belong or not to belong to a union was emphasised, and individuals could not be forced to join a union before entering employment, that is, the pre-entry closed shop. The post-entry closed shop was replaced by the idea of an 'agency shop', as a result of which a union could obtain sole bargaining rights if it secured the agreement of the employer or won the support of the workers in a secret ballot. Written collective agreements, unless they contained clauses to the contrary, were to be legally binding and the union could face prosecution through the NIRC if they did not prevent the breach of the agreement. The trade unions were also expected to register with a new Registrar of Trade Union and Employers' Association, whereby workers sacked unfairly could claim compensation, and union could force employers to recognise them through the NIRC.

The underlying assumption of the Act was that unofficial strikes represented the major weakness of British industrial relations. It was further assumed that union officials were failing to control the shop stewards. Consequently, it was decided that trade unions were abusing their freedom to strike in breach of voluntary agreements. The right to strike had, therefore, to be limited by an Industrial Relations Act. Strikes, 'the British disease', were to be faced head on.

Inevitably, trade unions objected to this challenge to the voluntary system of industrial relations which they so preferred. As the bill was going through Parliament in 1971, the General Council of the TUC held regional conferences and two special rallies in London. On 21 February there was a march through London from Hyde Park to Trafalgar Square. There was also a national petition against the intended act and the General Council called a Special Congress at Croydon on 18 March. The main decisions of the conference emphasised that trade unions were strongly advised not to register and to boycott the NIRC, and the already established Commission on Industrial Relations from which George Woodcock, the former TUC general secretary, resigned. Once the bill became law, the Labour Party pledged to repeal it.

By the end of 1971 the General Council was instructing its member unions not to register and to de-register if they had already joined. Nevertheless, 32 unions remained registered, to obtain tax advantages and to comply with their own rules and, as a result, they and their half a million members were suspended at the 1972 TUC Congress. Eventually 20 of these unions, who remained registered to the NIRC, were expelled from the TUC in 1973.

Without large-scale trade union registration and recognition there was little prospect that the 1971 Industrial Relations Act would create the more peaceful industrial environment which the Conservative Government desired. Indeed, the very presence of the NIRC provoked conflict. Most unions refused to put their case to the court and in cases, their presence was often assumed rather than real. The TGWU was fined £5,000 and further £50,000 for 'blacking' Heaton lorries and this led to the Court of Appeal and the House of Lords. NIRC also imposed a 'cooling-off period' when the railway unions decided to 'work to rule' in pursuit of an increased pay offer. The Court imposed a 14-day 'cooling-off period' and a secret ballot , the latter revealing that 130,000 members supported the union line and that only 24,000 were opposed. The union had won.

The whole fabric of the Act was further undermined by the problems on the docks which led to the case of the 'Pentonville Five'. This arose in July 1972 when the NIRC ordered dockers to stop 'blacking' vehicles using the Midland Cold Storage Company depot at Stratford in East London. When the dockers refused the order, five of them were arrested and gaoled, actions which resulted in a national strike of 170,000 dockers. The 'Pentonville Five' were released after only two days and, as Richard Barber has written, 'No sooner were the dockers in Pentonville than the Official Solicitor appeared like a fairy godmother to "spring" them from jail and in the process deal the Act a mortal blow.'[3]

Non-cooperation with the Act and the Court continued and it was effectively a failed experiment by 1972, the number of working days lost to strikes rising from about 11 million in 1970 to almost 24 million in 1972. After falling to just over 7 million days in 1973 this figure rose to 14.75 million days in 1974. Indeed, the conflict surrounding the NIRC and the Industrial Relations Act of 1971 provided the context in which many pay disputes were fought. This occurred with the pay demands of the railway unions and post office workers in 1971 and the pay dispute in coal mining in early 1972, which was settled by the generous settlement of the Wilberforce Inquiry. When, towards the end of 1972, the government imposed a 90-day standstill on prices, dividends and rents, followed by strict controls on pay imposed by a Pay Board from April 1973, the stage was prepared for further conflict. The 7 per cent pay limit imposed at the end of 1973 was immediately challenged by the coal miners who declared a strike from 10 February 1974, although this was settled quickly by the return of a new Labour Government at the end of February 1974. It was soon to be found opposing the Social Contract arrangement of the Wilson/Callaghan Labour Government of 1974–9 as it sought to impose the £6 guideline wage increase, accepted by the TUC conference in 1975 and subsequent percentage maximum increases. When the Labour Party failed to deliver on its commitment to social expenditure but expected continuing acceptance of the wage limits the pent-up frustrations and emotions of the trade unionists led to the numerous strikes of the 1978–9 'Winter of Discontent'.

The Communist Party of Great Britain and the trade unions

The CPGB played an important part in this industrial militancy and gave support in the post office dispute of 1971, the dockers' strike of 1972 and miners' disputes of 1972 and 1973–4. Indeed Bert Ramelson, who had become the Party's Industrial Organiser in 1965, helped organise the flying pickets during the seven-week miners' strike of 1972 and was deeply involved in the activities of the postal workers and dockers. He, and the Party, were encouraged by the fact that at this time the TUC lifted its 22-year ban on Communists attending conferences of the trades councils. In 1972, also, the Communist Jimmy Reid had led the eight-month work-in at the Upper Clyde Shipbuilders to force the Heath Government to keep the yard open with no redundancies and no closures. Reid said at the time that 'The workers of Britain are getting off their knees, getting on their feet and asserting their dignity'.[4]

The Party had extended its influence within the TGWU and the AEU at this time. To strengthen its links with these, and other, trade unions the CPGB had revived the LCDTU whose activities produced a major push for trade union support in 1973, when it identified potential supporters and ran a programme of meetings. Indeed, the Party recorded its links with 24 unions, listing both Party and Non-Party couples who might be invited to any meetings it organised. The AEU, for instance, had four married couples from the Party listed and three Non-Party couples, the most prominent being, the Non-Party, Mr and Mrs Hugh Scanlon. Scanlon had been a leading opponent of the Conservative Government's Industrial Relations Act of 1971, an act which had restricted the right to strike and led to the imprisonment of the five dockers. Although the list contained no Party members for the TGWU, it had Jack Jones, its secretary, and his wife down as its Non-Party representatives. As for the NUM, only Lawrence Daly, a former member of the CPGB who formed his own Marxist faction, was listed.[5] There were quite clearly some shortfalls in influence, which arose partly from the hostility of many trade unions to the CPGB in the late 1960s and to the neglect of workplace organisation in the late 1960s.

The prominent trade unionists on this list were invited to attend some, of what became a substantial series of, campaign meetings. On 30 March 1973 the CPGB circulated interested parties to organise a meeting of Communist comrades in the Post Office in order to take advantage of the poor industrial relations which had persisted since the Post Office workers' strike of 1971.[6] The CPGB also organised a meeting at the Social Centre, Birmingham on 12 May 1973 in order to encourage Communist delegates to attend the first conference of the Municipal and General Workers' Union under its new leadership, which was being held on 21 May.

By the end of October 1973 such campaigning culminated in the CPGB producing an extensive document in which it outlined the need to oppose the Industrial Relations Act (1971) and encouraged the TUC to instruct its affiliated unions not to appear before, or to be represented at, the NIRC. However, this action came rather late in the day for by that time the TUC had already taken the action the CPGB desired.

Nevertheless, the CPGB did contribute substantially to the opposition to the Conservative Government's industrial relations policies. It opposed the Industrial Relations Act and trade union membership of NIRC and fought for the release of the Pentonville Five. Indeed, Bert Ramelson told *The Times*, perhaps rather exaggeratedly, that:

> We proved that a law doesn't mean anything if everyone is against it. We got solidarity up and running – if we stick together they can't put us all in gaol.[...] We've never had a greater influence. Our ideas are getting generally accepted after a shorter and shorter period.[7]

As already noted, the Party also struggled along with other organisations to ensure that the Upper Clyde Shipbuilders, which was threatened with closure, would continue to receive government help. It had also worked through Mick McGahey, a prominent Party member and coal mining leader, to support the successful national miners' strikes of 1972 and 1973–4.

These actions were summarised and analysed on 31 October 1973 when the Party produced its 'Needs of the Hour' listings of the policies. This was a policy statement issued in the autumn of every year, from the mid 1960s onwards, by Bert Ramelson, the Industrial Organiser of the CPGB, and sent to a network of advisory committees each committee of which was connected with a major union. They were largely operating outside the Party but some, like the miners' committee, with Mick McGahey, and the farmworkers one with Wilf Page, had representatives on the EC of the Party. Ultimately, Ramelson would ensure that the main policies were discussed at the TUC the following September.

The 1973 the 'Needs of the Hour' document contained 52 statements, recording its policies from industrial relations to the Vietnam Settlement and apartheid in

South Africa. The first few policies, and indeed the most detailed sections, dealt with industrial relations, incomes policies and other industrial issues.[8] However, apart from the expected opposition to the Industrial Relations Act and NIRC these statements demanded opposition to the Housing Act of 1972, which led to the disqualification of the Labour Council at Clay Cross, equal pay for women now, rather than when the Act came in force in 1975, advocated a barrage of reforms to reduce the level of unemployment and encouraged the TUC to instruct its affiliated unions to recruit more women.

Indeed, the issue of women's rights became increasingly important during the 1970s, with the emergence of second-wave feminism. As a result, and from the perspective of industrial relations, the CPGB became involved in numerous disputes connected with both un-unionised male and female labour. In 1976 for instance, it provided a large number of people for the daily picket of the Grunwick factory, north London, where there was a largely Asian workforce for exploitive low wages in film processing.[9]

The CPGB participated in numerous industrial disputes, giving support to the workers both directly and in print, and became an irritant to the industrial policy of the Wilson/Callaghan Labour Government of 1974–9. In particular, it opposed the Labour Government's Social Contract, which had formed part of Labour's February 1974 general election manifesto *Get Britain Back to Work*. The Labour Party hoped that this new 'Social Contract' arrangement, which had been evolving since 1972, and approved by the TUC–Labour Party Liaison Committee in its *Economic Policy and the Cost of Living* statement, would remove the damaging impression that the Labour could not deal with the unions, and the new voluntary arrangement of wages control with the trade unions was outlined further in the election pamphlet *Britain Will Win with Labour*.[10] Such accord was short-lived once Labour was in office, even though Labour repealed the Industrial Relations Act in 1974.The voluntary arrangement gradually broke down when the government imposed a £6 wage limit, with zero increase for those above £8,500 per annum, even though it had at first been supported by Jack Jones (TGWU) and Hugh Scanlon (AEU). Jim Callaghan, gained some support for the policy when he replaced Harold Wilson as Prime Minister in 1976 but tensions increased in 1977.

At the 1977 TUC, Ken Gill, of the draughtsman's union TASS and a leading Communist since 1940, who had been on the TUC General Council for a number of years, put forward 'The Alternative Economic Strategy' adopted by the TUC which demanded social expenditure and tax reductions in return for the pay controls. He was supported by Mick McGahey, the prominent Communist miners' leader who was briefly on the General Council, and a flotilla of vaguely left-wing leaders such as Rodney Bickerstaff, of the public employees union, and Jim Slater, the seamen's leader and Bill Keys, the general secretary of the print union SOGAT. The Alternative Policy was widely supported in the trade union movement but it was clear that the Labour Government was going its own way with the Social Contract which most trade unions were prepared to abandon.

The CPGB became a leading opponent of the Labour Government's 'Social Contract' pay policy in the mid and late 1970s and encouraged the industrial action which led to the 'Winter of Discontent' of 1978–9. The Labour Government was not able to deliver its promised social expenditure and attempted to impose further wage controls, which were eventually rejected by the TUC which formally decided to return to free collective bargaining in the autumn of 1978.[11] The 'Winter of Discontent' began on 24 August 1979 with the Ford car workers putting forward a claim for a £20 per week increase and a 35-hour week, amounting to an overall claim of 25 per cent. Offered only 5 per cent they struck on 22 September, and won a 16.5 per cent increase five weeks later. Other unions followed suit. On 1–14 January 1979, 20,000 railwaymen held four one-day strikes; there were strikes by haulage drivers and petrol tank drivers. The former settled for 20–25 per cent and the latter for 15 per cent. Secondary pickets at the docks were accused of attempts to starve the country. On 22 January 1979, 1,250,000 local authority workers organised a national strike. Most notoriously of all there was the grave-diggers' strike on Merseyside.

Faced with such enormous industrial unrest the Communist Party began a round of national consultations on 9 December 1978. It was agreed that there would be district meetings to discuss new policies and that these would be held in London, the North West, Yorkshire, Kent, the East Midlands, South Essex and Surrey.[12] A summary of these proposals and decisions was prepared for the meeting of the PC of the CPGB, on 15 February 1979, by Mick Costello, the son of a New Zealand diplomat who had lived in Moscow between 1945 and 1950 and now Industrial Organiser of the CPGB. He had been President of the Student Union at Manchester University in the early 1960s and had become Industrial Correspondent of the *Morning Star* in 1969 before taking over as Industrial Organiser from Bert Ramelson in 1978. The policy was to focus upon current issues and particularly the trade union demands for a 35-hour week and wage increases which breached the Labour Government's incomes policy. By supporting such trade union policies, the Party hoped to build up factory branches, to promote a left-wing approach to industrial relations and to hold a national industrial conference in 1980. Once this strategy was approved by the PC, Costello prepared a seven-page report for the EC meeting on 11 March 1979.[13]

The Costello report was a detailed analysis of the 'Winter of Discontent' which had seen the Ford car workers break the incomes policy, followed by the lorry drivers, British Oxygen and the public service workers. It advocated the return to free collective bargaining and the raising of the standard of living, supporting the pay demands that would take lorry drivers beyond £65 per week and hospital workers to £60 per week and the 35-hour week. It rejected the new Concordat between the government and the TUC agreed on 14 February 1979 and, instead, offered progressive long-term policies for the working classes. This, Costello argued, necessitated the CPGB re-examining its own in industrial policy, last considered in 1963, before the proliferation of white-collar trade unionism and female trade unionism within the TUC.[14] Costello was instigating a pro-active and organised industrial policy rather than a reactive one which had no clear principles or purpose.

Costello's main recommendation in this report was , however, one of strategy. He observed that in the past the CPGB had supported defensive battles against injustice and in effect, any industrial conflict. This was, he felt, a reactive and un-co-ordinated policy which had to be replaced with the co-ordinated programme of trade union action and reform. The old policy was often disorganised or dominated by right-wing trade unionists and even 'The Left advances in the trade union movement were not accompanied by comparable growth in political understanding among the people.'[15] Indeed, the concern of the CPGB was to step up 'the *conscious* struggle for socialism' and it is clear that the CPGB saw the mass organisation of the trade unions as one of the most effective ways to achieve this goal.[16] It was to be achieved by facing up to the problems presented by New Technology and the de-industrialisation and rationalisation processes going on, and by supporting 'mini-alternatives' and campaigning for the Save Merseyside Campaign, the Corby steel town campaign and the Cut the Dole Queues Campaign in South Wales. Such activity would be part of the CPGB's Broad Democratic Alliance strategy:

> In fighting for progressive policies and leaderships to implement them we Communists are not alone. We have many allies on the Left. The building and development of broad left organisation in all industries is a must in order to weld together all who today stand for Left policies. The broad left is not something that starts or ends among the upper reaches of trade union organisations. We see it as based in the rank and file movement, providing forums for debate on policy and action; as, above all else, a fighting and campaigning living body.[17]

This meant that there needed to be more journals such as the *Engineering Gazette, Flashlight, Seamen's Charter, Building Workers' Charter*, the higher education's *Broad Left*, civil servants' *Broadside* and a much wider readership for the *Morning Star*.

In effect, Costello had continued the Ramelson policy of participating in the democratic processes of the trade unions through which they could influence the Labour Party and Labour Government. However, as will be indicated later, this had repercussions, for it suggested that the CPGB was buddying up with trade unions and their traditional demands and this left the Trotskyite parties to occupy the more left-wing ground in the trade union movement.

The whole strategy was further developed by the LCDTU which was working within the trade union movement, amongst the shop stewards, was discussing the implementation of New Technology and had taken action against *In Place of Strife* (1969) and the Industrial Relations Act (1971). Its purpose was to work with the rank-and-file in the factories and to get the political message of *The British Road to Socialism* across to the workers. However, Costello acknowledged that the CPGB had not always been so active and that 'We are paying a high price for long neglect of our workplace organisation and for the widespread failure to integrate the factory branches into the campaigning by the Party as a whole.'[18] Indeed, the Party had often antagonised trade unionists rather than worked with them, as for instance in the case of the *Morning Star's* attack upon Charlie Donnett in 1978, when it accused this Scottish union official of the National Union of the General and Municipal Workers as being right-wing when he had in fact given much help to the *Morning Star*. George Matthews wrote to Costello stating that 'It doesn't help relations with such a person to describe him in this way in the paper...'[19]

An old problem had returned to haunt the CPGB and it was felt that the corner on industrial policy could only be turned when the Party journals, such as *Marxism Today* and *Comment*, paid more attention to workplace organisation. As is evident in the Chapters 1 and 2, the CPGB had neglected its workshop and factory organisation and the Costello theme was that this had to be rectified by the Party as a whole turning to industry. Indeed, Matthews reminded Costello, who was well aware of the situation, that:

> In 1976 we held the first national workplace branch conference for nine years. It brought together 200 industrial activists. Subsequent conferences have seen a fall-off in attendance, primarily because the fight for understanding the role of organisation at the point of production has not been conducted nationally or in our Party districts. Organisational follow-ups to the conference have been almost nil. We cannot allow this situation to continue.[20]

Once again, then, the emergence of industrial conflict had encouraged the Party to turn to industrial action and to emphasise the importance of the factory branch. This strategy had been raised during the inter-war years, the 1940s and the 1960s. It had failed then and was to fail again in the 1980s when the Party was torn apart by conflict between the Eurocommunists and the old Stalinists, as the CPGB entered its final death throes. In the mean time, from the winter of 1978–9 to the mid-1980s, industrial conflict provided a basis for CPGB activities, before Thatcherism drew the sting of militant trade unionism.

The focus of CPGB activities in the late 1970s was the economic policy of the Callaghan Labour Government which it constantly attacked because it had 'succeeded in reducing the standard of living and real wages'.[21] Indeed, it reminded its supporters that 'It was the Labour government which formally abandoned the commitment to full employment' to which every post-war government, including the Tories, have been forced to subscribe for 30 years. It soon gave way to the need to tackle Thatcherism, which proved an even more considerable challenge. However, it was also drawn into promoting the rights of women through the second-wave feminism of the 1970s.

Feminism in the 1970s

Feminist theory, and activity, is commonly described as having gone through three 'waves' of intensity – first, second and third-wave feminism. First-wave feminism had challenged the idea that women were irrational beings who should be confined to domestic work and excluded from citizenship. This movement occurred in the early twentieth century and focused upon the vote for women, their financial independence and improved education. The second wave, often described as the WLM, developed from conferences held at Ruskin College, Oxford between 1970 and 1978. This movement demanded equality of employment and education for all women and, in 1974, added legal and financial independence, an end to sex oppression, the end of male violence and the right to a self-defined sexuality as its objectives.[22] These feminists felt that despite first-wave feminism the lives of women had not changed and that contemporary politics did not address the gender issues of reproduction, domestic violence and sexuality. The second-wave slogan thus became 'the personal is the political'. These second-wave feminists distrusted the state and demanded solidarity among women, the concept of 'sisterhood'. Added to this, in 1978, was a campaign against the discrimination practised against lesbians led by groups such as the Leeds Revolutionary Feminists' Collective, which went so far as to argue that heterosexuality and feminism were incompatible.

The second-wave feminism of the 1970s attempted to broaden its approach and cut across the ideological differences between women's groups, becoming less focused in its ideals by the late 1970s. Increasingly accused of presenting the concerns and images of middle-class white women, these new feminists began to recognise the diversity of the experience of women, unlike their counterparts in the 1950s and before. Black feminism developed rapidly as did the gay, lesbian and bi-sexual movement. As a result, and more in the 1980s, 'Queer theory' and 'third-wave' post-modernist feminism emerged. Feminist activity encompassed a range of activities from single-issue campaigns, such as the Greenham Common campaign against nuclear weapons in the 1980s, to involvement in the activities of political parties such as the Labour Party and the CPGB.[23]

In the 1970s feminists were often categorised by theory, and some were described as liberal, socialist, Marxist or Radical. In some cases this was because they affiliated themselves to such tendencies although in others they were attached by others to pre-existing traditions. Many groups began to attach themselves to the Labour Party, which was a large and amenable organisation for their development. Others associated themselves to the Marxist outlook, especially if they were intending to overcome the economic oppression of women. Yet others decided upon separatism in a quest to define women-only space. They began to associate with campaigns about women as housewives and added issues such as rape and pornography to their campaigns to improve the situation of women. By the early 1980s it was the opposition to nuclear weapons being stored at Greenham Common that dominated feminist campaigns. By that time there was emerging the view that women were different in many ways – being black or lesbian for instance – which challenged the impression that the problems of women were essentially those of white women and of a Western perspective. This idea that there were immense differences between the experiences of different women was associated with the third-wave feminism, a subject examined in Chapter 4, which challenged overarching theories and emphasised the differences put forward by post-modernist writers such as Jacques Derrida, Jacques Lacan and Michael Foucault.

In the 1970s, and indeed the 1980s, the CPGB was essentially associated with second-wave feminism, although in the 1980s, as will emerge in Chapter 4, there was some recognition of differences even though Marxist and post-modernist ideas were in conflict with one another. The revival of the feminist movement within Marxism was evident from the inauguration of the Women and Socialism conferences in 1971 but began in earnest in the spring of 1973 when the CPGB published the first issue of *Link*.[24] This was supplemented by *Women in Action*, a bulletin first published by the Women's Department of the CPGB in the mid 1960s.[25]

As previously noted, the CPGB had organised national conferences of Communist women since 1951 and Communist women had participated in the anti-war movement of the early 1950s and campaigned with a broad range of women's organisations on other social issues. By the 1970s Jean Styles was the Party's National Women's Organiser and was responsible for the National Biennial Conferences, and particularly the fourth to the seventh, held in 1970, 1972, 1974 and 1976, as well as the constant round of National Half-Yearly Women's Meetings. They discussed equal pay, published pamphlets, such as Rosemary Small's *Women: The Road to Equality and Socialism*, and lectures, such as Betty Matthews' one on 'Sex and Equality', the latter of which suggested the need for women to join socialist movements in order to 'win improvements in the economic and social status of women now'.[26]

The whole emphasis of the feminist and women's movement was changing. By the early 1970s the Party was claiming, with some exaggeration, that 'The Americans could not have been defeated in Vietnam without them. The advent of women in the Socialist countries has worldwide repercussions.'[27] Indeed, recognising that 9 million women were working, it began to demand equal pay for women, well in advance of the Equal Pay Act being implemented in 1975, and the end of discrimination in education, training and opportunities. It further demanded equality for women before the law and, indeed, the removal of such insulting inequalities as the need for the husband to sign for his wife to have a hysterectomy or for the fitting of an inter-uterine contraceptive device. The Party thus saw itself working with the WLM in securing these rights and the improvement of the lot of motherhood in British society and in its National Half-Yearly Meeting of 9–10 June 1973 took up the issues of tax credit and family allowances.[28]

It was, however, *Link*, the Communist Party Women's Journal, which wholehearted embraced the second-wave feminism of the 1970s on behalf of the CPGB. It was first published in the spring of 1973 and Rosemary Small's editorial declared *Link* to be 'a magazine of women's liberation' and that:

> More and more women, we believe, are realising that only a change of the system of society – only Socialism – can provide for their equality of freedom. The Communist Party recognises this and is the only political party with a planned programme of how this change can be achieved.[29]

The first issue also contained an article by Jean French stressing the importance of women joining trade unions and another by Irene Brennan which emphasised the importance of women becoming involved in politics, essentially as part of the Broad Left movement.

Much of what *Link* produced was based upon the need for socialism to replace capitalism and the desire to reconstruct gender family and gender relationships in terms of that social change. Marxist feminism was thus being firmly attached to second-wave feminism. However, it did not support those sections of the feminist movement who sought to separate the work of men and women – there was far too much emphasis upon Party and gender unity for that. Its emphasis was thus very much focused upon the predominant equal rights campaign. This was evident in

Margaret Bowden's article on 'Images of Women', published at the end of 1973, which stated that:

> The women's movement in Britain has reached a new stage. Previously women's activities have not attempted to radically change women's role in Society but have centred on traditional women's spheres – rent, prices and peace. New women though recognising the importance of these issues, are not content to have their life role determined by their sex. More and more women want to deal with women's exploitation, likening it to the exploitation of the working class.
>
> No longer content to be just wives, mothers and sex objects women are endeavouring to establish their own identities as independent thinkers and thus contribute to society. The contribution of the women's movement has been extremely valuable in raising ideological questions on the oppression of women in attacking the image of women put forward by capitalist ideology [and] in bringing the problem of women to the forefront.[30]

Bowden further suggested that women wanted free contraception and abortion, adequate child-care facilities and more direct participation in politics. Indeed, it is clear that equal pay for equal work, a long unfulfilled goal of the women's movement, was a driving force behind the attitude of the CPGB towards women.[31]

Link offered itself as a forum for all women who wished the position of women in society to be changed for the better and thus published articles on an immensely diverse range of topics. Mary Abbott, Secretary of the Rossendale Valley Textile Workers' Union, wrote of the trade union involvement in tenants' movements and the demands for better pension rights, emphasising that there were 2.5 million women trade unionists amongst the 13 million British trade unionists at the time.[32] Jean Styles, the CPGB's National Women's Organiser emphasised the importance of struggling to improve women's rights in 1975, International Women's Year. She listed the numerous local and regional events that were organised and noted the substantial manner in which many of the national bodies of the CPGB were taking up the issue of women's rights. Most important of all, the National Women's Advisory Committee held a conference at Conway Hall, London, on 12 July 1975 on the theme 'Women's Struggles – past, present and future'.[33]

Indeed, the year 1975 was a significant one in the development of women's rights because it was International Women's Year. Trade unions and trades councils were drawn into examining the rights of women, although some had begun to consider women's rights from the early 1970s. The London Trades Council, which had held two conferences on the issue of women in November 1973. Four members of the EC were elected to co-opt women trade unionists and, in 1974, they as a body produced a ten-point Working Women's Charter, which called for the increasing of family allowances, free contraception, abortion, equal pay for women and the equalisation of working conditions for both men and women.[34]

Nevertheless, there was some cause for concern amongst the CPGB for the lack of development at the national level. The London Trades Council's Charter provoked the

Women's Trades Union Congress of 1975 to produce 'The TUC Charter' with its '12 aims for Working Women'. This was, in fact, a revision of the 'TUC Charter for Women Workers' published in 1963, and, like its predecessor was criticised for making no mention of abortion, as the London Trades Council Charter had done, and upset some Marxist feminists who felt that it 'perpetuates the idea that the family and the home are the responsibility of women'.[35]

Many women members of the CPGB were critical of the TUC's policy and almost incensed at what they considered to be a 'bastardised version' of the London Trades Council Women Charter. At the beginning of 1976, Judith Hunt wrote:

> Let us face it, International Women's Year did not achieve a great deal for us and it was typical of the TUC that a Bank Holiday Sunday was the day chosen for trade unionists to celebrate the event. It is going to take a great massive effort from the whole trade union movement to ensure that the legislation now on the statute book – the Equal Pay Act, The Anti-Sex Discrimination Act and the Employment Protection Act – is fully implemented for the benefit of working women so that they can begin to play a big part in the movement.[36]

The CPGB found it a slow and protracted business to build up the rights of women within the trade union movement, which remained determinedly male in focus. The problem is that the prevalent view of trade unionists seemed to be that women were responsible for the home. The CPGB was barely more successful on the issue of women as property. *Link*, for Spring 1978, ran an issue on 'Women as Property', the front page of which contained a cartoon of a wealthy man and woman dressed in late eighteenth or early nineteenth century costumes. The cartoon balloons read as follows:

Man: Goldilocks Goldilocks, Wilt thou be mine?
Thou shalt not wash dishes
Nor yet feed the swine
But sit on a cushion
And sew a fine seam
And live upon strawberries
Sugar and Cream
Woman: NO! I BELONG TO ME!!![37]

The issue campaigned for women to be treated as individuals in their own right and not as the property of men. *Link* subsequently campaigned to ease the burden of women by advocating increased child care in 1979, the International Year of the Child.[38]

This increased concern about women edged their way into the debates and actions of the Party congresses. The fiftieth anniversary celebrations of the formation of the CPGB, in 1970, led the CPGB's National Women's Advisory Committee to circulate a listing of long-term women Party members with an apposite quote from V. I. Lenin at the front stating that 'There can be no Socialist Revolution unless women take part in it.'[39] The document listed 50 Communist women, although attempts had been made to block out the names, addresses and branch affiliations of three of them. The longest-serving member listed was Sarah Wesker of 7 Ashley Road, E 4 who had joined the Chingford branch in 1929, and the last to be mentioned was Helen Mason from Barking, who had joined in 1941. However, this seems to have been a random selection of women active in London and branches from the south east of England and drawn from the Barking, Becontree, Bexfleet, Billericay, Canvay Chingford, Chingwell, Dagenham, Gants Hill, Goodmayes, Grays, Leyton, Loxford, Park, Rainham, Southend, Walthamstow and Wanstead branches of the Party. A separate listing includes the names and address of 109 women comrades in London who had been members of the Party for 30 years or more – an incomplete list since the details of another four women were being investigated. The list included Noreen Branson, one of the Party's historians, Isobel Brown, who had once been a Party organiser with her husband in the Yorkshire area in the 1920s, and the wives of prominent Party officials, including Party activists, or wives of Party activists, such as Kay Beuchamp, Mrs Dash and Helen Falber. There was real pride in the association of women in the activities of the Party on the eve of the Party's greater involvement in the feminist cause.

Indeed, throughout the 1970s the Party congresses continued to support the CPGB's involvement in the women's movement, even if this was more support of a ritualistic type than one of positive action by the Party as a whole.[40] The 1971 Congress demanded women's equal rights in society and welcomed the WLM 'in which Communist women have worked wherever it is possible for them to do so' in order to remove the subjugation of women 'which originated from the division of society into classes'. The 1973 Congress saw the fight for women's liberation as 'a vital part of the struggle to unify and mobilise the mass movement to end this Tory government's anti-working class policies and the build the movement for an advance to socialism'. The 1975 Congress, which took place in International Women's Year, 'reaffirms present party policy which supports the aspirations of the Women's Liberation Movement' and discussed the need for the Party to give 'socialist leadership to the women's movement' to demand equal pay and to oppose the James White Abortion Amendment Bill and the National Abortion Campaign, which threatened to reduce the freedom of abortion. It also supported the activities of Women Aid Groups in aid of battered women and the demands for the extension of child-care facilities for children under five and after school hours and during school holidays.

Throughout the 1970s the Marxist feminists had been part of the second-wave feminism or the WLM. Its representatives contributed to the feminist debate and also attended the Women and Socialism conferences that were held from 1971 onwards. The Marxist feminists of the CPGB were happy to work within this broad arrangement. However, the WLM began to break down in the late 1970s, particularly at the Party's National Women's Conference held at Manchester on 1978 and at the London Women's Conference of 1979.

At the Manchester Conference it was clear that Joanna de Groot was addressing about 1,000 women, only 300–400 were expected to turn up, who were largely non-aligned socialist feminists. According to the March 1978 minutes of the National Women's Advisory Committee of the CPGB they were:

> Old hands and new people. 30 workshops around relationship of socialist–feminists to broad women's movement, to Left groups, to campaigns. How to campaign socialist–feminist way against violence and rape – aggressive reaction from radical feminists, should we respond differently. Nevertheless to be persuaded by the Scarlett Women Collective.[41]

This indicates that there was clearly disagreement between socialist–feminists and feminists about the political and social direction that they should be taking and that there was a clear move towards the socialist–feminist position within the CPGB. Indeed, two months later the Committee was discussing the need for women to take part in their actions against oppression but expressing some discussion and concern about the narrowness of *Link:*

> That *LINK* reflects the political situation within the CP and the difference of opinion there. That many CP women find *LINK* is irrelevant to them and want a more campaigning paper. That *LINK* attempts to satisfy women with many different needs/interest/issues/theories which result in an uneasy balance; trying to realise this problem will offend some readers whatever they decide to do. That there were insufficient links with women in the Districts and no reflection of WACs. That we must not polarize between action and theory, it is possible to decide to have both in *LINK* though articles need to be better.[42]

This debate ran deep within the Party and as the socialist–feminist conference was about to meet in London the 'possibility of split' within feminist ranks was considered.[43] It was evident that many women members of the Party were unhappy at the general and broad approach of the WLM and wanted a much more focused political campaign, as some had advised for *Link*. The WLM was simply not seen as very outward going and regional organisations were often seen as more effective than the national one. There were also discussions about the way in which many trade unions were taking up women's issues, such as abortion, but that the Party needed to act as an intermediary between the trade unions and the WLM, since the latter did not send delegates to trade union meetings.

It is clear that these developments were part of the problem of decline and change that the whole Party was facing. The Party's falling membership and dwindling industrial base was provoking a discussion on inner party democracy and what the broad democratic alliance meant. Women Party members felt that this was an opportunity for the Party to ensure that, like the WLM, the structure operated from the bottom upwards rather than from the top downwards and that such a change might allow the hostility to feminism within the Party to be defeated.[44] In line with this the National Women's Advisory advocated changes which would reduce the frequency of national meetings and enhance local and regional developments.

By the time of the socialist–feminist London Conference the whole tenor of the women's movement had clearly changed. From 1971 until 1978 the CPGB had been willing to work with the WLM in a loosely-based broad alliance of women's group. However, the 1,500 women who met in London on 24–25 March 1979 were mainly non-aligned socialist feminists who were active in campaigns such as the National Abortion Campaign or Women against Racism and Fascism. In the view of Caroline Rowan, who wrote a report of the Conference for *Link*, the move towards creating a socialist–feminist movement was wrong even though it was probably favoured by the CPGB. Indeed, she wrote that 'Most Communist women I have spoken to do have reservations about an organised tendency – although this is not the CP policy and open to debate – mainly because it could divide the women's movement.'[45] The fact is that she feared that, whilst a socialist–feminist tendency would work well with the broad democratic alliance and better than was the case with the WLM, it would mean a narrower base of support for the Feminist movement. Such fears were partly realised in the 1980s, although the CPGB and *Link* took up some of the 'third-wave feminist ideas' of variation such as Black Feminism whilst rejecting the post-modernist tendencies which challenged overarching theories such as Marxism.

The fact is that the CPGB and its women's section cultivated the broad democratic alliance in the 1970s with the WLM and with the non-aligned socialist feminists. *Link*, edited by Rosemary Small and an editorial board which included Beatrix Campbell, Margaret Cartwright, Mary Davis, Jean French, Jean Styles and Jenny Welmark, did a remarkable job in pressing forward the second-wave feminism and raising women's issues beyond the objectives of the National Conference of Communist Women in the 1950s and well beyond the emphasis upon rents and peace emphasised by the broad alliance of the National Assembly of Women.[46] These women, and others, made their mark in establishing links between the women's sections of the CPGB and the broader women and feminist movement. Indeed, it is worth noting the interconnectedness of some of these women.

Jean Styles, born in 1928 was, for instance, Women's Organiser for the CPGB and a London trade unionist, who used *Women in Action* to raise the issue of equal pay and the removal of sex discrimination. Jean French, born in 1924, was also from London and Chairwoman of Women in Action. At a lower level there was Yvonne Reynolds, who was a London teacher strongly connected with women's groups in Haringay in London, Norma Costello from Seven Oaks in Essex, who was branch secretary of the local National Union of Teachers, and Joanna de Groot, of York, a lecturer at York University who was a prominent branch member of the University Teachers' Association. These, and many other Communist women, worked within the Feminist movement and then trade union movement in a broad democratic alliance which favoured the improvement of the rights of women as well as serving the Marxist cause in Britain. However, as will become evident later, their views were not always fully represented in the Communist Party structure and at Party congresses. In addition, it is clear that the declining membership and weakening structure of the Party was seen as a barrier to improving the lot of women. Indeed, at the Seventh Biennial

National Women's Conference of the Party held at Birmingham on 23–24 October 1976 it was stressed that there was a need for a bigger party:

> A bigger Communist Party and a stronger *Morning Star* are essential if people are to be won to socialist ideas and for policies which break the capitalist ideas of Thatcher and Callaghan. Many women who are in action could be won for membership if we had a vigorous and lively women's group constantly feeding into the Party material specially directed to this and assist us to develop theory and policy on a number of... issues.[47]

Political performance and membership

Given the level of industrial activity and protest activity for women's rights it is surprising that the CPGB did not move significantly to the Left. Instead, the Party remained a fairly moderately left-wing Party before drifting towards the right in the late 1970s. Its policies in the early 1970s did win it some support but one has to ask why the Party's participation in industrial conflicts of social campaigns did not bring a significant rise in membership and wider political support? Membership figures improved a little in the early 1970s but began to fall from the mid-1970s, at a time when MT and other Trotskyite groups seems to have experienced a rise in membership. There was also disappointment for the Party when it came to elections. In both local and national elections, the Party won only derisory votes and at the 1974 general election almost all communist candidates lost their deposits. Even the famous and charismatic Jimmy Reid polled a mere 2,000 or so votes in his parliamentary contest. Indeed, the obvious point is that the CPGB message was simply not getting through to the working class. In order to appeal, the CPGB continued with its broad democratic left approach and its attempts to work within the Labour Party. However, these policies were also failing to produce results and as new young activist and intellectuals, such as Martin Jacques, came into the Party there was an increasing questioning of existing policies and the value of applying Lenin's policy of democratic centralism since it seemed to have stifled discussion within the Party.[48] Indeed, such support as the CPGB had gained was quickly lost in the mid and late 1970s by the conflict between the pro-Soviet wing of the Party and the newly emergent Eurocommunist wing who fought over the influence and value of issues such as the Soviet model of communism, *The British Road to Socialism* and the democratic centralism.

The British Road to Socialism and inner party democracy 1978–9: 'time is not on our side' and the Party at the crossroads

The declining membership of the CPGB in the mid-1970s provoked further discussion within the Party about the way in which that decline could be arrested. Inevitably, this led to the debate about the importance of democracy within the Party and the value and continuing relevance of *The British Road to Socialism*. This was modified and partly re-written in 1977 and finalised at the 1977 Congress with changes which suggested that a future Labour Government would not be a socialist government committed to social transformation but a government committed to minor democratic reforms. It raised a sub-debate about whether or not Stalin had written part of the original version, which provoked a flurry of letters between Monty Johnstone and George Matthews and debates in *Tribune* and *Marxism Today*.[49]

The membership problems of the Party, and particularly the emergence of Eurocommunism and the CPGB's internal discussions on *The British Road to Socialism* and democratic centralism occurred at a time when a three-part documentary 'Decisions: British Communism', directed by Robert Graef was being prepared. Filmed over 18 months at a turning point in the history of the CPGB, when the Party was considering policy changes, these documentary films were based upon 50 hours of filming distilled into about three and a half hours of television time.[50] The first part, shown on 25 July 1978, was a 'fly-on-the-wall' filming of the redrafting of *The British Road to Socialism* entitled 'Liberty'. The second, broadcast on 1 August, was entitled 'Equality' and continued with the same theme. The last, shown on 8 August, was about relations with the Soviet Communist Party and was entitled 'Fraternity'.

The first programme contained the internal discussions of the Party on the issue of democratic centralism and the redrafting of *The British Road to Socialism*, although it did not include the 1977 Congress's decision to form a commission into Inner Party Democracy. The second programme was very much based upon meetings of *The British Road to Socialism* committee with Bert Ramelson, who was at that time the Party's Industrial Organiser, in the chair.[51] Indeed, the programme recorded the conflict between Ramelson and Renate Simpson, a committee member, and was couched in terms of the impact of Eurocommunism upon the CPGB. The Party was keen to reveal the process of internal discussions at first hand. The third programme, which focused upon CPGB–Soviet relations, noted how the Soviet Union kept the *Morning Star* viable by taking 12,000 copies a day.

The filming captured the mood of this formative period in the history of the CPGB. It occurred at a time when between 500 and 700 pro-Moscow members of the Party, referred to as the 'tankists' because of their support for the invasion of Czechoslovakia in 1968, split to form the NCP in July 1977. It was led by Sid French, a party veteran and the Surrey District secretary, who believed that 'When the Soviets went into Czechoslovakia they saved socialism and world peace.'[52] Their split was recorded in the first programme and, though there was no detailed examination of their views, the second programme referred to their criticism of the 'left social democratic' nature of the 'British Road'.[53] Indeed, the second programme, in particular, revealed the emerging internal conflict within the CPGB. On this, one newspaper article on 'The British Road Map', a cutting in the Communist archive and almost certainly from a non-Communist paper, reflected accurately upon the revelations of the 'Decisions' programmes.

We see the opposing strains from the Moscow and Eurocommunist camps. We see the balancing act of leadership in their attempts to ride both horses. We witness an intense debate: 'I was surprised by how much argument there was about some fairly basic questions like the definition of the working class or exactly how the process of social change would take place.' But probably the most remarkable feature is the bizarre way the debate around the 'British Road' was conducted. There were an enormous 2,600 amendments from all over the country, which we see Industrial Organiser Bert Ramelson patiently, but obviously, selectively, processing. Only nine went before the Congress. The absence of any right to form organised political tendencies on a political footing with the leadership left delegates with no clear and coherent choice as to political strategy. It is from this that the confusion, the wrangles and the weakness of the oppositions emerges.

It is ironic that we hear the Eurocommunists inveigh continually against the invasion of Czechoslovakia. Yet it is no coincidence that three days before the invasion, the Czech Communist Party had voted to grant the right of tendency and faction within the Party – the first Communist Party to do so since 1921! But still the Eurocommunists do not demand the elementary rights themselves.

But the last word must go to Roger Graef:

> You could say from the beginning that the 'British Road' would be passed. Whether or not it was passed is not the subject to make a film about. *How* it was passed was. True, you don't learn a lot about the 'British Road' itself but you do learn *how* they took that decision.[54]

The 'Decisions' programmes were clearly a timely record of the internal battles going on within the CPGB. They showed how Ramelson, and Irene Brennan, an ex-nun who was in the chair of the 1977 Congress arrangements committee, controlled discussions and limited the changes to *The British Road* document of the early 1950s. The old style leadership certainly emerged when Brennan asked 'Why all this discussion about inner party democracy rather than cuts in social expenditure?'[55] Indeed, another report noted that:

> The two people who swiftly emerged as the stars, or the villains, of the films, are Bert Ramelson (then Trade Union organiser and Chairman of the 'British Road to Socialism' committee) and Irene Brennan. (Chairman of the 'Congress Arrangement' committee.)
>
> *Party bureaucrats:* These two epitomise the Party bureaucrat: they know what they want and they know how to get it. Not that they are wholly unpleasant. Bert 'I move from the chair. Right, that's unanimous. Ramelson, a Canadian-educated Ukrainian is positively endearing at times with his ear-to-ear grin, expansive gestures and battered face that tells a hundred different stories.'[56]

The old pro-Soviet section of the Party was attempting to restrict the onslaught of the Eurocommunists led by the likes of Martin Jacques, who was editor of *Marxism Today*. It also reflected the continuing Party affinity with the CPSU and the Soviet Union, for the third programme saw the arrival of a top-ranking Politburo member for the Congress, a development which compelled the Party leadership to remove critical references to the Soviet Union from their previously agreed statements. Moscow's views still carried weight.

The series was therefore an exposure of the CPGB's policy-making procedures which revealed the immensely complex nature of decision making in the Party. Despite agreeing to 'Rules of filming', which included the deletion of 'All personal, diplomatic and personal secrets', Graef was not in fact asked to remove any material from this 'fly-on-the-wall documentary'.[57] The booklet *Decision: British Communism*, produced by Granada Television to accompany the series, was also frank in its representation of the CPGB as a party dominated by the old Party leadership which was now facing change. It noted that the self-perpetuation of the Party leadership was evident for all to see. For instance, the PC consisted of 16 members, 12 of whom were full-time Party officials, of whom seven had worked for the Party for over 29 years. The Party Congress, which met every two years, also served to emphasise this continuity of control for whilst the delegates were elected by the branches the EC of 42 members, elected at every Congress, was drawn up by the outgoing PC, a sub-committee of the EC. In effect 'the new Executive is approved by the *old* Executive which in turns selects the *new* Political Committee'.[58] Therefore, whilst there was an element of democracy within the Party the leadership was pretty much self-perpetuating and gave no opportunity for 'factions' and 'tendencies' to develop. As in 1956, any move to challenge the leadership was likely to be defeated and the factions driven, or forced, out of the Party with the implementation of the principle of democratic centralism.

Despite such caution and control, British Communism was at the crossroads in 1977 and 1978 and the *Decisions* series recorded these changes. But one wonders why the CPGB allowed its internal discussions to be recorded? It is clear that the filming produced heated controversy within the Party and that some of the hardliners refused the Granada team the right to film because they felt that it would violate the democratic centralism objective of maintaining a united front in the Party. However, with Party membership falling, *Morning Star* in financial difficulties and the Party's poor electoral performance in the general election of October 1974, when it polled an average of a mere 600 votes per candidate, change had to be contemplated. In addition, and despite having a couple of members on the General Council of the TUC and gaining some support amongst trade unions for its industrial policy in the early 1970s, its influence within the trade union movement was less impressive than Costello and the leadership wished for. The CPGB was also, as already noted, losing members to other Marxist organisations such as the Socialist Workers' Party. It was also failing to make headway within the Labour Party, even though there were Communist–Left Labour alliances operating as part of the 'Broad Left' strategy, and the Labour Party general secretary rejected the offer of a Labour–Communist pact, stating that 'The Labour Party has no desire to have any discussions or contact whatsoever with your Party.'

Clearly there was need for more publicity and a greater need for transparency of the CPGB was going to win greater support for its 'Broad Left' approach. However, the rapid rise of Eurocommunism within the CPGB is a factor in the greater degree of openness which cannot be discounted. The influx of new and young students in the 1960s and the influx of young members since 1968, many of who believed in Eurocommunist ideas, began to change the complexion of the Party. The CPGB had hitherto held to the principles of Lenin and advocated the dictatorship of the proletariat and democratic centralism to be essential to society before full communism emerged. Eurocommunism challenged these ideas by asserting that a Communist party could define its own brand of socialism, work with whatever capitalist enterprises it wanted, work with whatever foreign societies it wished and criticise other Communist parties including that in the Soviet Union.[59] There was clearly struggle within the CPGB and the changes that were occurring were clearly part of the loosening of the ties which kept the old leadership in power.

Within a few years the Eurocommunists were able to gain control of the Party and use the old mechanisms to eradicate the old leadership and many of the old Party faithfuls. Nevertheless in 1977 and 1978 the old Party leadership, committed to Moscow, was still in power although its influence was dwindling fast.

Faced with its declining fortunes the Party's Thirty-fifth Congress (1978) decided to set up another commission on Inner Party Democracy, much as it had been done in 1957 after the crisis of 1956.[60] It was declared that its 'Main objective [was] to eliminate role of Party branches in foundations of policy and take discussion on political questions out of committee to floor of Congress.'[61] In other words, there was a desire to widen discussion and allow the rank-and-file to discuss issues, although how this was to be accomplished when the Congress delegates were largely representing the branches and the Congress programme was vetted by Ramelson and Brennan is not at all easy to grasp. And when it appeared, it is clear that the report of the commission on Inner Party Democracy did something of a whitewash job by reiterating the broad and general statement that the declared objective of *The British Road to Socialism* was to:

> create new and close relationships within its own ranks – between different section of the workers, between men and women, black and white, young and old, workers and intellectuals. Only in this way can the Party overcome the experience among its members of sectionalism that divided the working people.
>
> The Party needs to be centralised, be capable of fighting, struggling and intervening as a disciplined united collective once policy is decided. It is this, among other things, which makes the Party capable of acting in a unique way.
>
> These points enhancing the principle of democratic centralism which combines the democratic participation of the membership is centralised leadership capable of directing the entire Party (Aims and Constitution of the Communist Party).

It further explained that all the major committees were elected, that higher committees were more important than lower committees, which would carry out their wishes, that there would be discussions and that the majority view would prevail.[62]

In effect, the report did little more than describe how democratic centralism operated, through the EC of the Party, the District Committee and the PC, and elaborated how the PC was responsible for enacting the wishes of the EC. It outlined the scope and limits of the Party branches and the role of full-time Party workers, the role of the *Morning Star* and other Party organs – *Marxism Today, Link* and *Communist* – and the importance of Congress 'as the highest authority of the Party'. Unremarkably, it proposed that 'expressions of differences to take place within the

Party organisation and press. No factions of forms of association outside or across the structures of the Party to be permitted.'

What emerged then was a set of procedures and responsibilities designed to create an opportunity for democratic discussion within the Party whilst instilling authority. It noted that the EC could mention minority views but could not pass these views downwards in the Party; the EC and District Committees had to be elected by secret ballot, and this could be accepted by the city, area and borough committees; sub-committees were to be advisory, not policy-making committees, accountable to the EC or District Committees; Congress regulations were streamlined and all the Party press were to be accountable to the EC. Democratic centralism was thus endorsed almost without demur. It is not clear that many of the contributors to the work of the commission were at all convinced of its value, some wanting clearer direction from the Party and others being less than enamoured of the restrictive nature of Party decision making.

There were a number of relatively minor criticisms which suggested that the Party structure was fine, perhaps needed strengthening and was rather more democratic than it was presented as being. Pat Devine, in his 'Notes on Discussions, Decisions and Actions' stated that:

> The new *British Road* emerges [as] a broad democratic alliance, led by the working class, built around the underlying themes of extending people's democratic control over every aspect of their lives at all levels. It requires a Party capable of effective political initiative and intervention in all movements of the people, whether specific or general, local or national. It involves a continuing process of democratically determining policy, working together to carry it out.

Additionally, and alternatively, he stressed that:

> The quantity and quality of the pre-Congress decisions has been of concern in the Party for some years. The difference prior to the last Congress, with the much fuller debate around the redrafting of *The British Road to Socialism* only served to highlight the problem of the earlier pre-European periods.[63]

Thus minor changes were required.

Similarly, Dave Priscott, Yorkshire district secretary of the 1970s and 1980s, was concerned about voting in the Yorkshire District for the list of candidates at the Congress and, in a letter to Reuben Falber, the Party's assistant general secretary, stated of the results of voting for the recommended list of candidates that:

> What these figures do NOT show is how many comrades voted for the list, the whole list and nothing but the list. To get that information you have to go through the actual ballot papers. I did that at out last District Congress in 1976 and at that time, although the rec. list, only 18 comrades actually voted for the whole list and nothing but the list. This time, of 114 ballot papers, only 8 voted for the list and nothing but. It is clear that many comrades varied their voting for the list, quite a number did not use all their votes.[...]

My own conclusion is this, as a result of changes taking place in the Party, our system is working quite well. Delegates do take notice of recommendations, as they should after all that goes into them; but they use their own judgement in the end, as they should do. Too many anti-list arguments seem to me to start from the assumption that the delegates are just a bunch of sheep who will let themselves be talked into voting for whatever is past before them. This is particularly untrue. There is after all one final statistic that is also of some importance: [...] after a ballot in which each individual delegate can vote as s/he thinks best, no one can ever be elected unless a majority of the delegates vote for them.[64]

Most of the correspondence to the Party was slightly more critical. A letter from the Communist History Group, written in December 1978, suggested that 'Specialist groups have a large measure of autonomy', that the History Group elected its committee annually, and that the status of specialist groups should be written into the Party rules'.[65] The South Essex District of the Women's Advisory Committee also noted that:

An undemocratic feature of the [Women's Advisory Committee] of the CP at the moment is our failure to involve women comrades in the life of the Party at all levels. Of particular concern is the under-representation of women on our policy-making bodies.[66]

It added that 'The Party has failed as well to develop a feminist perspective to its theory and practice, an example which is the current "Cut the Dole Qs" campaign which has been criticised by our women comrades'. The solution it suggested was to develop both national and district women advisory committees, which would involve women in the Party at all levels, lead to the publications of pamphlets and leaflets, and develop connections with non-Party feminists. It also suggested the formation of a National School for Women. Rosemary Small, who wrote to the Party on behalf of *Link*, also reflected upon the necessity of every Party journal to carry discussion material on Party policy:

The fact that *Link* was overlooked when decisions were being taken on the discussions of the draft of the BRS is, we feel, indicative of the attitude of women which is clearly related to the question of Party democracy. Just as work amongst women should be seen as central to the life of the Party, so the CP women's journal should be seen as one of the central organs of the Party.

Jean Styles, of the North West Area Committee, Denise Walshe of the Central Political Committee, and Freida Park, of the Glasgow University Branch, endorsed such views.

By and large such letters and responses to the Commission on Inner Party Democracy were supportive of the Party, although a larger role was being demanded by specialists, women and other interest groups. However, there were significant critical responses from some sections of the Party about the undemocratic nature of what had occurred before. The Commission received more than 30 letters from far more severe critics. They came from the Becontree, Brixton and Hackney branches of the CPGB and many others. Becontree noted the 'self-perpetuating nature' of the elections for the EC and PC which encouraged the election of safe candidates and the 'lack of competition for full-time appointments'. David Waddington, of Watford, reminded the Party that 'time is not on our side' and that he had had reservations about the Party throughout his 48 years of membership and that the last discussion on inner party democracy in 1956–7 had resolved little. In a powerful attack upon democratic centralism he suggested that it had 'proved unsuitable and unworkable':

> It mitigated against fuller democracy and open politics needed for Party growth and the only kind of British Road developments standing a chance, The impact of the last sixty years of centralism, may be suited to illegality elsewhere, has left its mark.[...] A branch – as with all 'higher bodies' – may take decisions but membership of a voluntary organisation will generally respond how they feel inclined, hopefully on the basis of conviction. Many will express their different viewpoints, if they have them, in public. What exactly is the role of 'discipline' in our interpretation of democratic centralism?[67]

One of the most detailed critical analyses of the concerns about democracy and discussion within the Party came from John Baruch, of Bradford, in a 14-page typed statement written on 3 January 1979, and reflecting upon the declining support for the CPGB, the 1977 version of *The British Road to Socialism* and the question of Inner Party Democracy. He argued that democratic centralism was right in theory for the conditions in Britain at that time but felt that it ignored the organisation and structure of the Party 'which impeded the practical application of our programme and our internal democracy'.[68] Centralism, from the top down, was sensible, he argued but the democratic flow of ideas from the bottom up was faulty as a result of the ineffective Party structure that existed. This, he maintained, was made worse by the fact that the Party leadership demanded action on a number of major national issues at the same time as the local branches were being swamped with the need to deal with more parochial but essential, local issues that might arise. Thus, he argued strongly in favour of the amalgamation of branches into one or two city branches in order not to disillusion the rank-and-file members with an onerous burden of work. He also argued that since the 17 district organisations – other than Wales, Scotland and London – were barely involved in the struggle for a broad democratic alliance they should be encouraged to become 'centres of theory and education'. However, his main concern was that ever since 1922, when the Party adopted democratic centralism, the different industrial backgrounds of the towns within a district often emphasised differences within a district rather than any sense of unity. Indeed, in Yorkshire, where textile and chemical industries dominated in Bradford, Halifax and Huddersfield and the steel industry dominated Sheffield, differences abounded. He wrote that:

> Typically, there was a recent resolution from Huddersfield calling for anti-tory committees in the factories. After a considerable debate it was rejected because it was totally inapplicable to Sheffield. [A] Halifax comrade recently suggested

a touring agitprop group to be sponsored by the district for a month or so. Every one was enthusiastically in favour. In reality it was left to Halifax to organise [it] itself. If there is any area of importance for Yorkshire, it is the coalfield, Harry Pollitt said so in his day and yet 30 years later there were only two miners at the recent Yorkshire district congress (total delegates 145) and hardly any miners active as communists in the coalfield. If the argument that the district helps the weaker branches, more than a city based district would, has any validity, this 30 year failure must undermine such illusions. In fact as long as the miners think that district might do it for them they will not get down and do it themselves. Similarly in Sheffield hardly any of the factory branches bothered even to elect delegates to the district congress, this must reflect the view that the district is irrelevant to their needs.[69]

Few of the 40 or so letters and responses to the debate on inner party democracy, which survive in the Communist Party archives, are fully supportive of democratic centralism. Some, like that from Baruch, endorsed the principle, if not the practice, of democratic centralism. Most felt that democratic centralism, as practised, had denied the rank-and-file and women the right of being heard. Undoubtedly, most Party branches gave their unquestioning support to the Party leadership, mainly through resolutions to the Party Congress, although few seem to have sent letters to the Party directly indicating their support. One exception to this rule was the Sunderland branch of the CPGB which endorsed the hard line position of the past. It wrote that 'We believe that the prime need of the present time is for the party to strengthen the working of democratic centralism in the party, and to reject attempts to modify democratic centralism out of existence.' It added that 'We view with alarm the campaign being waged by a small group of party intellectuals in France to abolish democratic centralism in favour of an 'open' discussion of all party decisions.'[70] Most branches and writers were not so adamantly looking backwards and Willie Thompson, Party activist and writer from Glasgow, referred to the reforms in the Party being 'profound and far reaching'.[71]

Betty England, of the Lewisham Women's Group, gave perhaps the most balanced assessment of the debate and its significance. In an extensive 11-page letter she wrote that:

> Why are we discussing inner-party democracy now? Primarily because of the poor shape the party is in – a long-standing decline in membership when we ought to be growing, the apparent cluelessness of the leadership as to the reasons, a lack of confidence as we claw the way forward and continuing divisions.
>
> This is quite a different situation from 1957, when the last inner party democracy commission (IPDC) was set up. The background to that was the shock of the twentieth congress of the CPSU and the events in Hungary and much of the fight was about the right to criticize. By and large the right to criticize is not an issue now.[72]

The redrafting of *The British Road to Socialism* in 1977 and 1978 and the discussion of inner party democracy in 1978 and 1979 provoked an enormous outpouring of concern for the structure of the Party. In the end, all that occurred is that some rules and regulations were changed to provide more opportunity for lower committees and bodies to express their concerns. Whilst the democratic process was tweaked, the centralism, from the higher committees downwards, remained in place and largely untouched. Essentially, the Party was unchanged and given the extent to which the Party became divided over the issue of Eurocommunism and the dominance of Soviet Russia it is hardly surprising that the old adage that the process was one of re-arranging the deckchairs whilst the ship was sinking comes to mind. At the least, critical decisions were made by the IPDC before the full force of critical comment had been made and such views were certainly not listened to.

Eurocommunism and Marxism

In the early and mid-1970s Marxist parties throughout Europe began to re-assess how they could achieve power. The CPGB had already worked out a programme, *The British Road to Socialism*, which envisaged a peaceful transition to socialism through parliamentary activity and pluralistic democratic socialism. This approach had become necessary since the Seventh Congress of the Comintern, in 1935, when revolutionary means of bringing about change had been abandoned to the need to form a popular front of all anti-fascist forces, to defeat fascism. By 1976 the French, Spanish and Italian Communist parties, and others, had developed this strategy further. They stressed the need to develop policy, to extend democratic liberties and human rights and to win an electoral mandate to achieve socialism, thus relating their approach to the conditions of 'advanced capitalism'. They particularly advocated the need to diverge from the communism of Moscow.

The word 'Eurocommunism' was probably first used at the end of 1970, although it may have first emerged in 1975.[73] At first most leading European communists rejected the term and what it represented. Indeed, in June 1976, at the Berlin Conference of the Communist Parties of Europe, Sanitiago Carrillo, general secretary of the PCE (Spanish Communist Party) declared that it was a most unfortunate term and 'That there is no such thing as Eurocommunism'.[74] The general secretary of the French Communist Party (PCF) also avoided the term at that meeting but his equivalent in the Italian Communist Party (PCI) accepted it and referred to the need for communists in Western Europe to 'seek new answers to the problem of transforming society in the direction of socialism'.[75] In the wake of this conference, however, the term became more widely used. Indeed, by the end of 1976, Santiago Carrillo had launched the idea of 'the Eurocommunist road to power' in *Mindo Orbrero*, on 16 December 1976, and his views were further set out in his book *Eurocommunism and the State*, which was published in 1977.[76] In this book, Carrillo sought to produce a programme that was 'neither vote-catching nor revolutionary, but based upon an assessment of modern capitalism'.[77]

The newly emerging Eurocommunists stressed the need to extend democratic liberties and human rights as well as winning the electoral mandate to achieve socialism, thus relating their approach to the conditions of 'advanced capitalism' and diverging with the communism of Moscow.[78] They decided to remove the 'dictatorship of the proletariat' from their phraseology, a phrase which had referred to Marx's democratic state ruled by the representatives of the working class based upon the principles of democratic centralism bridging the interval between the overthrow of bourgeois rule and the establishment of a society of abundance which would have no need for state rule of any sort: 'rule over men' would be replaced by the 'administration of things'. To Marx and, indeed, Lenin, the dictatorship of the proletariat and democratic centralism were the twin principles of the state of society before the arrival of full communism. Eurocommunism emerged to challenge these Marxist–Leninist ideas with the belief that a communist party could define its own brand of socialism, participate with whichever capitalist brand enterprise it wished, work with whatever foreign powers it desired, and criticise other communist parties, including that in the Soviet Union.[79] Eurocommunism thus came to represent a view that any communist party could pursue whatever policies seemed appropriate for the creation of a communist state in a particular country. The primacy of the Soviet Union and the 'dictatorship of the proletariat' were no longer to be the defining qualities of communism in the future. Those who supported Eurocommunism often referred to the Gramscian idea of gaining political hegemony through alliances, compromises and the gradual extension of communist ideals.[80]

The British Road to Socialism, adopted in the early 1950s appeared to advocate a distinctively British route to socialism and an element of independent action.[81] However, the CPGB followed closely the Soviet line and identified itself with the Soviet invasion of Hungary in 1956, although it later formally distanced itself from the Soviet invasion of Czechoslovakia in 1968. But the pro-Soviet elements within the CPGB were, as already noted, beginning to lose control of the Party in the late 1970s and throughout the 1980s, in such a way that the Party was split between the Eurocommunist and Soviet factions.

Many of the older members of the CPGB, the faithful supporters of the Soviet Union, disagreed with the new Eurocommunist ideas, which they saw as being unfairly critical of the Soviet Union. The *Morning Star*, through its editor Tony Chater, acted as a conduit for their criticism of the emerging Eurocommunist trends within the CPGB.[82] From 1977 onwards, then, the *Morning Star* led the Stalinist backlash to Eurocommunism, although weakened by the defection of the pro-Moscow faction, led by Sid French, who formed the NCP in 1977.

What is amazing is how quickly 'Eurocommunism' gathered strength within the Party and how much discussion there was about it. Gerard Streiff published an article on the topic, entitled 'Is it possible to talk of Eurocommunism' in February 1977, and this circulated around the Party.[83] In it, he noted its undeveloped state but emphasised that it favoured a policy of broad alliances. Gerry Pocock doubted the ability of Communist parties to be self critical and agreed that 'it is important to approach the differences in the situation in the countries of Western Europe'.[84] On the other hand, Gordon McLennan, the new general secretary of the CPGB, suggested to the *Morning Star* that 'I don't agree with the term and therefore don't use it. Those who use it are referring to a process that is taking place in the development of policy and strategy in a number of Communist Parties in capitalist countries.'[85] In other words, he did not like the term but emphasised that the process of accepting differences between countries had been going on for some time and could be recognised in Harry Pollitt's book *Looking Ahead*, written in 1947, and in the first edition of *The British Road to Socialism*, published in 1951, which had embraced the concept of achieving socialism without civil war and through the democratic traditions and political institutions of Britain. He hoped that the divisions, evident in the conflict between the Soviet *New Times* and the Spanish Communists, and marked at the summer 1976 meeting of the European Communist Parties in Berlin, would not widen. Indeed, he felt that this was not necessary since in future there would be international or regional centres of communism for 'each individual party is independent and sovereign and responsible for the development of its own policy and strategy'. In essence, then, he didn't like the term but supported the ideas which had been developing for more than a quarter of a century.

Clearly, however, the Eurocommunist approach gathered pace within the Party. Disillusionment with the Soviet model of communism and the changing composition of the Party, which saw a move from an industrial base to the Party to one increasingly dominated by intellectuals who had come through the student movement, led to its growth. It was partly encouraged by Martin Jacques, editor of *Marxism Today*. A university undergraduate, Jacques had joined the EC of the CPGB in 1967 at the age of 22, as 'a recognition that the youth culture of the sixties could not be ignored'.[86] He was certainly a contrast to the older leadership of the CPGB but rose quickly, despite being a full-time lecturer in economic history at the University of Bristol, and became editor of *Marxism Today* in 1977 following the death of James Klugmann in 1976. Jacques' academic supporters also ran the Communist University of London each year, using it to press forward Eurocommunist ideas. This was particularly evident at its conference week in March 1979. With up to 280 speakers attempting to broaden the appeal of the Party, Sue Slipman suggested to the EC of the Party that industrial action, a feature of the old Communist practices, was isolating workers from each other: 'The building of the Broad Democratic Alliance is the mechanics of democratic political change.... At the moment we are tail-ending those involved in wage struggle, unable to intervene in a process which may be politically disastrous.'[87] The point being made was that anti-monopoly alliances and strikes were leading the workers into conflict with their political allies in the then Labour Party. In effect, the Party's Eurocommunists were attempting to abandon the class approach to politics in what was a rightward move away from the leftward class politics of the old Communists. Indeed, under Eurocommunist influence the Party was no longer gearing itself to become the mass party of the working class, which it had sought to be since its founding convention in 1920. Now only the old Stalinists clung to the 1920 goals, still orienting themselves towards the organised working class. Jacques' 'broad democratic alliance', of the working class, the middle class, women, gays, ethnic minorities and intellectuals, was now firmly in conflict with class warrior approach of Tony Chater, *The Morning Star* and the old pro-Moscow members of the Party. It was a conflict which the Eurocommunists won in the 1980s, which is the basis of Chapter 4.

These conflicts in the 1970s were, however, of seminal importance to the development of the CPGB. In 1996, five years after the demise of the CPGB, Edmund and Ruth Frow, examined the rise of Eurocommunism in their pamphlet

The Liquidation of the Communist Party of Great Britain. The Frows were old-style members of the CPGB, and Edmund had been a prominent figure in the engineering industry. They strongly objected to the dominance of the Eurocommunists in the Party in the 1980s and complained that the revolutionary dialectic of Marxism had been stripped away by *Marxism Today* and Martin Jacques. For them this process had begun in 1977:

> At the Party Congress in 1977 a resolution was passed critical of the contents of the *Morning Star*. The Executive Committee (EC) set up a Sub-Committee to examine the whole question. Although the Report of the Sub-Committee was critical of some aspects of reporting and use of space on the issues covered basically it was agreed that the paper was doing a good job with limited resources despite declining circulation....[88]

Battle thus ensued.

In the process of change there was also, as already mentioned, discussion of the legitimacy of democratic centralism in the Report on Inner Party Democracy which simply justified the higher committees imposing their will upon the lower committees, thus endorsing the *status quo*.[89] However, the report's objective of greater discussion to end factionalism did not work. Indeed, Party rules on democratic centralism were used by the Eurocommunists in the 1980s to root out the opposition of the old Stalinist and pre-Moscow type of communists, much as the Stalinists had acted against the dissidents in the 1950s.

The convulsions of internal conflict meant that the CPGB missed out on the opportunities that arose to make connections with the Labour Party. In May 1979 the Labour Party had been defeated in the general election and was divided over the selection of its leaders. Tony Benn and the Bennites favoured the development of a college system based upon the votes of MPs, trade unions and constituencies whilst other sections of the Labour Party favoured the old system of selection by the Parliamentary Labour Party. James Callaghan, the Labour Prime Minister, having lost the general election decided to pre-empt the new college system by resigning and thus provoking the selection of a new leader under the old system of a vote taken by the Parliamentary Labour Party. The CPGB, whilst it did not make much noise about it, preferred to keep the old system since the new one would raise issues about trade union block votes and the influence of the Communist Party in the selection of a Labour Party leader, something which would undermine the Labour Party and the CPGB's opportunity to influence it. As a result the CPGB missed the opportunity to link up with the Bennite Left and truly broaden the broad democratic left strategy.

Further to this, the tensions between the Eurocommunists and the pro-Soviets began to mount in 1980, at the very moment when there were further discussions being held about inner party democracy. Indeed, there was an internal policy review in which, in a clear reference to Russian intervention in Afghanistan in 1979, it was stated that: 'The battle for peaceful co-existence and for the application of the principle of non-interference in the internal affairs of other countries is a base class position.'[90] Later in the document there was an even more explicit reference to the EC of the CPGB objecting to Soviet intervention in Afghanistan.[91] By 1980 the Eurocommunist view was becoming dominant.

Dissent and Trotskyism

Eurocommunism did lead to dissenting groups of communists peeling away from the CPGB as their traditional values were challenged. Most obviously, there was the creation of the NCP in 1977, led by Sid French. The Party was concerned, and Reuben Falber, a long-standing Jewish member of the Party who was the Assistant general secretary, informed the EC in a letter dated 18 July 1977 that:

> I am writing to put you in the picture regarding the Party (formed on the previous Sunday). It does seem from the information which has come in during the last few hours that the organisers of the breakaway party have overestimated their likely support. Comrades from Sussex and Surrey, on seeing the report in the *Star*, have been phoning in asking for guidance and from other Districts indicate that even some of those who were contemplating joining the breakaway organisations are having second thoughts.
>
> We have considered the question of calling an emergency meeting of the Executive Committee but at the moment feel that we should not take a decision as it does not seem that the E.C. is called upon to take disciplinary action, as those who are associating with the breakaway organisation have automatically put themselves outside the Party. We think that any statement issued by the E.C. would tend to be a repetition of what the Political Committee has already said. There is also the consideration that an Emergency E.C., and subsequent statement would elevate the importance of the issue and give splitters more press publicity than they would otherwise obtain....[92]

Indeed, the NCP was not given the oxygen of publicity and the fragmentation and collapse of both the CPGB and Trotskyites groups in the 1980s and 1990 did not help its cause. Throughout the 1980s it regularly purged its members to guarantee political purity, survived on handouts from Eastern Europe, and by the mid 1990s it was down to about 200 members and published a paper, *The New Worker*, dedicated to the uncritical support of China and North Korea.[93]

Although the dissenting NCP did not thrive, it is clear that the larger Trotskyite organisations did pick up some support from the fragmenting CPGB, although such success was fleeting and did survive far into the 1980s. The most significant, sonorous, Trotskyite challenge came from the SWP (formerly the International Socialists or IS), which was claiming about 4,500 members in the late 1970s. It had focused its efforts upon the workers in industry and trade unionists. It had also attacked the CPGB since its attempts to influence trade unions had made it appear to be a representative of traditional trade union values and it abhorred the effective abandonment of class conflict by the Eurocommunists. The SWP tactic was to set up 'Rank-and-File Organisation' within each union and to suggest that there was a large body of workers who were prepared to overthrow capitalism but for the restraint of the bureaucratic trade union leaders who the CPGB were increasingly supporting. The *Socialist Worker* spent most of its time attacking the CPGB in the late 1970s and at that time had about fifteen 'rank-and-file' newspapers in various, mainly white collar, trades. These included the *Hospital Worker*, *Journalists' Charter*, *Rank and File Teacher* and, in the civil servants' union, *Redder Tape*. These, as with their parent newspaper, attacked the secret deals and corruption of CPGB trade union officials who, it was alleged, had duped their own members. These wild charges were made without any real evidence. However, the SWP influence soon dwindled and the number of rank-and-file newspapers fell to six by 1982, with each of their circulations being down by about two thirds on their heyday in the 1970s.[94]

The IMG also claimed some success in the 1970s but, in an attempt to win more support from manual workers, had removed Tariq Ali from its leadership in 1972. It then made a call for a general strike which received almost no support.[95] The Workers' Revolutionary Party (WRP formerly the SLL run by Gerry Healy) was convulsed with disputes connected with Healy and had made little progress. Indeed, Alan Johnson, looking at the internal, almost Stalinist, workings of the WRP quoted one of the Central Committee members reflecting upon the dominance of Healy at a Central Committee meeting in 1974:

> In line with the politics of Healy a further decision was taken of some importance. Without a single word of discussion, the meeting to recruit 3,000 new members in the next ten days. This item took literally thirty seconds. To have spoken or have voted against such a position would have meant certain branding as anti-party and opposed to building the party. No one did so. In spite of the resolution the WRP continued to decline.[96]

MT (founded in Liverpool in the 1950s by Ted Grant as the RSL) was probably as damaging to the CPGB in the late 1970s and early 1980s as it was to the Labour Party. It challenged the very fundamental policy of the CPGB for its constitution stated that 'unlike the reformists, centrists and Stalinists, the Marxists decisively reject the theory of the Parliamentary road to socialism...'[97] Its policy of entrism into the Labour Party is well documented but like the Communist Party, MT played a fringe role in the Labour leadership crisis of the late 1970s and early 1980s as the Bennites within the Labour Party promoted the idea of an electoral college selecting the Labour Party leader.

Trotskyite organisations of the 1970s were critical of both factions within the CPGB. They disagreed vehemently with the Eurocommunist ideas, which were seen to be unfairly critical of the Soviet Union, despite their own views, and the abandonment of Marxism–Leninism and the class struggle. However, they were barely more successful than the CPGB, taking some of its dissident members but doing little to improve the performance of Marxism in Britain. The SWP and MT probably exerted a damaging impact upon the CPGB, challenging both its trade union orthodoxy and its lack of commitment to the class struggle. Yet set against the decline of support following the defeat of the Heath Government in 1974 and the rise of Eurocommunism, the Trotskyite impact appears minimal.

Conclusion

The CPGB began the 1970s in great hope as it sought to widen its support in the face of the blatantly anti-trade union policies of Edward Heath's Conservative Government. It also hoped to attract the support of women's organisations as it openly embraced second-wave feminism. However, after an initial blush of success and some evidence that its broad democratic alliance was beginning to work the Party's hope of widening its influence waned rapidly. It is clear that after 1974 the Party could not cash in on the trade union support to the extent it could when opposing the Industrial Relations Act of 1971. Even though the social contract was still a potentially potent force in the Party's attempt to maintain its trade union influence it was not easy to win support for it was always easier to oppose the Conservatives than a trade-union based Labour Party. No matter how offensive Labour policies were to the trade unions the fortunes of the Labour and the trade union movement were inextricably intertwined. The Communist Party also lost some of its trade union supporters, most notably Jimmy Reid. However, the real problem for the CPGB was that it ran out of time.

The constant failure to develop and to even recapture its Second World War membership peak and influence meant that some of the new members of the Party, many of them young middle-class academics who had joined as students in the 1960s, began to feel that even the broad democratic alliance needed to be widened further and that the features of the old Communism – a reliance upon the Moscow model, notions of class conflict and the dictatorship of the proletariat – were no longer relevant to a new Communism which had to emerge. Eurocommunism was the result.

Yet even before Eurocommunism emerged, the Party was already examining its more moderate and right-wing credentials. For instance, the CPGB's 1977 version of *The British Road to Socialism* declared that a future Labour Government would not be a socialist government carrying out a socialist transformation of society but only be carrying out minor democratic reforms to British society. Nevertheless, the Party still hoped to win support from the trade union movement in order to increase its influence in the Labour Party. However, even here it missed its opportunities when it came to the changes in the procedures for selecting Labour Party leaders and failed to support the college system advocated by Tony Benn and his supporters. Indeed, at this moment the CPGB appeared to many workers, as a smaller version of the non-revolutionary Bennite Left operating within the Labour Party which proved to be a stronger poll of attraction for many workers. And the emergence of Eurocommunism made the Party look even more right wing.

How important, then, was Eurocommunism in dictating the decline of the CPGB and in softening its line against the industrial policy of the Labour Government in the late 1970s? It is certainly likely that it led to the CPGB playing a less prominent role in the trade union struggles, in the late 1970s than it had earlier in the decade.

In the late 1970s the Eurocommunist approach gathered rapid support within the CPGB because of the disillusionment with the Soviet model of communism, and the move from the industrial base of the Party to one increasingly dominated by intellectuals who had come through the student movement of the 1960s. The Russian invasion of Afghanistan in 1979 only served to increase the disillusionment felt by many with the CPGB and Eurocommunism was an attempt, which was not fully successful, to abandon Marxism–Leninism and the Party's class approach to politics. Nevertheless, to the disgust of many Trotskyite parties, the Eurocommunist CPGB abandoned its goal of becoming a mass workers' party, an objective established at its founding convention in 1920. Only the old pro-Soviet wing of the Party clung to the 1920 goal. The Revolutionary Workers' Party, and other Trotskyite organisations, looked aghast at these developments, unrelentingly committing themselves to bringing about revolutionary change and workers' control and reflected upon the failures of both sides of the CPGB from their own position of powerlessness.

Eurocommunism thus divided the CPGB and Marxism deeply in the late 1970s and provided the platform for the internecine conflict within the CPGB that occurred in what Frances Beckett calls 'The Awful Eighties'.[98] The 'Decisions' programmes produced by Granada caught the very moment of change but also revealed the extent to which the old Party faithfuls could limit discussion as they debated changes to *The British Road to Socialism* and revisited debates about inner party democracy. Conflicts between the Eurocommunists and old Communists dominated the 1980s and played a major part in the demise of the Party in 1991. In comparison the challenge of Trotskyism, to both factions within the CPGB, was of limited importance.

4 The challenge of Thatcherism, the triumph of Eurocommunism and the collapse of 'Stalinism', 1980–91

Throughout the 1980s the bitter conflict between the pro-Soviet wing of the Eurocommunists, both inside and outside the CPGB, became more intense. This conflict was fought out against the background of the Thatcherite offensive against the trade union movement and, from 1983, an increasingly reformist Labour Party. The internal conflict, which had emerged in the late 1970s, weakened the ability of the Party to respond more positively to Thatcher's offensive and Britain's falling industrial output, thus limiting its ability to respond effectively in the miners' strike of 1984–5. However, there was no doubting this threat with the Labour Party deflated and the trade union movements losing about a third of its members in the 1980s. Divided and retreating, the CPGB and British Marxism were faced with a perilous decline which they could not easily survive once Marxism collapsed in Eastern Europe and the Soviet Union. By the early 1990s, then, the end of the CPGB and the practical irrelevance of Marxism in British politics seemed almost guaranteed and it is doubtful whether it could have developed a viable alternative other than to have developed the Socialist Alliance movement further.

Declining political fortunes

By 1980 the CPGB was looking to be a spent force even in its natural position on the margins of British politics. Its membership was declining rapidly, it had done badly in the general election of May 1979, and it was divided between the rising Eurocommunist influence and the old pro-Moscow sections of the Party, normally dubbed the 'Stalinists'. The mood of the Party had already shifted somewhat in 1976 when John Gollan, the general secretary since 1956, was replaced by Gordon McLennan, who was much more amenable to the rising Eurocommunists and prepared, as he did in 1981, to go to Moscow to tell the Soviet leaders that they were wrong to try to dictate policy to communists in other countries, and particularly in Afghanistan at that time. Indeed, McLennan in the late 1970s had gone so far as to attempt to stop the secret financial subsidy from Russia, which had run to about £100,000 per year in the 1960s but was down to about £14,000 per year in the mid-1970s. It was apparently stopped in 1979, although there is a suggestion that some money was still being provided in the 1980s.[1]

'Stalinists' versus Eurocommunists in the 1980s

The internal conflict within the CPGB produced a bitter harvest in the 1980s, particularly from the old class-based party members who were gradually being driven out of the Party. Indeed, the main contention of Eddie and Ruth Frow, in their pamphlet *The Liquidation of the Communist Party in Great Britain*, was that the new Eurocommunist leadership of the CPGB colluded with *Marxism Today* in the 1980s to abandon scientific socialism, as outlined by Karl Marx and Frederick Engels in *The Communist Manifesto*. The abandonment of revolutionary Marxism:

> was promoted on the pages of *Marxism Today* under Martin Jacques' editorship. Non-Party academics and journalists were invited to contribute. Their main line of attack was on the decline of the working class, the autonomy of the State and the need for Labour Party members to distance themselves from their traditional basis. The article which made the position abundantly clear was a vicious attack on shop stewards by Tony Lane in a September, 1982 issue.[2]

Tony Lane, a sociologist from Liverpool University, portrayed the shop stewards not as hard-working men who were vulnerable to victimisation because of their activities but as foremen and managers in waiting. They were corrupt and seeking to take advantage of the trade union 'gravy train'. Lane added that:

> Here we are simply observing the creation of a new working-class élite which has the opportunity (and too often take it) of sharing in the expense account syndrome: the franchise of perks and fiddles which has often been widened.
>
> Shop stewards and full-time officers have had other opportunities. Some stewards have used their position as a stepping stone to promotion to charge-hand and foreman. A favoured few, usually convenors and full-time officers, have gone on to become personal managers and even industrial relations directors. Such routes of progression, to say the very least, induce a mixture of cynicism and resentment among the rank and file. Other stewards have simply used the role as a means to an easy life, an opportunity to get off the job and out of the plant with spurious excuses of 'union business'.[3]

To their criticism the Frows added a further concern about the security services: they believed that Harry Newton, a Communist who was an agent of MI5, and many others were operating to undermine the unity and principles of the CPGB. This had led to false accusations that there was a red plot top encourage strike activity and that the 'liquidators' had, in a deliberate move, acted to expel in a most undemocratic and dictatorial manner many of those members who still believed in Marxist–Leninist ideas. The end product of this was that:

> At the 43rd Congress of the CPGB held in November 1991, the Eurocommunist majority formed the Democratic Left which abandoned the theoretical basis and principles on which the CPGB had been formed. It became a loose, amorphous organisation functioning as a pressure group.[4]

The basic outline history offered by the Frows is correct although the precise events were far more complex and subject to different interpretations. It is clear that they were looking at the events from the perspective of the old Communists, who were often dubbed 'Stalinists' by their opponents. It was they, and their type, who were being driven out by the Party they had helped to shape.

The *Morning Star*, which was pro-Soviet, was similarly critical of Eurocommunism. The official daily paper of the CPGB, the *Morning Star* was run by a cooperative society registered as the People's Press Printing Society (PPPS), which had been formed in 1946 and included CPGB representatives. Relations between the Party and the paper did not always go well and glimpses of these could be seen in the 1970s. However, it was during the emergence of Eurocommunism in 1977 that the *Morning Star* came under severe criticism and a subcommittee was set up to examine the question of its content. Nevertheless, the Eurocommunist influence within the Party was not yet entirely dominant and the subcommittee reported that the paper was doing a good job with limited resources and falling circulation. The Draft Report, written by Dave Cook, despaired of the fall in circulation and asked 'Is the political situation and capacity of the Party such that we cannot reverse the downward trend in circulation?'[5] The report noted, however, that the CPGB and the *Morning Star* were separate and distinct units and that it would be wise for it not to be run by the King Street headquarters of the Party.[6]

It is clear that the increasingly 'Eurocommunist' Party did not accept this view for in 1981 two *Morning Star* journalists wrote to *The Guardian* suggesting that the PPPS was a 'Communist Front' and attacking the increasing Party control of the paper. Shortly afterwards a CPGB spokesman was reported in *The Guardian* as suggesting that the two reporters were wrong and that the PPPS operated according to its own wishes, although Communist Party representatives did express the Party views.[7] Nonetheless, it is clear that the Party was trying to influence the paper at a time when they were diverging over the issue of the Soviet model for communism.

The tensions between the Party leadership and the *Morning Star* became more pronounced when the former criticised the latter at the 1981 Party Congress. Tony Chater, editor of the *Morning Star*, felt betrayed by the criticism that the paper was not commercial enough in its approach since he believed that the paper should be a pure Labour paper and not a capitalist venture. The situation worsened in December 1981 when the *Morning Star* was critical of the EC's condemnation of the Soviet-inspired takeover of Poland and the suppression of the Solidarity movement. The *Morning Star* suggested that the Soviet actions were correct because the Polish people had forgotten their class destiny.

By this stage the conflict between the rampant Eurocommunists and the retreating old 'Stalinist' within the Party was overt. Mick Costello, the Industrial Organiser of the Party, was by this time almost isolated on the EC of the CPGB as a sceptic of Eurocommunism. He felt that the Party was playing down its industrial and class role which he had emphasised since his campaign in 1979 to win positions of 'trust and understanding' in the trade union movement. Temperamentally, Costello was very close to Tony Chater, editor of the *Morning Star*, which was pro-Moscow although it had journalists such as Chris Myant and Franks Chalmers who were not.

Thus, Costello and Chater became the two main defenders of the very much pre-1977 Marxist–Leninist principles of the Party.

Lane's article was published in the September 1982 issue of *Marxism Today*, which had appeared on the bookshelves the previous month. As already indicated, Lane examined the growing isolation of the trade union movement in British society and referred to the petty corruption and expenses fiddles in which lower levels of union officials and shop stewards sometimes indulged. As a result of this Mick Costello met Tony Chater at a Wimpy Bar, in the so-called 'Wimpy Bar Meeting', and decided to produce a statement in the *Morning Star* to rebut the allegations. This simply widened the split within the CPGB beyond repair. One report states: ' "Mick thought the article would isolate our comrades in the TUC", says Chater, "He wanted to put a statement in the *Star*. Everyone ought to know this was not the view of Communists." '[8] In response, Mick Costello criticised Lane in an article which appeared on the front page of the *Morning Star* on 26 August 1982. He claimed that Lane's article was an insult to trade unionism, 'a gross slander on the labour movement' was being used by the anti-left *Daily Mirror* and was helping the Tory Government to 'undermine the self-confidence of the working class'.[9] Costello was defending the trade unionists and shop stewards whom he and the CPGB had defended for many years and Ken Gill, the Communist leader of the draughtsman's union TASS, poignantly reflected that 'This was the watershed, when the Party fell into the hands of those who had no working-class base.'[10]

Tony Lane responded to Costello's criticism in a letter written to the EC on 26 August, maintaining that the issue of perks and fiddles had been mentioned in a gentle way and that 'I hope it will not seem immodest if I say that I think the article in question is one of the best analytical pieces I have written and raises a host of serious questions.'[11] Jacques later reflected that the fuss was a surprise to him and that he felt that Costello was in fact responding as a result of an article he had published in *Marxism, Today*, by Roy Medvedev on the lack of democracy in the Soviet Union.[12]

When the EC of the CPGB met on 12 September it gave a mild rebuke to Martin Jacques, editor of *Marxism Today*, for printing the Lane article without fuller consultation.[13] However, it was stated that 'the executive committee does not accept that it was gross slander on the labour movement', whilst it did reaffirm its belief in the importance and integrity of the shop steward movement.[14] It was far more critical of Chater, Costello and David Whitfield (the *Morning Star's* deputy editor), for forming a cabal to attack another Party journal and for using the Party's name without reference to the EC. Strictly speaking, of course, the *Morning Star* was not a Party journal, although it had Party representation, and needed no such permission. But it is clear that the CPGB was now dominated by the Eurocommunists and that those who opposed the dilution of 'class politics' had received a rebuff. Interestingly, however, Chater took an extended trip to Moscow and appears to have brokered some arrangement whereby the press in the Soviet Union became less critical of the *Morning Star*.

The files of the EC of the CPGB contain around eighty letters expressing various concerns about this internal conflict. They were pretty evenly divided between those favouring Lane, Jacques and *Marxism Today* and those favouring Costello and Chater. The Hastings CPGB branch attacked Costello and asked for self-criticism within the trade union movement whilst Willie Thompson expressed the view that Martin Jacques had done a good job and made *Marxism Today* 'an asset to our Party'. On the other hand, the Sheffield CPGB resented the 'Lane smear' and favoured censure of the editorial board of *Marxism Today* and the Newcastle City branch did not consider *Marxism Today* to be a Marxist journal. Vic Allen, the famous Marxist lecturer at Leeds University, wrote an article in *Morning Star* stressing that Eurocommunism had gone too far in shaping foreign policy and thus welcomed Mick Costello's intervention.[15]

Relations between the increasingly Eurocommunist-dominated Party and the pro-Soviet *Morning Star* began to worsen as the PC of the Party attempted to secure Chater's removal as editor. The Party continued to work with the *Morning Star* and helped it in its January campaign to increase daily circulation. However, relations became more difficult when Costello resigned as Industrial Organiser of the CPGB to become Industrial Correspondent of the *Morning Star* in November 1982, according to the Frows, thus widening and hardening the split within the CPGB. According to Willie Thompson, however, Costello became Industrial Correspondent of the *Morning Star* seven weeks later.[16] Beckett's account states that:

> A few weeks later [after the debate about the Lane article] Costello came into McLennan's office to hand in his resignation. He explained that following the breakup of his marriage he needed to be more often at home with his children. McLennan said: 'The one thing you mustn't do, Mick, is go back to the *Morning Star*'. He was furious when he heard this was just what Costello did, and thought it was part of a plot.[17]

As the *Morning Star's* circulation campaign failed each side blamed the other and relations worsened still further. Gordon McLennan, now an increasingly Eurocommunist general secretary of the Party, offered to meet Chater to resolve differences but nothing happened. The Party could not sack Chater, Costello or Whitfield from their posts at the *Morning Star* because the PPPS was an independent and self-governing body, as it had been since 1946. Nevertheless, it bitterly complained that these individuals had been appointed to the *Morning Star* without the EC being in a position to express its opinion and decided to put forward a recommended list of candidates of the forthcoming election of six representatives to the management committee in 1983.[18] The list included George Matthews, a former editor, Bert Pearce, the Welsh district secretary, David Priscott, the Yorkshire district secretary, and, for decency's sake, Tony Chater, the errant current editor. Yet matters grew worse when the *Morning Star* complained in June 1983 that a 'powerful outside body' was attempting to take over the paper. It was not immediately obvious to many Party members that this meant the Party itself. Despite the offence this created the Chaterite candidates defeated the EC nominees in the AGM elections for the *Morning Star*.

The movement was now even more deeply divided between the Eurocommunist dominated Party and the pro-Moscow *Morning Star*. The Eurocommunists and rank-and-file members of the Party objected to Chater's action in hijacking the *Morning Star*. On the other hand, Chater and his supporters appealed to those of the left, including the 'Straight-Leftists', who wished to protect the Party's working-class heritage. Indeed, Chater and Costello attempted to present the Eurocommunists, Party leaders and *Marxism Today* as both anti-trade unionist and anti-working class. The Straight Leftists claimed to represent working-class interests and to be defending the Party and movement against dangerous revisionism. Chater endorsed this by publishing articles of a pro-Soviet nature in the *Morning Star*.

There was a hostile reaction to this within the Party. Beatrix Campbell wrote a letter of criticism to the *Morning Star*, repeated her criticisms in *City Limits*, and sent similar comments in a letter to the EC of the Party.[19] Of course, the EC accepted her rejection of the old line and powered forward with its own criticisms. The Party leadership emphasised that the development of political consciousness required compromise and realignment if the historic mission of the Party, the securing of working-class power, was to be achieved.

In 1984 there was an even more determined attempt to remove Chater as editor. The Party decided to appeal directly to the PPPS, who owned the paper, to remove Chater. It was unwilling to do so. Ken Gill, the Marxist trade unionist, reflected upon the situation, stating that:

> The *Morning Star* was not the organ of the Communist Party. They behaved as though it was and ordered us to sack the editor. If they had said to Communists on a trade union executive, get rid of your general secretary, that would have been an unwarranted interference in the affairs of the union.[20]

Failing to gain the response it sought, the Party, and McLennan its general secretary, set about trying to ensure that its supporters were elected to the PPPS management committee. The Party produced numerous circulars of advice to their members on how to use their votes and power and published *Focus*, a monthly magazine, which acted as the reservoir for readers' letters that were critical of Chater.

As a result of such campaigns, hundreds of people turned up to the PPPS regional meetings in 1984. Five hundred people went to the Scottish meeting at Woodside Hall, Glasgow, and fights broke out before a Chaterite majority was declared on the management committee. At the London meeting Gordon McLennan tried to muster the vote for Chris Myant, the Party's candidate, in a forlorn attempt to replace Chater. As a result of this offensive by the Party, the *Morning Star* removed from its staff pro-Party writers such as George Matthews, the former editor who wrote opera reviews, and Bill Wainright, the science correspondent and former deputy-editor.

Meanwhile, and rather markedly, the Party continued to favour *Marxism Today* and noted, favourably, that this monthly journal had increased its sales from 4,500 in 1978 to 11,500 in 1983 under Martin Jacques's editorship, which it praised.[21] The journal, in turn, stressed the need for the Labour left to review its policies.

The Straight Left faction, named after the journal *Straight Left*, which first appeared in 1979, also entered the debate with a 34-page pamphlet entitled *The Crisis in Our Communist Party: Cause, Effect and Cure*. It was allegedly written by Charlie Woods, an 83-year-old retired miner but was possibly written by Fergus Nicholson or Brian Filling. It rejected both sides in the dispute and called for 'a new leadership with new principles'.[22]

The conflict of opinion between all three factions – Eurocommunists, 'Stalinists' and Straight Left – spilled over into a major debate throughout the Communist press. Most obviously the major battle was going to be fought at the Thirty-eighth Congress of the Party in November 1983. In the build up to this Congress, Costello placed a critical article in the Party's monthly bulletin *Communist Focus*, raising issues which he considered might be tackled at the Thirty-eighth Congress in November 1983. In reply, Chater was inexorable in his attack upon the Eurocommunists through the *Morning Star*. The Chaterites and the Straight Leftists, although antagonistic towards one another, also produced a clandestine recommended list for the EC. However, this was undermined by the fact that the Straight Leftists also produced a personalised bulletin called *Congress Truth*, which attacked both the Chaterites and the Eurocommunist-dominated EC of the Party.

The EC of the CPGB responded by getting Congress to condemn the actions of all opposition factions. Congress also censured Chater and Whitfield and then removed them, and most of their supporters, from the EC. There was also further criticism of the fact that four members of the Election Preparation Committee were involved in putting forward a 'Political Alternative List'; Barry Johnson later withdrew his name from this list and the other three – Brian Topping, Bruce Allen and Barbara O' Hare – asserted that they had done nothing wrong.

At the Thirty-eighth Congress (1983) the Eurocommunists were also confirmed in their control of the Party. Thereafter began a witch hunt in which the Party machinery and rules were used to remove the Chaterites and the old pro-Moscow faction. In May 1984 the EC adopted two statements attacking factional activity at the previous Congress. One, 'Factional' and other 'Unprincipled Activity' at the Thirty-eighth Congress condemned Wood's pamphlet and expelled him from the Party. Also, on 17 July 1984, those who had produced the 'Political Alternative List' were expelled from the Party although Johnson was only expelled for three months.[23] The EC's statement also noted that the PPPS was now facing an annual general meeting and declared that the Party was putting forward five candidates for the management committee – George Bolton, Tricia David, Ron Halverson, H. Mitchell and Chris Myant.

The disciplinary action of the EC drew widespread criticism. The east Midland district and the Carlisle branch both complained about the expulsions, the latter stating that 'The expulsions were in fact an attempt at stifling the widespread criticism within the party of the present leadership and its policies, by administrative methods.' This was seen to be an example of 'the retreat of the leadership of the party from the revolutionary Marxist–Leninist past and an open avowal of their revisionist socialist–democratic stance'.[24] At this time the British trade union movement was faced with its biggest challenge for almost a century as the Thatcher Government took a determined stand to scale down the coal industry. It was not a propitious moment for the Party as Thatcher emphasised the need to destroy trade unions as part of her strategy of rolling back the welfare state, 'nanny state', and releasing the forces of privatisation. Distracted by its own internal convulsions the CPGB failed to fully respond to the challenge of 'Thatcherism' and was unprepared for her assault upon the coal miners.

The coal miners' strike of 1984-5

The immediate context of the coal miners' strike was the decision of Ian MacGregor, and the National Coal Board to offer the miners only a 5.2 per cent wage increase in October 1983. The NUM rejected this and imposed an overtime ban on 30 October 1983. Matters came to a head when MacGregor proposed to cut coal output and employment in the mines. There were spontaneous strikes, such as that at Cortonwood, where pits had been informed of their immediate closure. The coal strike began on 9 March 1984 at the pits in Scotland and Yorkshire where notifications of closures had been made. However, there was to be no national ballot. Instead, the NUM sent flying pickets from Yorkshire to Scotland and Kent to persuade the working miners, particularly those in Nottingham and the Midlands, to join the dispute, despite a high court injunction forbidding such action.[25] This led to mass picketing and violence, notably at Ollerton in Nottinghamshire, where a Yorkshire striker on picket duty was crushed to death in the demonstration outside the pit, and at Orgreave coke plant near Sheffield. There were many twists and turns throughout this dispute. On 14 March the High Court gave the National Court Board (NCB) an injunction against flying pickets, though the NCB chose not to use it. The Thatcher Government also maintained a police presence to stop the movement of flying pickets. At this stage, trade union support for the miners was mixed, although Arthur Scargill drew immense personal support at the 1984 TUC Conference.[26]

Yet as the strike ground on, court action by the government began to take its effect. The South Wales Mineworkers were fined £50,000 for contempt over picketing and when this was not paid the £707,000 of their funds were sequestrated. The NUM was also fined £200,000 on 10 October for breaking an order declaring their strike unofficial, and when it failed to pay, its assets were also seized – at least those assets which had not been salted away to Luxembourg, Dublin and other financial centres.

There was much violence and many incidents of high emotion during the strike. Arthur Scargill was heavily criticised for his refusal to hold a national strike ballot, and there was much criticism by the NUM of the decision of a substantial proportion of the Nottingham miners to form the Union of Democratic Mineworkers (UDM), which sought to do business with the government. Scargill and the NUM were also intensely hostile to the decision of the National Coal Board to offer a Christmas bonus pay-packet to any miner who worked for full time before Christmas. The violence which ensued included the much publicised incident when a concrete block was dropped from a motorway bridge on to a taxi taking a miner to work in South Wales, killing the driver and leading to two strikers being sent to gaol for twenty years. Despite the NUM's opposition 15,000 miners did return to work under this offer.

Eventually the strike came to an end, in a ragged fashion, and without any settlement, when a special delegate meeting of the mineworkers decided to return to work without agreement on 3 March 1985. The government had remained firm, the strike had not forced any power cuts throughout the winter and at the end of February 1985 the Welsh miners had returned without accepting an offer. There was no other outcome available, unless the NUM was willing to force the dispute through to another winter. At the end of the dispute it was clear that the power of the NUM had been irrevocably destroyed and that it would be unable to prevent the rapidly developing pattern of pit closures which reduced the number of miners to half over the next six years. In sum, 10,000 miners were arrested during the strike, 1,000 people were injured and three killed. Eventually 100 pits were closed, 100,000 miners lost their jobs and the NUM was left divided and almost bankrupt. Scargill, with little to clutch to even when negotiation would have been a more sensible course of action, reflected to his members that 'The greatest achievement is the struggle itself.'[27] This was a rather bland and unrewarding comment for those who had suffered for a year and seen the NUM virtually destroyed. In the face of such disaster the CPGB gave the false impression that it was united behind Scargill when a close inspection of the record suggests nothing of the kind.

The Communist Party of Great Britain and the coal miners' strike

During the miners' strike the factionalism of the CPGB meant that there was rather less activity and support for the miners than might have otherwise been the case, although a pretence of unity emerged. Indeed, as will be seen, there was some significant effort from Communist feminists although conflict and concern about the role of Ann Scargill and others in the WAPC movement meant that this was also less effective than might otherwise have been the case. Indeed, the Eurocommunists seemed almost hostile to the miners when one looks beyond the facade.

The Party did work with support groups for the miners yet it, and *Marxism Today*, were much criticised for their lukewarm attitude to industrial and class conflict. Indeed, it was accepted that 'the Party is deeply divided and in crisis'.[28] Not surprisingly, *Marxism Today* published only three articles on the miners' strike throughout 1984–5. Indeed, the Party's condemnation of Arthur Scargill's tactics as the defeat of the miners became imminent and was seen by some critics as evidence of the lack of support for the miners by the Eurocommunist-dominated Party.[29] The *Morning Star*, Chater and Costello went to the other extreme. Indeed, it supported the miners so strongly that Scargill commented that 'The *Morning Star* is guilty of one act, it supports working class politics and socialism.'[30]

Instead of being the opportunity for the CPGB to demonstrate its unity with the most obvious well-organised section of the working class, the miners' strike had become part of the conflict between the two major factions. The NUM was, after all, the union which the mid-1970s Party had rested its hopes on. The Vice-President of the NUM was Mick McGahey, a leading Party member, and Arthur Scargill, the President, had at one time been a Communist.

At the beginning of the strike McGahey had attempted to use his influence upon the CPGB to get it to accept the Scargill line that there should not be a mass vote on the strike and gained it without dissent. However, it is clear that that decision was not popular and the cause of much debate within the Party. Indeed, the Party's lack of resolve was recognised by Jim Cowan, the chairman of the National Coal Board, who observed in June 1984 that 'the Communist Party is ready to settle'.[31]

The fact is that the Party wanted a quick settlement since it felt that a protracted strike would be a disaster and that this might reflect badly upon the Labour Left. Indeed, Gordon McLennan, the Party's general secretary, and Scargill were embroiled in a fierce private row and the Party called Bert Ramelson out of retirement to mediate. This was a blatant attempt to influence Scargill who had been greatly influenced by Ramelson in his youth. However, Ramelson wrote a detailed analysis of the situation but Scargill rejected it and accused him of betrayal.

At this point Margaret Thatcher described Scargill as 'the enemy within' – a term used almost thirty years before by Bobby Kennedy in the title of his book about the similarly troublesome Jimmy Hoffa, the leader of the American Teamster's Union. As a result the miners bought T-shirts with those very words emblazoned upon them. In this situation, it was difficult for the Party and McGahey to pressure Scargill further in their attempt to bring an end to the dispute.

Nevertheless, Bill Keys, of the Print Union, arranged for McGahey to meet Willie Whitelaw, of the government, for a secret meeting in Edinburgh in the hope of brokering a settlement. McGahey also talked to Ned Smith, the NCB's director of industrial relations. However, these moves came to nothing as Scargill was unbending and Thatcher scented victory. Indeed, the futility of attempting to gain a settlement faced with Scargill's obduracy led to heated exchanges between McGahey and Scargill.[32]

Once the strike was ended it was difficult for the Party to maintain the impression of unity it had with Scargill and the miners. Indeed, Peter Carter, who had replaced Costello as the Party's Industrial Organiser, produced a statement in which he criticised Scargill's failure to hold a national ballot of the miners and mass picketing. This was suppressed by the Party and Gordon McLennan provided the veneer of unity by organising a meeting between himself, Scargill and Peter Carter, which was allegedly less friendly than it was presented as being.[33]

Scargill, for his part, denounced all those who had attacked him during the dispute. He thanked the *Morning Star* for the support it had given but condemned the Party for considering the Carter criticism and *Marxism Today* for the way in which it had traduced the miners' leaders. Scargill belonged to the old pro-Stalin tradition, having supported the Soviet Union in its invasion of Hungary in 1956. He was a trade union leader who used the Party machine for his advantage but operated industrial conflict in his own way and the fatal weakness which many have detected is that he was almost religiously committed to believing that nothing could be won unless it was achieved by industrial struggle. According to Beckett:

> He told the *Observer* after the strike that his father was a Communist: 'Not the Eurocommunist variety, not the New Realist variety, but the real Communist who wants to see capitalism torn down and replaced by a system where people own and control the means of production, distribution and exchange.... I'm more passionately in support of that view now than I was then.'[34]

The miners' strike of 1984–5 simply enforced and endorsed the differences between the two major factions within the Party but, to some extent, it also hid the way in which the Eurocommunist-dominated Party had moved away from its old industrial and class roots. It also revealed tensions between the Party's feminist movement and the wider feminist movement.

Feminism, women, Greenham Common and the miners' strike

The Women's Section of the CPGB was greatly affected by three developments in the 1980s. One was the change within feminism which saw third-wave feminism emphasise the diversity of the woman's experience and cut across the increasingly socialist aligned feminism that was emerging in Britain in the late 1970s. This came, of course, just at the time when, as indicated in Chapter Three, the WLM was fragmenting and just as the Party was generally moving towards the more focused political campaigning envisaged by socialist feminists. A second development was the conflict between the Party women and the women's support campaign for the miner's strike, which led to some further fragmentation of the women's movement. A third development was the rapid decline in the influence of Marxist women as the CPGB collapsed in the late 1980s. The overriding point in these developments was the fragmentation and rapid decline of the influence of feminism both inside and outside the CPGB.

Link, the 'communist party women's journal', began the 1980s with an article entitled '50 years of Strength: Women and the *Morning Star*'.[35] It emphasised, rather exaggeratedly, the influence of the women's groups of the CPGB. Nevertheless, in the early 1980s it is clear that the Marxist women's movement remained staunchly committed to widening the rights of women and protecting their interests against the predatory Thatcher Government's attack upon housing, health and education. Indeed, in the winter of 1980 *Link* campaigned against the tendency to make part-time teachers, who were mainly women, redundant as part of the education cuts. It also added that 'The cuts in in-service training are bound to have a particular affect on women. After even a short break in teaching, short in-service refresher courses are very important. The likelihood of going on such courses is getting less and less.'[36] It also expressed a concern about the high levels of perinatal and neonatal mortality rates. There was also a continuing campaign to extend the right to work, to women who were part-time workers or lost their employment as a result of strikes and pregnancy.[37] However, the big issue which arose in the 1980s was that of the position of black and lesbian women feminist groups, the emergence of which led to the further fragmentation of feminism and the WLM.

The concept of difference, which drew from the work of French post-structural theorists Jacques Derrida, Jacques Lacan and Michel Foucoult, impelled feminism to its third wave. Whilst these ideas linked up nicely with postmodernism they did not easily dovetail with overarching and universalistic theories such as Marxism and socialism. Postmodernism rejects the idea of searching for an underlying truth and threatens the idea of the collective action based upon share identities, objectives and class consciousness which Marxists and socialists normally demand.

Notwithstanding this problem *Link* and the women's group within the CPGB attempted to embrace new initiatives at the beginning of the 1980s. Most obviously, they provided an outlet for the emergence of Black women groups. Shortly after the Brixton race riots of April 1981 *Link* focused upon the Black Women's Centre in Brixton which was formed by the Brixton Black Women's Group, which emerged in the mid-1970s:

> The Group started about seven years ago and from the start defines itself as black 'in the political sense'. It therefore includes both Afro-Caribbean and Asian women, and two Chinese women have also been involved, since all non-white people share the experience of racial oppression.[38]

The Group produced its own newsletter *Speak Out* and met every Sunday. One meeting per month was open to all black women in the hope of attracting new members, two were given over to study group work on imperialism, racism, police harassment and the fourth Sunday was given over to the discussion of community affairs. The Black Women's Centre provided a library, playgroup and Easter play scheme for black women and was, at that time, planning to provide contraception and pregnancy advice and a Care Assistance Programme for teenagers. Its schemes were partly financed by the government's Inner Area Partnership Scheme which provided it with enough funding to employ one full-time worker and it was run by a management committee which included representatives from consumer groups such as the Abeng Community Centre, the Consortium for Ethnic Minorities in Lambeth, the Care Assistance Project, the Black Women's Group, and other bodies. It was also involved in work on the legal representation, with the Brixton Legal Defence Group, in connection with the 'April uprising'.

From the start, the CPGB was aware that the Black Women's Group was something different which cut across the second-wave feminism which it had been involved in. *Link* noted that:

> The Black Women's Group's attitude to the women's liberation movement was described as one of 'critical support'. Although willing to cooperate with the WLM the Group identifies more closely with the black community. The WLM has fought for valuable gains for both black and white women, but the priorities of black women's groups are different from those of the mainstream of the women's movement. There are differences even in the treatment of issues central to the WLM, such a contraception, abortion rights and sterilisation. The role of the black women's groups in the campaign against the contraceptive drug Depo-Provero is an example of this.
>
> Moreover, while the WLM has created a favourable ideological climate for setting up new groups, the black women's movement in this country draws on its strong tradition of women organising politically, especially in Afro-Caribbean societies.
>
> This tradition is clearly very much alive in the Brixton Black Women's Group, which is playing an increasingly prominent role in the black community, as an organised force. Only a year after it opened the Women's Centre is seen as a major advance for black women and has led to similar initiatives in other parts of the country.[39]

What clearly perturbed the Communist Party was the fact that very little of this effort carried over into its organisation. Indeed, the subsequent issue of *Link* reported an interview between Mary Davis, of the editorial team, and Margaret Tonge, a young West Indian woman then living in Tottenham, North London, who came to Britain from Montserrat in 1959. The main question as stake was 'At a time when few blacks are turning to the Communist Party (despite their mounting militancy on many questions), why has Margaret chosen this organization?'[40] The answer appeared to be that she had lived in Montserrat, England and Canada and was aware of the class nature of capitalist countries and felt that the Communist Party, unlike the Labour Party with its parochial attitude towards politics, offered the right international solution to the problem. However, this hardly explained why the CPGB was failing to attract black support.

The subsequent edition included an article on 'Black Women Unite' written by Neehm Zabit, which was far more enlightening. It particularly pointed towards the opposition of the 'white left' and the 'ultra-left too' to issues which affect black people.[41] In effect, it is argued, that there were two trends at work. One was that autonomous black organisations were emerging and they felt, since the time for working in mixed groups was over, they needed to strengthen the links between black communities. This had begun in 1978, when the first ever National Black Women's Conference was held, and had moved on to the formation of OWAAD (the Organization of Women of African and Asian Descent) and the formation of the first ever Black Women's Centre in Brixton in 1980. This was partly a response to the second trend, which was for white left organisations to ignore the issues of black people. The article argued that:

> In the past the struggle against racism was not a priority on the agenda of most white left organisations – it was seen as a diversion away from the class struggle – or there was token reference to it without meaningful work around raising the consciousness of the indigenous working class for fear of alienating them. Instead criticism was more often than [not] misdirected against black people's reluctance to join parties, trade unions, campaigns, etc. or to the disunity amongst the black organisations themselves. This has clearly been shown to be a myth, and a racist myth at that.

After that there seems to have been remarkably little discussion of the black women and the black community in relation to the CPGB. The exception was in 1984 when the Women's Conference was on racism, although it was admitted that 'We need to sort out what we mean by solidarity and support, and what black women want from us. Also we mustn't lose sight of the sharp differences between black activists, as in any movement.'[42]

It is possible that the raging internal conflicts within the Party distracted attention away from the issue, that the Party's rapidly declining membership posed more immediate problems, or that the Party could not come to terms with the fragmentation of the WLM that black women's politics presented but it is clear that inertia set in.

Link made occasional references to black women but women's unemployment, a serious issue in the early 1980s, and the feminist opposition at Greenham Common against the United States nuclear air base, attracted more interest.[43]

Initially, and much more serious in the minds of Party members, was the issue of whether or not feminism could survive the 1980s. Jackie Heywood, dealing with 'The Moving Left Show' expressed concern at the state of socialist feminism and Anna Coote, in a call for action, felt that the feminists had let the left get away with too much. Surrounding this were the constant issues surrounding women's conferences, the People's march and women's unemployment, which rose rapidly in the early 1980s.[44] Throughout these events the CPGB's National Women's Advisory Committee and the Women's Network continued its work tirelessly, if narrowly, on issues more associated with second-wave rather than third-wave feminism. There was no clear and categorical line on lesbian feminism, except for a general waft of support in its direction, but there are hints that the Party was coming to terms with black feminism, albeit in the form of a National Aggregate Meeting of Black members in May 1991, but this was only six months before the end of the Party.[45]

The fragmentation of the WLM, as black feminists, socialist feminists and other feminists began to go their separate ways tended to produce a feminist movement which fought upon specific issues without any real sense of overall unity, purpose and coherence. Indeed, some of these particular issues served to divide the movement further. This was particularly evident in the case of the miners' strike of 1984–5.

The year-long miners' strike led to the formation of the WAPC movement, to which the CPGB was deeply attached. This organisation, formed during the dispute, was supported by the National Women's (Advisory) Committee of the CPGB.[46] This body invited Betty Heathfield to its July 1984 meeting, although she could not come and Tricia Davis, of the CPGB, organised an appeal to support the 11 August demonstration of WAPC. There was widespread discussion of the work of the women's groups against pit closures in Sheffield and Yorkshire and the need to have a meeting with the Party's miners 'to talk about how they can support the women's organisations at more than just a superficial level'. A meeting of women in the coalfields was also organised on 4 August.[47]

Unfortunately, the Party's criticism of Arthur Scargill's tactics during the dispute led to a cooling of relations between the NUM and the CPGB which meant that the Party had limited influence over the WAPC campaign. Indeed, this became abundantly clear in the months following the end of the dispute when the CPGB exerted an obviously limited influence over WAPC. The Sheffield meeting of WAPC on 20 September 1985 reveals the tensions that had emerged. According to the CPGB account Ann Lilburne, the Chair of WAPC, had organised the morning meeting badly, especially when it came to voting, and the meeting had been rescued in the afternoon by Ella Egan, who was the Vice-Chair, a delegate for Scotland and a member of the CPGB. The CPGB report on the meeting suggested that it was not clear what role the WAPC would be playing after the strike, that there was a lack of consultation between the National Committee and local groups and that there was dismay that the NUM would not allow women associate membership and seemed to be wanting to create the WAPC as a political organisation in its own image. Above all, the report complained that the non-elected ex-officio members were undermining the authority of the National Committee, citing Betty Heathfield, Ann Scargill, Jean McCrindle, Kate Bennett, Kim Young and Shelley Adams as acting in this role controlling the machine of the WAPC and producing the strategy documents. The report noted 'Just two examples of what happened over the weekend. Ann Scargill left for Bulgaria with 20 hand-picked women and Jean McCrindle went to Paris for the meeting of the new international miners' organisation.'[48] The latter action was apparently objected to by the National Committee.

The fact is that the CPGB and WAPC were largely in conflict with each other and the CPGB report indicates its approach and concerns. Indeed, the report noted that:

> We have two comrades on the National Committee: Ellen Egan (Scotland) Vice Chair and Lorraine Bowler (Yorkshire). They are operating in a difficult climate between the general hostility between the NUM and the Party resulting from our analysis of the strike, and because they challenge... what is currently going on. There is a strong anti-party feeling mainly being promoted by ex-officio members.[49]

This conflict extended to the CPGB opposing an early conference and the power and influence of the ex-officio members but it was noted, by the CPGB reporter, that:

> The problem we have at the moment is that most of the women on the National Committee support the ex-officios. The influence of Ann Scargill and Betty Heathfield is still powerful and they are able to assert a kind of authority on the movement via Arthur Scargill and Peter Heathfield.

It is quite clear then that the issue of Black feminism and third-wave feminist development plus particular events, such as the miners' strike, did nothing to maintain any sense of unity within the feminist movement which became increasingly fragmented in the 1980s. Nevertheless the CPGB did try to maintain its contribution to the women's movement but with diminishing results.

The CPGB maintained much of the programme of the 1970s, organising its National Biennial conferences and it half-yearly meetings. Throughout the 1980s, particularly after the demise of *Link* in 1984, it was the Party Women's Conference that kept the diminishing and fragmenting women's movement alive within the Party. Its Women's National Conference, of 2–3 October 1982, warned of the ideological and political stance of Thatcherism and the way in which Thatcher's administration had increased unemployment, particularly amongst women who faced twice the level of unemployment as did men.[50]

The Women's Conference of 1–2 October 1983 was even more dramatic though, focusing upon 'Tory Family Policy' and 'Women and Peace'. Mary McIntosh, who wrote *The Anti-Social Family* with Michele Barratt, put forward her views on Tory family values in a paper discussed at conference, suggesting that women members should also read Jean Coussins and Anna Coote, *The Family in the Firing Line*. Her aim was to provide an opposition to the Tory 'family policy' which was not simply reactive and designed to oppose the impact of Thatcher's social cuts but geared towards creating a communist society 'in which family will not be so central to people's lives'.[51] This was in line with the writings of Engels and Marx who wrote about 'abolishing the family' but, as McIntosh observed, was rarely discussed today. Yet it was an answer to the degrading system, that of the ' "family wage" system of breadwinning husband and his housewife [which] makes women economically dependent and therefore less powerful and lacking psychological independence'. This was the basis, she argued, of domestic violence. She envisaged the abolishing of the family system of income with the abolition of the class system.

The issue of 'Women and the Peace Movement' was also discussed in reaction to the 1983 general election when Thatcher used the Falklands War, 'Falkland Factor', to win a new term of office and put forward her resolute stand on the nuclear arms race and 'standing up to the Russians'. Jean Turner presented her views at the Conference of the need to work with the Soviet Union and for Britain to adopt a non-aligned peaceful role in world affairs'.[52] Following the anti-war waves of the Stockholm Peace Appeal against the dropping of an atom bomb on North Korea in the 1950s, against the war against North Vietnam in the 1960s, and the 1970s anti-war movement against the installation of the neutron bomb in Europe, she argued that the women's movement needed to be involved deeply in the anti-war wave against the installation of Cruise and Pershing II missiles in Britain and Europe. In addition the Soviet offer to destroy the SS-20 missiles in equivalent numbers to those destroyed by the USA and British was promoted. Inevitably, this led to support for the action of the Greenham Common protest in 1984.

The Party also organised a conference on 'Women in Trade Unions' on Saturday, 10 December 1983 and followed this up on 8 December 1984 with a 'Women and Work Conference.'[53] In February 1983 Tricia Davis, of the Birmingham Trade Union Resource Centre, also followed up the work of the Labour Research Department survey on unemployment, discussed the work of Unemployed Workers' Centres and stressed that women were unrepresentative amongst the unemployed as well as unrepresentative in unemployment statistics. She therefore encouraged women 'signing on campaigns' at employment exchanges. The National Women's Committee of the CPGB also attempted to challenge the problem of 'invisibility' of women.[54] Trade unionism and low pay were targeted, and the need for more training for women was emphasised.[55]

There had, indeed, been a major shift in the work and the attitudes of the CPGB towards women between the 1960s and the 1980s. Instead of generally supporting women's rights the Party had moved towards a more pro-active and co-ordinated policies of second-wave feminism. At the 1979 Party Congress it was stated that 'The 36th Congress reaffirms that the basic right of women to decide if and when they would bear children, is central to our current campaigning and closely linked to The British Road to Socialism.' At the 1981 Party Congress it was emphasised that women were losing rights and facing increasing exploitation under capitalism and Thatcherism to which was added the issues of violence and sexual harassment. Indeed, in a movement from the external relationship to the internal, 'the personal becomes the political', Congress asked all members to examine their own family relationships in the light of the 'second-wave' if not 'third-wave' feminism the CPGB had adopted.[56] Nevertheless, it was international peace rather than domestic arrangements that became of paramount importance and one of the most important activities of Communist women was to support the Greenham Common protest against nuclear weapons.

Greenham Common was the United States Cruise Missile Airbase at Newbury. In 1981 a women's peace camp was established there, which was attended by hundreds of women, despite prosecutions by both the civil and military authorities. In December 1982, 30,000 women encircled the nine-mile fence and in 1983 women invaded the base and danced on the missile silos. Protests continued until the end of the Cold War when the base was closed. Despite an enormously hostile press, Greenham became a symbol of women's rejection of war and violence. Throughout the Greenham Common years the protest was exclusively by women; men were asked to stay away. It was emphasised that there were no leaders, meetings were often held on the first Saturday of each month, there was planting, picnicking, singing, sharing experiences and non-violent direct action.[57]

The Party received letters of support for the Greenham Common women from the Soviet women. One dated 12 May 1984 demanded the prevention of nuclear war and opposition to the deployment of Pershing II and cruise missiles in Western Europe.[58] This was passed on to the Greenham women but the main activities of the Party seems to have been to support women who were arrested. For instance, it took up the case of 'TWO GREENHAM WOMEN WHO FACE TRUMPED UP CHARGES'. They were Gloria Delmont and Jill Morony who were charged with pulling down a section of the nine-mile perimeter fence at Greenham Common in a major demonstration of 2,000 women on 29 October 1983.

> Only when Gloria and Jill presented themselves in Newbury Magistrates Court on the 15 March 1984 to face trial on a charge of causing criminal damage worth £25 were they and their counsel informed that the charge had been amended to the value of £5,397·65 regarding 81 sections of the perimeter fence. The women elected to be tried on the new charge in Crown Court, and were committed to this on 12 April 1984.[59]

The Party campaigned, with others, to expose these charges, noting that the damage they were charged with did not correspond in location with the original grid reference given for the fence. It also stressed that some of the alleged questioning by the police had never taken place and complained that other women arrested with Gloria and Jill had never been charged. They stressed that Gloria and Jill had been singled out for a 'blatantly manipulative charge' and that the Ministry of Defence police wanted scapegoats.

Such unity as engendered by the events of Greenham Common did not revive the women's movement within the Party nor remove some of the disenchantment within the Party produced by its internal conflicts. Continuing internal conflicts seem to have taken their toll on the influence of the Communist women's movement in the late 1980s. The National Women's Advisory Committee complained about not understanding the language of *A Manifesto for New Times*, the new Party documents being circulated in 1989 and there were ineffective discussions about feminism and its relationship to the Green Movement.

Further internal Party conflict: London and the North West

At the time of the miner's strike and Greenham Common, the Party was becoming more deeply involved in internal conflict. The Chaterites began to widen the internal conflict by seeking to use the district organisation to oust the Eurocommunists who were entrenched at the top of the Party hierarchy. Initially, they won some support in London and later in the North West. However, their actions led to a witch hunt by the Eurocommunists which led to such serious splits that the Party faced horrendous divisions by the late 1980s.

London, where there was a strong Chaterite and Straight Left presence, saw the first engagement. In November 1984 Bill Dunn, the London district secretary, died and the EC of the Party moved to replace him with Ian McKay, the National Organiser, who was to be acting secretary. On 24 November, McKay then used some previous allegations against the Hackney branch to forbid the London District Congress to elect a new district committee. He argued that there were at least ten delegates to this Congress whose representative right to be there was questionable. When the dominant Chaterite supporters present at the meeting refused to accept this ruling, Congress co-chairman Gordon McLennan, the general secretary of the Party, declared the Congress to be closed and walked out, accompanied by the loyal Eurocommunist and Straight Left delegates, declaring that 'All those who support the Communist Party of Great Britain will now leave the hall with me.'[60] Regardless of this action, the Congress continued with Mike Hicks in the chair.[61]

The action of the Chaterites in continuing the London District Congress, allowed the Party to discipline those members for breaking Party rules. Indeed 22 of those who participated in the continued Congress were summarily suspended from the Party at a Special EC meeting on 30 November 1984. The Party also issued a statement on the need to *Unite the Party for the British Road: Defeat the Factionalists* at the Special EC meeting.[62]

The Chaterite leaders of the London District issued collective statements and refused to follow the Party line and the CPGB reacted by sacking the full-time organisers of the London District. In their place, the Party co-opted a provisional London District Committee of their own choosing and closely scrutinised the membership returns of those branches where there was significant opposition to the Party leadership. At the January 1985 meeting, the EC expelled from the Party, along with Chater and Whitfield, the four most defiant of the London 22 – Mike Hicks (later the general secretary of the CPB), Tom Durkin, Roger Task and Ian Beavis – and continued the suspension of 6 others and barred the remainder from holding Party office. From January 1985 the Party also circulated the periodical *Focus* free to every

Party member in the hope as part of its campaign to counter Chaterite ideas and to justify the expulsion of such dissenters.

This period of expulsions saw the Party cut many of its links with trade unionism. In the process Ken Gill, general secretary of the draughtmen's union TASS and soon to be chairman of the TUC, was expelled alongside Chater for promoting candidates for the PPPS management committee who were not supported by the Party. Other top officials from the engineering, building and tobacco workers' industry were also expelled. John Foster, the famous historian, was also expelled from the Party along with his Govan Branch which had refused to accept his expulsion. Kevin Halpin, one of the Party's key industrial militants, fought on within the Party avoiding expulsion but finally resigned from the Party in 1988 to join Mike Hicks and others in forming the CPB.

The Party's EC also took control of the meetings of the North-West District Committee, which had ignored the Party's list of recommended candidates in the election of its new committee. Suspecting factional activity the EC appointed Gerry Pocock and Dave Priscott to attend the district committee meetings and to report their findings to the EC.[63] However, in the face of stubborn resistance from the North-West District the Party's EC dissolved the North-West District Committee in July 1985 and imposed a provisional committee made up of its own candidates. Confident that it now had control, the EC organised a Special National Congress in May 1985.

Meanwhile, the Party demanded that the PPPS of the *Morning Star* call a special general meeting to discuss the actions of Chater and Whitfield. Initially, Chater managed to stave off this attack. However, the EC moved stealthily to expel those who openly protested against the further dilution of Marxist–Leninist ideas and still held on to a faith in the dictatorship of the working classes.

Matters were now coming to a head. The London expulsions attracted most attention and the Party's Special Congress in May 1985 was organised in such a way as to give the 'right revisionists', or Eurocommunists, control. Indeed, the Brent branch with 104 members and Clapham with 107, both active centres of opposition to the EC of the Party, were allowed to send only one delegate each while the more supportive Lewisham East, with 45 members, was also allocated one delegate.[64] Monty Goldman, who had already been expelled from the Party, reflected that 'It means that the Congress is being packed by Executive delegates elected by the gerrymandering of the selection process.'[65] Indeed, the result was that at the Congress there was a 2 to 1 majority in favour of the Eurocommunists. This Congress thus inevitably rejected the appeals against expulsion of the expelled London members, including that of Chater, and those that had already taken place in the North West. During the Congress a new 45 member EC was elected and consisted largely of Eurocommunists, or 'right revisionists', as they were dubbed.[66] In the North-West District the Party's actions went further. In November 1985 the Party set up a North-West Provisional Committee of 23 unelected members, 10 representing Manchester, 8 Merseyside and 5 from the counties.

The Party was now truly and irrevocably divided. Ironically, the Eurocommunists, who had for so long challenged the machinery of democratic centralism were now using it to remove the old pro-Moscow communists. The Party demanded allegiance and used the old 'Stalinist' Rule 22 of the Party Constitution to allow it to dissolve difficult branches and make their members re-apply for membership. On the other hand, the old pro-Moscow communists were attempting to use technical points to defy the implementation of the principle of democratic centralism.

Not surprisingly, membership of the Party plummeted further as a result of all this internal dissension – falling from 20,638 in 1978 to 12,711 by 1985.[67] The London District had only 2,141 members by 1985, nor surprisingly 400 down on 1983. The Yorkshire District membership fell from 1,020 to 920 between 1983 and 1985.

The rapid decline of membership provoked almost panic stations within the Party. It therefore decided to produce a new weekly paper, *7 Days*, producing the Chris Myant edition, in October 1985. The PC of the Party also discussed plans to revive the Party fortunes in December 1984, the main focus being the arrangement of a meeting with 45 trade union organisations in 1985.[68] Ironically, this was at a time when some of the Party's leading trade unionists were being expelled.

The Party's unity was somewhat improved by the fact that in 1985 Mikhail Gorbachev rose to power in the Soviet Union. This forced Straight Left and the Chaterites to support *perestroika*, *glasnost* and an altogether more reformist type of communism, even if only because they were committed to the Soviet Union.

Nonetheless, Party membership continued its inexorable decline. However, by this time the CPGB was even less radical than the Labour Party on some policies. This is evident in the articles on John Grahl and Bob Rowthorne (who was a prominent Eurocommunist and on the Board of *Marxism Today*) in which they rejected the public ownership policies of the Labour Party in the 1983 general election as too radical. Abandoning the struggle for a socialist economic system, they argued that the Labour Party had to be realistic in aiming for minor reforms within the realms of a capitalist economy: 'It means, of course, accepting the continued importance of capitalist enterprise in our economy, but there is really not much alternative.'[69] Rowthorne later wrote, in *The Guardian*, that 'I've become a left reformist. The crisis has been long and drawn out, but I can't see the agencies of change and I'm not convinced about the socialist answer any more.'[70]

Given this prevailing mood amongst leading Eurocommunists, many members felt that there was no point continuing with the CPGB. By 1987 there were only 10,350 members and this figure had fallen further to 7,615 in 1989. Gordon McLennan, touring the United Kingdom in 1988, said, 'The more I travel round the country the more I am convinced that unless we fight for membership of the Communist Party with greater tenacity, perception, confidence and élan than at the present, the decline in membership will continue.'[71] The PC of the CPGB therefore discussed the need for a fundamental realignment of the Party in February 1987. There was intense disagreement at this meeting. Dave Priscott admitted that 'the ground had shifted from under out feet'. He added, 'My own position is a very simple one. As a Party of socialist revolution we may have had hard times (nothing particularly new in that) but we can survive and fight our way forward. As a Party of radical democratic left reformism there is absolutely no future at all for us; this particular slot is already full.'[72] Priscott, and indeed Monty Johnstone were at odds with those members of the Party who were moving towards a democratic left perspective and Priscott eventually left the editorial board of *Marxism Today* as a result of the stance he adopted.

Nina Temple, the future and last general secretary of the CPGB who was born on a North London council estate in 1956 and was a close friend of Martin Jacques, also gave her views to the PC. She sent off a set of notes to the PC Meeting of 14 February 1987 because of her absence due to illness and having to look after her baby. In 1986 she had informed the EC that 'First, of course, we are a Marxist Party. Not a Party of dogmatic, fossilised quotation-based Marxism, but a Party with a tradition of the creative development of the British Marxist tradition.'[73] However, this trend, it must be said, was one which had not developed until the 1970s. Nevertheless, the five pages of notes she sent to the 1987 meeting indicated that she had moved further towards democratic reform and broad socialist alliances and away from the socialist revolution she once proclaimed. These comments were a pointer to the future. Noting that the Party membership had declined rapidly, that *7 Days'* circulation was down from 10,000 to 5,800 and that municipal results had been poor, Nina Temple admitted that the old Party had never become part of the mainstream of British politics but that it had an identity and militancy which made it attractive to British socialists. Indeed, she added that:

> In recent years we have embraced a wider political agenda, feminism, anti-racism, alliance politics, and largely through the success of *Marxism Today* have established ourselves as relevant to the thinking of the realigned left. But these developments have coincided with our glaring weakness in membership, electoral activity, trade unions, youth, & loss of *Star* which have greatly hindered our ability to conduct struggle.

Temple felt that the Party had to go forward with this fundamental realignment of its political orientation, particularly on issues such as feminism and anti-racism, which it had recently rejected or ignored. She felt that recent political distractions and the lack of accountability were the reasons for the Party's decline. In order to develop the Party she believed that there had to be vision and identity. A relevance to British politics had to be developed as well as the ability to affect events and develop an attractive Party life. She also listed a number of her personal interests and concerns, and emphasised the need for the leadership to work together.[74] Temple, a rising figure in the Party, was clearly veering to radical democratic reform and alliances with other labour and socialist groups – developing the idea of networking which became the dominating characteristic of the DL which replaced the CPGB in 1991.

The two main of the concerns at this stage were winning members and responding to the challenge of Thatcherism. The former could be seen in the moves to strengthen CPGB organisation within student bodies, where the Party still had 508 members in March 1987.[75] The latter presented an insuperable challenge as Thatcher's trade union and employment legislation reduced the trade union power base and pushed

British politics to the right by making high taxation, and with it a developing welfare state, a politically dangerous option for the Labour Party. Thatcher's attacks upon high public expenditure and 'nanny state' were fought against a weakened Labour Party and a declining Marxist movement just when the traditional working-class base for both organisations was declining.

Falling membership was increasingly a problem and a Special Emergency EC Meeting was held on 28 June 1987 to discuss the future of communism in Britain. There were many contributions to this debate and Nina Temple, following up her advice to the PC, suggested that the Party was still committed to removing social inequalities through *The British Road to Socialism* and the transformation of Parliament. Temple also stressed the importance of *Marxism Today* in analysing and countering Thatcherism even as the Party was 'consumed with inner divisions and disciplinary questions'.[76] Indeed, the truth is that the internal conflicts within the Party meant that the major conflict with Thatcherism was in terms of press criticism for there is little evidence of a concerted trade union policy against Thatcherism, as was demonstrated by the CPGB reaction to the miners' strike of 1984–5.

Nevertheless, this meeting was greatly taken up with discussion about the Broad Democratic Alliance of the Left and the need to work with the CND and other protest organisations. At the same time, Dave Cook, a committed reformer, suggested that even given the changes to *The British Road to Socialism* in 1977–8 it was now in need of an update. Others demanded more unity within the Left.

The meeting was, however, remarkable in one sense for it revealed the increasing recognition that Eurocommunism in Britain was no more successful than the old pro-Moscow approach because of its reluctance to adapt and change. Dave Cook attacked the EC, which had been dominated by Eurocommunists since 1977, for not allowing 'a more thoroughgoing transformation of the Party'. On the other hand, David Priscott had modified his position from the previous six months and was less critical of the Eurocommunist-dominated EC, suggesting that 'our Party can learn from other CPs but for us there are no models, neither Socialist nor Euro-communist'.

With Communist failures in Spain and other Western European countries, the term Eurocommunism was in fact becoming irrelevant by the late 1980s. Pragmatism and broad-based socialism became the order of the day and this is what emerged from the Special Meeting. The Party decided that *The British Road to Socialism* would be redrafted and that henceforth the Party's approach would be to seek new alliances with the Greens, anti-racist bodies and students. The Party remained wedded to democratic centralism but stressed the need for more democratic participation by the membership in Party life and an elected central leadership capable of directing the entire organisation.

None of these changes appealed to the old non-Eurocommunist Party members and the Chaterites. The *Morning Star* suggested, quite rightly, that the 'Communist Party is being hijacked by a right-wing revisionist faction' which aimed to destroy 'the Marxist basis and class approach of the Communist Party'.[77] As a result the Communist Campaign Group was formed in June 1985 in an attempt to oppose revisionism within the Party, and was particularly active in Brent.[78] It consisted of Party members and some of those who had been expelled and contained quite a number of those who had opposed the revision of *The British Road to Socialism* in 1977 but had not joined the breakaway NCP. Gordon McLennan, the general secretary, suggested that this group would also become as obscure as the NCP if it broke away but complained, as did others, that they had 'hijacked' the *Morning Star*. Indeed, when the *Morning Star* kept reporting upon how the Communist Campaign Group was breaching CPGB rules, the Party leadership became concerned and acted to meet and remove the challenge.[79]

Eventually the supporters of the Communist Campaign Group met together to form the CPB in April 1988 in the hope that it might become a mirror image of the pre-1977 CPGB.[80] Chater and the *Morning Star* contingent joined the new organisation as did some of the old Party faithfuls who had hung on in the CPGB. Kevin Halpin, who had once chaired the LCDTU, joined. He explained that 'We wanted to stay and fight the right-wing opportunity position. We had a good chance of winning the Party. If we had been a majority we would not have been expelling people.'[81] The CPB published, annually, *Needs of the Hour* to inform trade unionist about the policies they needed to pursue.

The CPB appointed Mike Hicks, who had been expelled from the Party because of his actions in the London District of the CPGB, as its general secretary. The son of a docker and a printer who was active in the print room SOGAT, he had become a member of the EC of the CPGB. However, as already noted, he was expelled from the Party in 1984 for chairing the London District Congress against the wishes of the Party. He later reflected of the Eurocommunists that:

> They knew we could beat them democratically, so they went for a purge. They used the sort of administrative methods which they condemned the Soviet Union for using. If they had not we would have won the National Congress and removed McLennan and that lot. Nina Temple and those people made it clear that they were not Marxist-Leninists. But they stayed in the Party and therefore had the benefit of money, £4 million of it. They were like bees round a honey pot.[82]

In 1986 Hicks was arrested in the mass demonstrations outside the Wapping plant which Rupert Murdoch set up to rescue trade union power and was imprisoned for three months.

The CPB held its first Congress in November 1989 when it updated *The British Road to Socialism*. Even that was an admission that this organisation was much less radical than the CPGB of the 1930s and very much in line with the CPGB of the 1950s and 1960s.

As the CPGB contemplated its end in 1991, the NCP and the CPB held a 'communist unity' conference at the beginning of 1991. This attracted 250 delegates of whom about 50 spoke, including Tom Durkin Mary Davis and Jean Turner (CPB) and George Davis and Ian Gunn of the NCP. What was revealed was that unity was unlikely as the two leading dissident Marxist parties ploughed their own furrow. The New Communist Party's general secretary, Eric Trevitt, appealed for unity but insisted upon such unity being based upon a Marxist critique and wanted a vanguard Marxist–Leninist Party based upon democratic centralism working with surviving

Communist countries such as Cuba, Vietnam and North Korea. However, this was challenged by Ron Bellamy of the CPB who said that Trevitt's proposed ideological unity was abstract and asked 'what is *the* Marxist critique of capitalism?' [83] In any case, the presence of the CPB at the conference was an unwilling one since the leadership were opposed to holding the conference but had been forced to organise and attend after a resolution they opposed was passed at their recent congress. However, Derek Robinson (CPB), who chaired the conference, refused to take resolutions and thus avoided decisions being taken.

Mike Power (CPGB), in his critical report of the conference, suggested that it was more about raising £2,000 for the *Morning Star* which was running an £800,000 per year deficit after losing the Soviet order of 12,000 copies a day as the Soviet Union and communism in Eastern Europe collapsed in 1990 and 1991. Power noted that issues of racism, environment and current concern were particularly avoided since the NCP and the CPB disagreed on many of them. He believed that the two organisations, with about 1,000 members between them, might unite but that 'If they do join, they will embody all the most negative elements of communist history that the CPGB left behind at its congress last December.'[84] However, the CPGB was also going nowhere with its more moderate policies.

The beginning of the end

Ignoring its opponents the CPGB meandered onwards towards political oblivion. It had lost much of its trade union support to Chater and the *Morning Star* faction and it is to be remembered that amongst those who left was Ken Gill, general secretary of the draughtsman's union TASS, a member of the TUC General Council and chair at the 1984 TUC conference. Such a loss, and indeed similar losses, could not be recovered easily. The CPGB failed in municipal elections, with the number of councillors coming down to single figures by the mid-1980s. In parliamentary politics the situation was even worse. In March 1983 the Party put forward a candidate against Labour's Peter Tatchell at the Bermondsey parliamentary by-election and received fewer votes than the Official Monster Raving Loony Party candidate.

With the exception of *Marxism Today*, whose sales blossomed in the 1980s, the Party faced one disaster after another in the 1980s. However, *Marxism Today's* sales success was something of a mixed blessing because its articles demolished many of the political icons of the CPGB and the labour movement. It attacked some of the institutions of trade unionism and undoubtedly lost the Party support. Increasingly it was read by non-communists, rather than just communists, and by the time of the 1987 general election its broad and irreverent approach led it to suggest the need for an anti-Tory electoral pact – almost a popular front against Toryism. However, it became so prone to compromise in the process that it accepted the importance of the European Economic Community for Britain and stressed that a socialist Britain could not cut contacts with capitalist nations. The political views of *Marxism Today*, which pushed the Party even further towards the right, won the day and were expressed through the redrafted version of *The British Road to Socialism* which became *Manifesto for New Times* at the November 1989 Congress. This *Manifesto* recognised the end of the old forms of industrial and class conflict, addressed issues such as feminism, gay and green politics, and anticipated a significant remodelling of the Party.[85] However, the 1989 Congress was a bad-tempered affair. Two resolutions were passed condemning *Marxism Today* and the *Manifesto of New Times* was only passed by a narrow vote.

The 1989 Congress also saw a change of Party leader. All the factions within the Party had potential leadership candidates to replace Gordon McLennan. There was Ian McKay, the National Organiser, a Scot who embodied the old Party virtues. Those connected with *Marxism Today* favoured Martin Jacques, its editor, and former Eurocommunists supported Nina Temple. Party members throughout the country were asked for their advice but Temple, 33 years of age at the time, became general secretary by default when the other two candidates elected to remain in their existing posts.

Temple was born in London in 1956, worked for the YCL and stayed in the Party in 1982 only through loyalty to Martin Jacques, whom she later became disillusioned with. In 1982 she became responsible for the Party's press and publicity. Once she assumed office she began to remove the icons of old Communism, symbolically removing the bust of Karl Marx from the general secretary's office. With the Party down to about 7,500 members in 1989 she helped reduce the CPGB office staff from more than 20 full-time staff down to 6 and removed the almost legendry Reuban Falber, a Jewish Communist who had joined the Party in the 1930s, from his part-time post in charge of Party finances. Her own brief was to establish a free form of communism, especially after the rise of Gorbachev in the Soviet Union and the decline and collapse of the old type of 'Stalinist' regimes in Eastern Europe. She recognised that the old Communist Party had been declining for decades and that a new direction was required, although there was the danger that the new approach would lack the clear definition of the old and emerge as an amorphous organisation lacking any sense of purpose and direction. But as she came to office the Party was so weak that it even gave up ground to the relatively weak Trotskyite organisations in campaigning against the Poll Tax and was finally forced to face its end.

Trotskyism

It was the remnants of the Trotskyite groups, not the CPGB, who made the running with the poll-tax issue of 1990. The Party no longer had the energy, membership or inclination to lead this event torn as it had been by thirteen years of serious internal conflict. Yet even the Trotskyite Left seemed to be breaking up, although that was hardly an unusual event, and facing serious opposition from the Labour Party in some areas.

The great success story for Trotskyism in the late 1970s and early 1980s had been the success of MT in infiltrating the Labour Party and some of the local authorities it controlled. Committed to a vast programme of public works, MT had gained ground amongst the younger members of the Labour Party. The Labour Leader, Michael Foot had campaigned against them in the early 1980s but had failed and two Militant supporters – Terry Fields and David Nellist – were elected as Labour MPs at the 1983 general election. In addition, Militant supporters won control of the

Labour group on Liverpool City Council, led by Derek Hatton. However, Neil Kinnock, who replaced Michael Foot as leader of the Labour Party in 1983, ensured that the fortunes of MT began to decline. At the 1985 Labour Party conference, Kinnock declared his disgust at the action of the MT leaders in issuing redundancy notices to all its city council workers in order to place pressure on the Thatcher Government to remove its capping of council expenditure. This had annoyed the trade unions and at the Conference Kinnock made his famous statement that:

> I'll tell you what happens with impossible promises. You start with far-fetched revolutions. You are then pickled into a rigid dogma, a code, and you go through the years sticking to that, outdated, misplaced, irrelevant to the real needs, and you end in the grotesque chaos of a Labour council hiring taxis to scuttle round a city handing out redundancy notices to its own people [Applause]... You can't play politics with people's jobs... [Applause and some boos].[86]

One front bench Labour MP stated that 'with one speech he lanced the boil'.[87] This was not quite the case as MT got three of its members elected as Labour MPs in the general election of 1987 – Pat Wall, Terry Fields and Dave Nellist.[88] However, Kinnock waged war against the 'Loony Left', as Militant was referred to, and by the late 1980s and early 1990s it was in serious retreat from its Labour ranks. Other Trotskyite organisations were also facing difficulties.

The WRP accused its leader Gerry Healy, now in his seventies, of 'sexual debauchery' – using young female members of the Party as sexual playthings – and the Party split in two. The IMG was split between the 'right wingers' who supported Tony Benn and Arthur Scargill, and purists who considered both Benn and Scargill to be too reformist.

The party is over, November 1991: change or die – the end of Marxism–Leninism and Democratic Centralism and the emergence of federalism

Gordon McLennan was formally replaced by Nina Temple as general secretary in mid-January 1990.[89] He handed over a Party with 7,625 members, a small fraction of the 27,000 or so members he had inherited when he became general secretary in 1976, and allegedly about £4 million in assets, mainly in the form of property.[90] It was a Party which, by now, had shed many of the old Stalinists and pro-Soviet supporters but it was further divided into two main tendencies. On the one hand, there were the *Marxism Today* supporters who were pragmatic, oriented towards 'consumerism', willing to explore a variety of political actions, and prepared to work with capitalism. On the other, there was the more inchoate tendency towards adopting a politically moralistic stand on such policies as Green politics, feminism and anti-racialism. The leading figures in this strand were Nina Temple, formerly YCL national secretary and Communist Press and Publicity Officer and now general secretary, and the London district secretary Dave Green. Temple, in fact, was committed to a process of renewal and reconstruction within the Party aimed at transforming the landscape of left politics by reorganising the Party and developing left alliances and networks. Her views, at this time, did not go quite as far as those of Tony McNally, another representative of this tendency. He envisaged an ex-socialist movement based upon *Marxism Today, Manifesto for New Times*, the centrality of people's power, and the promotion of a new movement: it would be a group of associations rather than a Party, committed to uniting socialist and Green groupings in alliance based upon 'ecologically sustainable development at home, democratised, decentralised, pluralist, non violent, multi-racial and with humanitarian internationalism'.[91]

The events in Eastern Europe, where neo-Stalinist regimes were collapsing in the face of the demands for more democratic systems, began to challenge the Party to consider further its future role, especially as it had opposed popular domestic movements such as the mass campaign of non-payment organised by the All Britain Anti-Poll Tax Federation. Tommy Sheridan, its chairman who was a Glasgow councillor for the Scottish Militant Labour, played a leading part in the famous Trafalgar Square demonstration of 31 March 1991, a meeting of 150,000 to 200,000 people which led Thatcher to abandon the poll tax. The CPGB could claim no success in this popular victory, partly engineered by Trotskyite groups.

As a result of the poll tax agitation in Eastern Europe and other circumstances, the EC threw open the debate about the Party's future at its January 1990 meeting. Three main lines of argument were pursued. First, the Eurocommunists, now gravitating towards the moralist standpoint of Nina Temple, wanted the Party to disband and to use its assets to create a different type of party based upon a more democratic approach associated with broad left issues. This associationist line was supported by both Martin Jacques and, ironically, by the *Morning Star*. Second, the old traditionalist Party members wanted any new organisation to retain the name 'Communist' in the title, with some semblance of older Communist values. Third, the Straight Left, which had avoided separating from the Party, unlike the Chaterites, and had built up a base of support in London, attacked Stalinism even as communism was collapsing in Eastern Europe and maintained the belief that there was no need for far-reaching changes in the Party as it existed in 1990.

In order to reconcile these three positions – a looser more democratic party, the pre-1977 party and the party of 1990 – Temple suggested that there was a need to transform the Party while at the same time setting up a left-wing association to broaden the appeal of communism. This was known as the 'twin-track' or 'dual-track' approach. It was strongly suggested even though the Party lacked the resources to implement this solution. Throughout the following 12 months the old traditional Communists and the Straight Leftists supported the idea of transforming the CPGB while keeping the basic beliefs of the past. However, Jacques and the associationists wished simply to create a new and different organisation, as they, Temple, and others had originally proposed.[92] As a result of these tensions a special meeting was called to discuss the Party's future and it was agreed that there would be a Special Congress in 1991.[93]

In the meantime the situation in the Party worsened with membership continuing to decline and even prominent figures such as Hywel Francis, the Welsh historian, leaving. At the September 1990 EC it was also announced that John Peck, a long-time member of the Party and Eurocommunist who had built up a base of support in Nottingham, had left to join the Green Party.[94]

The CPGB was simply collapsing and was down to about 6,000 members by the autumn of 1990. In the September EC meeting the largest single block of votes (13) favoured dissolution but Nina Temple combined with the 'twin-track' supporters advocated both the reorganisation of the Party and the formation of broad alliances. They defeated those favouring dissolution by 19 votes.

In this crisis the Special Congress, originally called for the spring of 1991, was brought forward to December 1990. At the main Saturday debate five alternative positions were discussed. The suggestions that the Party should dissolve and be turned into 'The Communist Association' was rejected. The dissolution group were defeated. The simple restructuring of the Party deleting the EC sections on 'Transforming the Party and Starting a New Formation' was also dismissed along with the idea of reverting to an older Communist tradition. A third suggestion to delete all references to 'association' and 'formation' from the draft resolution was also rejected, thus thwarting the Straight Left and some of those committed to the revival of the old Communist Party. The idea of going for a revised version of the 'new formation' alongside a transformed CPGB, putting the emphasis on local, regional and national initiatives was also dismissed. In the end the Congress opted for the final 'dual-track option' of a new broader political association aiming at the development of a New-Times left, recognising that the continuation of the existing CPGB was no longer helpful. This was voted for on the Sunday by 2 : 1 on a hand vote.[95]

Nina Temple got her way on the 'twin-track' proposal because of the support she gained from the Scottish section of the Party, who sent 58 of the 200 plus delegates who attended. She got the Scots to agree that the 'association' proposal alone, which would have ended the existence of the Party, would not be accepted and that the 'twin-track' proposal would be accepted with vague concessions to the 'association' proposal. It was also stressed that the restructured Party would be a federal organisation with virtually complete autonomy for the Scottish and Welsh elements.

The Forty-second Congress of December 1990, which had convened in the TUC premises in Great Russell Street to the accompaniment of shouting and chanting 'Stalinists' outside the building, was thus a seminal moment in the history of the CPGB. It determined that the old CPGB would be replaced by a new broader party which Nina Temple argued would have a crucial role to play in renewing the progressive politics of the New Times. In her address she stated that:

> 1990 has seen the Bolshevik era end in disaster. Perestroika and glasnost have exposed and opposed what it had become; stagnant, corrupt and repressive. Gorbachov's [sic] revolution had broken the old system, but the initiatives of the new... appear inadequate to stem the engulfing chaos. [...]
>
> So what of the Communist Party's future? What role are we going to play in defining a new popular socialism?
>
> 1989 represented the end of the epoch in which the Communist Party was cast. We were set up to organise revolution, overthrow capitalism and create a Soviet Britain.

From 1956 onwards the party suffered crisis after crisis as the majority broke away from authoritarian socialism while a vocal minority saw any criticism of Eastern Europe as anti-socialist and criticisms of our own labour movement, such as the lessons the party drew from the miners' strike, as class treachery.

The party today is largely inactive. Many party organisations have ceased to function... There has been a natural reluctance in the party to face full square the position we are in. Largely because we all wish it were not so. But there has also been an attempt by conservative forces... to play down on this reluctance in order to avoid change.... Now we have a simple choice – cling to the past and carry on dying, or break with that authoritarian tradition, examine and learn from our history and seek new living forms for our politics. Change is unsettling, but it is a lot more pleasurable than certain death.[96]

The message was very clear and blunt: the CPGB was not going to be a major player in British politics but it could, if it changed, play a part in helping to shape future British politics. Bluntly put, it was change or die. Therefore, Nina Temple completed the task which Martin Jacques and *Marxism Today* had undertaken in the hope that communism, 'the cause', would outlive the collapse of Eastern European regimes, the disintegration of the Soviet Union and the apparent demise of international communism.

It was at the Forty-second Congress, in December 1990, that the decision was taken to change the structure and politics of the Party, along the lines recommended by Nina Temple, Martin Jacques and *Marxism Today*. The idea of the Party going out of existence was rejected, as were several other variants, in favour of the Party changing its name and strategy.[97] Marxism–Leninism was finally abandoned, along with the policy of operating democratic centralism, which meant that the Party would move more towards federalism. The recommended list system of selecting candidates for the EC was also abandoned and 107 candidates contested the 35 places on the new EC. Twenty-two of these were retiring members from the old EC and there were 13 new members.[98]

The removal of the recommended list left delegates free to decide matters at the next congress, including the name of the new party from the list of 21 different names put forward, including the British Communist Federation, the Party of Democratic Socialism, the British Socialist Party (a potential move back to the title used before the Great War) and the Democratic Communist Party of Great Britain. Indeed, on this issue it was possible that the future delegates would be able to keep the existing name.

A handful of Straight Leftists were elected to the new EC at the end of this Congress but the majority of delegates were moderate old traditional communists and old Eurocommunists willing to accept the compromise arrangements that were emerging. As a result many of the pure 'associationist' advocates left the Party, including Brenda Kirsch former Assistant Editor of 7 *Days*, Sion Barrow (who was quickly replaced by Mike Power) the editor of its modest replacement, *Changes*, and Dave Green, the London district secretary. Some had been members of the previous EC.

Yet Nina Temple and the New Times faction had got their way and drew some comfort from the fact that the Forty-second Congress (1990) indicated that the new Party could be a wider movement. Indeed, of the 237 delegates who were due to attend 40 could not make the Saturday because of the winter blizzards and only 4 of these absentees arrived on the Sunday. It was disappointing that of the 204 delegates listed as being present 46 were women (a third of the Party membership were women) but 102 were, or had been, members of trade unions; MSF had 26 members present, NATFHE 23, NUT 21, NALGO 16 and the TGWU 12. Delegates listing membership of other organisations indicated that 80 had CND membership, 58 were in Co-ops, 51 were connected with Anti-Apartheid, 22 associated with environmental groups, 14 with friendship organisations, 8 with other peace organisations, 7 with anti-poll tax groups, 7 with community groups, 7 with tenants' associations and various other interest groups.

It was with some confidence, then, that the new EC circulated its proposals for the 'transformed party' in March 1991. They amounted to little more than the rejected proposals of the previous year and it was suggested that the new party organisation – to be known as the DL – would be formed but left the final decision to the November 1991 Congress.

On 23 May 1991 the draft constitution for the new party was circulated by the CPGB, from its new headquarters at 6-9 Cynthia Street, London. It was declared that the Party had decided to 'drop Marxism–Leninism and embrace politics drawing from creative Marxism, feminism, anti-racism, ecology and other progressive traditions, and to replace democratic centralism with an open and democratic structure, involving the move towards federalism'.[99] It stated that its aim was:

> to achieve a society in which people are free from oppression based on gender, race, age, sexuality and disability. We are committed to the transformation of society which will put power in the hands of the people, enhancing their lives both on an individual and collective basis. Our ultimate goal is a classless society where all people are free and equal.

The old Marxist–Leninist views of class conflict, the dictatorship of the proletariat as an interim measure along the way to full communism, and ideas of democratic centralism were going to be swept away.

In the next few months there was intense discussion about the constitution, the structure and, above all, the name of the new party. Arthur Mendolsohn, from London, favoured the name Democratic Socialist Left.[100] Bill Laughlan, from West Lothian in Scotland, maintained that 'Political conditions now made an independent Scottish party necessary', adding that 'The history of the communist party in Scotland over its 71 years provides all the evidence needed to still doubts about the correctness of deciding for a separate and independent party for Scotland ... to serve the best interests of the Scottish people'. Paul Webb felt that 'The draft constitution is a brilliant synthesis of the familiar and the innovative....' Andy Croft of Teesside reflected that 'The party ... is over' and felt that there was no alternative to the DL. Jim Fyrth felt that the new party would become known as 'the soggy left'.[101]

A stronger touch of realism came from Willie Thompson, the historian of the Communist Party who came from Glasgow, who wrote that 'The unhappy fact is that the Communist Party has collapsed.' He added that 'The CPGB never became a major party... it never succeeded in spite of constant efforts, in adapting itself to the character of British political culture,....'

Changes also conducted a vote on the 21 names proposed for the new organisation that were being touted. There were 1,011 responses from Party members, as well as 161 from the DL mailing list who were asked to give their first, second and third preferences.[102] Although 71 per cent (726) preferred a name other than the Communist Party of Great Britain this received the most individual preferences, 370 votes with 285 (28.2 per cent) as first preference. DL was the second favourite name with 290 voters and 204 (20.18 per cent) first preferences. However, it was clear that much of the support for Democratic Left Party, Democratic Socialist and Democratic Socialist Left would ultimately fall to the DL in a final round of voting.

In September 1991 the PC suggested the need for a sustained campaign to launch the DL and debated the procedures for setting up the DL after the Congress.[103] There were some strong objections to the title though, most obviously from David Priscott of Leeds, who suggested that its new name should be Democratic Socialist.[104] However, there were distractions *en route* to the Congress.

Shortly before the Congress was held, however, R. Davison, the *Sunday Times* reporter, wrote an article based upon a ledger found by the paper's Moscow correspondent, which showed two sums of £15,000 being paid to 'Comrade Falber' in 1978. When confronted by this evidence Reuban Falber had rejected the claim that the Soviet Union had been underwriting the CPGB but Temple, in telephone conversations with him, began to get at the truth of the situation. Eventually Falber told Temple the whole story and she insisted that he prepare an article for publication in *Changes*, a new party journal. After considerable haggling between Falber, Temple and McLennan the article was published. Falber began with the statement that in 1958 he had been given a package by John Gollan containing £14,000 and referred to subsequent packages of money which he had handled. However, the *Changes* editorial team did clarify matters and suggested that as much as £100,000 had been received in one year in the 1960s.[105] It appeared that this financial provision and was not given in return for the CPGB's support for the Soviet Union but once McLennan replaced Gollan as general secretary in 1976, he did not wish to continue with the money and called for it to be stopped. The impression given was that it was phased out by about 1979, although Nina Temple did note that there were a large number of legacies received in the 1980s. According to Falber, only John Gollan and David Ainley, chief executive of the *Morning Star*, were aware of the money although it seems pretty clear that both McLennan and Temple knew something about it before the issue was made public. It appeared that the money was laundered through the CPGB's pension funds and provided money for the *Morning Star* and various Party activities.

The revelations had been forced out of Falber and the CPGB by virtue of an article in the *Sunday Times* and Falber's article confirmed the murky secrecy of the financial arrangements between Moscow and the CPGB. Apart from the obvious, and exaggerated, outrage of the British capitalist press a shock wave went around the Party and Marxists in Britain. Martin Jacques resigned from the Party the day the article was published and Sarah Benton, an ex-Party member, wrote a bitter article in *The Guardian* attacking 'The dour men in grey suits' who drew 'funny money and directions from Moscow'. Those who might well have reacted with less vitriol – Mick Costello, Tony Chater and Mike Hicks – had already left the Party in 1988 and so it was to a Party no longer committed to the class struggle that the news of 'Moscow money' was revealed. The Party arrived at its denouement in a mood of shock and outrage.

At the Forty-third Congress of the CPGB in November 1991, the Eurocommunist/New Times left majority formed the DL. The theoretical base and principles of the CPGB were now totally abandoned. By a majority of roughly two to one it was decided to dismantle the existing Party structure and to replace it with a loosely organised federal body. About a third of the 220 delegates fought against the changes and applauded the recently revealed evidence that Moscow had provided money to the Party between 1959 and 1979. The final voting on the name and rule book revealed that 72 delegates wanted the old CPGB rule book, 135 were for the new draft and that three abstained. Bill Laughton, from Glasgow, speaking in favour of the old constitution, argued that the DL added up to having 'an ideology you make up for yourself'. He wanted a Marxist party with 'communist ideological certainty' to it. Kate Hudson, of London, was also critical of the new developments and suggested that DL offered 'a travesty of effective organizational structure'. Steve Howell, of Sheffield, felt that the DL was full of 'bland platitudes that David Owen would be able to accept'. Pat Turnbull pointed out that 21 of the 108 branches who had made returns had favoured the old, not the new, draft. Yet, despite such criticism, the majority favoured the DL and the new pluralistic policies that were being offered.[106] Indeed, Nina Temple's opening speech to the Congress captured the new mood of the Party when she stated that:

> We must recognize that the era of Communist Parties is at an end. Our own party cannot be revived by nostalgia, discredited ideologies, rosy views of history or unaccountable command structures. Only an honest appraisal and a rupture with the past undemocratic practices can take the best of our traditions forward with integrity.[107]

The DL, now took up the mantle of the defunct CPGB at a time when the character of British politics had changed dramatically.

Conclusion

The CPGB went out of existence in November 1991, after 71 years, partly, perhaps even largely, because of the divisions between the new Eurocommunists and the old class-based pro-Moscow/Stalinist sections of the Party. The former group had quickly gained widespread support throughout the Party and sought a broad alliance with environmental groups, feminists, anti-racist and peace groups and organisations.

Opponents of the new orthodoxy split away and formed their own parties. The NCP had done so in 1977 and the CPB did so in 1988. Yet these two organisations probably robbed the CPGB of only about 1,000 supporters. The haemorrhage of Party membership was far more serious than that and arose from the whole broad democratic alliance approach which emphasised networking and alliances rather than the certainties of Marxist–Leninist ideology, class conflict and democratic centralism.

By dropping its class base the CPGB effectively lost much trade union support. Indeed, this was most marked in the case of the coal miners' strike of 1984–5 to which the Party gave little more than token support. It was the independent Marxist paper *Morning Star*, not the Party and its journal *Marxism Today* which did most for the miners.

Yet, despite advocating new alliances, associations and networks, it is ironic that the feminists in the Party generally favoured socialist–feminism and its class and gender approach, rather than a broader approach to the feminist movement. In addition, the women's movement within the CPGB was never able to embrace the third-wave feminism of the 1980s with its emphasis upon the different experience of women. Feminists in the CPGB were largely fighting the political issues of the 1970s, in a more class-based way, than addressing the third-wave issues of the 1980s which cut across the approach of broad theories such as Marxism. Feminists in the CPGB never truly came to terms with the emergence of black women's groups, barely recognising that their experiences were different from those of their white members, and lost influence within the wider women's movement just as the Party, obsessed by its own internal problems, turned its attention away from women's issues beyond passing resolutions at its congresses which offered token support to the demand for women's rights. In the end, the CPGB responded to the events at Greenham Common and the work of WAPC rather than initiated action.

Willie Thompson was thus right when he suggested, of the CPGB, that '...it never succeeded in spite of constant effort, in adapting itself to the character of British political culture....'[108] The Party adapted in the 1980s by dropping its distinctive political character in a vain hope of mounting effective alliances against Thatcher and winning broad support.

It is ironic that in making its attempt to adapt the CPGB was, for the first time since its formation and despite some continuing financial support from the Soviet Union, truly free from the domination of the Soviet Union. Eurocommunism had undermined Soviet influence from the late 1970s, although Soviet influence was, in any case, diminishing from the 1960s onwards. Yet once the Soviet influence was undermined, once *perestroika* and *glasnost* emerged and the Soviet and Easter European communist regimes collapsed, the Soviet Union ending in 1991, the CPGB became almost rudderless. The reason for the CPGB's existence was filched and its successor, the DL, was faced with networking groups supporting minority issues. This became the focus of DL policies in the 1990s as it searched for a new purpose to unite the individualised policies it fostered.

During its last decade the CPGB had looked less and less like the old CPGB as it came to place its hopes on the revival of the Labour Party, moving its support to Labour leadership in opposing Thatcherism, in opposing the Lambeth and Liverpool councils against the infiltration of MT and Trotskyite organisations, and in supporting Labour councils against government rate capping. It became so right wing that even some of the Labour Party policies appeared too radical for it. As it moved in the direction of 'associationalism' with green politics, racial issues and women's issues, and the like, its socialism looked more and more 'pick and mix'. As the 'new Marxism' of the Party catered for the individual needs of its members it threatened the certainties of the past and its policies increasingly lacked clear definition and shape. This was to be the main problem for its successor in the 1990s.

In the end the CPGB was torn apart as it was unable to come to terms with the two major challenges of Thatcherism, which it barely challenged because of its internal schism, and the collapse of Stalinism in Eastern Europe. Sections of the Communist movement in Spain and Italy have successfully reformed themselves as left of centre political factions. This raises the question of whether or not the CPGB was doomed to political extinction. Could it have pursued other political avenues in the 1980s? On the basis of what occurred it seems doubtful whether anything could have been done. The Party was divided at a time when Eastern European and Soviet Marxism was ailing and its own internal conflicts made it incapable of effectively facing up to Thatcherism as its splits drove out trade union supporters and limited its influence within the embattled trade union movement.

5 Postscript

The re-emergence and reconstruction of Marxism in Britain or 'All dressed up with nowhere to go?'

It could be argued that the demise of the CPGB saw the death of a meaningful Marxist movement in Britain. Indeed, Willie Thompson has suggested, in the world wide context, that:

> Now destroyed, it is inconceivable that world communist movement could ever be re-created (though Trotskyite organisation continue to preserve the fantasy, seeing themselves as a purified version of global communism). The movement's basic presuppositions have been too emphatically demonstrated to be false, its record and ideological tenets have been thoroughly discredited. An entire historical era has in effect sunk beneath the waves. [...] It stands as a foredoomed and heroic though destructive attempt to emancipate humanity from the contradictions of modernity and to pass, in Engels's words, 'from the realm of necessity to the realm of freedom'.[1]

However, despite the pessimistic comments of an active member of the CPGB and with more than a glimmer of optimism, it might also be maintained that the 1990s saw some rebirth of Marxist and socialist organisation in new forms although not yet on the scale of the CPGB and Trotskyite organisation before the 1980s. This lengthy postscript examines the decline and re-emergence of the Marxist tradition in Britain which, although it has had some successes, mainly in Scotland, still remains a marginal, if possibly growing, force in British politics even though it may not be the class conflict Marxism of the past.

Indeed, the collapse of Stalinism in Eastern Europe in the late 1980s and early 1990s exerted a major destructive impact upon Marxist organisations throughout the world. In addition, social democratic parties began to question the relevance of socialism; the British Labour Party abandoned Clause Four in 1994–5 embracing the market economy and the 'Third Way' and the DL became more a social networking organisation than a political party. As a result of these political shifts, in many countries there has been a realignment of Marxist and social democratic parties which have united to form a non-sectarian form of Marxism. In Spain the United Left emerged from the old communist party and the left wing of the socialist party. In Italy Communist Refoundation is a mass party which has been a junior partner in government. What is happening in Britain?

The Democratic Left

The DL, which replaced the CPGB, never made the same impact as the CPGB although its activities will undoubtedly be examined, and re-examined, in far more detail by a future generation of historians as its records (deposited in the John Rylands Library Labour Archive and Study Centre in June 2000) become fully available. As it is, most of their records are still closed for the foreseeable future. Its few available surviving records means that its history is inevitably sketchy, as is the history of some of the other Marxist and Trotskyite organisations, for more obvious reasons. Nonetheless, there is little doubt of the minimal impact of the DL in the 1990s.

The DL took over the property and holdings of the old CPGB, in the 'First Wave Transformation' of November 1991, and continued to use the old CPGB headquarters of 6 Cynthia Street (London N1 9JF) throughout the 1990s. It seems to have had around 1,600 members in its early days, considerably less than half the number of members of the CPGB it replaced. By 1995, it was down to about 1,200 members and in February 1998 it was claimed to have 836, even though occasional estimates gave it figures of between 1,000 and 1,400. Although it was the 'constitutional successor' to the CPGB, and inherited both its assets and the copyright to its name, it was in fact only one of several Marxist groups making that claim in the 1990s. However, the DL owes more to the CPGB of Gordon McLennan, who didn't join, and Nina Temple, who did, than to the Marxist–Leninist tradition of Harry Pollitt and John Gollan, many of whose supporters can be seen in other organisations such as the NCP and the CPB. Some of those who did join, who belonged to the older Marxist tradition, clearly had some doubts about the DL. Mick McGahey, the miners' leader, joined the DL with little enthusiasm stating that 'I reject Martin Jacques and the intellectuals who don't even know what class struggle is.'[2] He added in January 1994 that 'I'm not a member of the Communist Party at the moment, but Mick McGahey is a Communist.'[3] McGahey eventually joined the Communist Party of Scotland in April 1994. George Matthews shared similar misgivings, although he joined largely to ensure that the Communist Party archive was prepared for the historians who were going to inspect it (Table 2).

Table 2 The membership figures of the DL 1991–2000[a]

Year	National figures	Scotland
1991	1,600	
1995	1,200	
1998	836	114 (down on 1996)
1999		
2000		

Note

a Democratic Left archive, contains some of the nine copies of *Futures*, which was published to seek views on the future of the DL in from the end of 1997 and the beginning of 1998 until December 1999 when the DL became the New Politics Network. Most of these figures are quoted in the various letters printed in *Futures*.

The DL inherited *Changes*, the CPGB fortnightly paper, which immediately became the *New Times*, its journal. It produced its first issue on 28 December 1991 and in the 1990s it was intended that it would be reformed in 2000 although the formation of the NPN in December 1999 overtook events.[4] The DL was, from its beginning in 1991, mainly concerned in trying to create a sense of unity and purpose within the Party and quickly adopted an accommodating and networking style.

The first major decision the DL made was to agree its position on the general election of April 1992. In fact, this proved to be easy since its members inherited the CPGB's fervent commitment to bring down the John Major Conservative Government at all costs. Indeed, Chris Myant advocated tactical voting in March 1992.[5] This approach was re-emphasised by *New Times* at the beginning of April in an article entitled 'Turn the Tory Tide – Vote Tactically'.[6] It was no surprise then that the DL announced that it would not stand candidates for the 9 April 1992 general election – even though it proposed policies which were not supported by the other opposition parties – and advised its members to vote for whichever candidate was likely to beat the Tories be they Labour, Liberal Democrats or candidates of the Scottish National Party (SNP). Nina Temple, the general secretary, defended this decision by stating that: 'We are trying to create a new culture of politics.... Vanguard revolutionary politics has had its day.' This undoubtedly reflected the general policy of the left at this time, that is, it was more about defeating the Tories than of pushing Labour to the 'commanding heights'. However, Helen Taylor, the assistant secretary of the DL, put the position of the Party more clearly when she suggested that it intended to:

> work across traditional divisions to develop a new pluralistic and radical left based upon cooperation and not confrontation. DL is composed of the best strands of the old CP with the desire to seek a transformation of society which puts power into the people's hands and is free from oppression and exploitation. The constitution of the DL is different from other parties as it seeks to empower its membership by recognising the right to self-organisation and autonomy.
>
> She said DL celebrates diversity, aiming to take forward the best of the women's movement, green and black issues and left politics. Resource centres are still operating in Scotland, Wales, Leeds, Birmingham, London, Manchester and Merseyside to facilitate activity. And work is being encouraged around the specific issues of democracy, social policy, international relations, black, environment, trade unions and women. [DL is attracting young people.] There was a massive response from women following an insert card placed in Everywoman and 40% of members who were not in the Communist Party are under 30.
>
> [The DL is realistic about its size and makeup.] We know we haven't got all the answers but by working with others we aim to create a new space for political activity.[7]

This statement is very revealing for it demonstrates how the DL was continuing the developments in the CPGB of the late 1980s in abandoning Marxist–Leninist ideas. It admitted that the DL was really acting as a citizen and community activist group, with little real intention, or possibility, of gaining direct political power at either the local or national level. It had thus become an enabling organisation for political action. It was aiming to find a niche in British politics which the old CPGB could not establish.

It has been suggested that the financial legacy of the CPGB was about £4,000,000 but even if this estimate is on the high side it is clear that the DL did have significant assets. Nevertheless, most of the assets were tied up on property and with its diminishing base it was soon faced with cuts. In 1992, the first full year as the DL, its expenditure was about £477,000, according to its Strategic Resource Group. However, almost immediately cuts were made in advertising and in the number of days of employment of officials and office staff. In 1993 the DL was reduced to ten paid officials. There was a secretary (Nina Temple) and assistant secretary (Helen Taylor), a secretary for the DL in Scotland (Bill Laughlan), a Black, Women and International Officer employed for 2 days a week, a Scottish development officer for 3 days a week (the Development Officer, all other workers and network officers were cut), a finance worker employed for 3 days a week (formerly 4), and a membership officer for 2 days. The Connections Unit, including *New Times*, employed a home editor, a deputy editor for 4 days and a business manager for 2 days. As a result of pruning, the annual expenditure of the DL fell to £259,586 in 1993, almost half the level of the previous year.[8] Undoubtedly this reflected the enormously scaled down, indeed declining, fortunes of the DL. The hoped for revival in the CPGB/DL support was clearly not occurring. By its Fourth Federal Conference in June 1999, its fortunes had diminished further. According to an audit for 1997 and 1998, its assets totalled £1,996,486, the most important item being the office at 6 Cynthia Street which was allegedly worth £976,868. It also held £592,605 of investments, mainly in Treasury stock. Apart from a small carryover, its income for 1997 and 1998 was £340,637 which, despite appearing substantial, was considerably down on the annual average income it gained and expenditure levels of even the early 1990s.[9] The DL was visibly shrinking.

This is not to suggest that the DL was not making enormous efforts to exert a political impact. The DL's policy of acting as an enabler was, by now, well established and as a result it became involved in a variety of campaigns. It fought to establish 'New Times trade unionism in the 1990s', encouraging the much diminished British trade union movement to develop a strategy for the unemployed.[10] Nina Temple, the Federal Secretary [of] DL Britain by the autumn of 1992, began a positive Federal Europe Debate aimed at generating a vision of democratic Europe.[11] Rosemary Bechler, DL International National Officer, also began a debate about opening up Europe, noting that many Socialists said yes to Europe but no to the Maastrecht Treaty and suggested that the Treaty was too negative but that the DL and socialists should be examining what room for manoeuvre existed. The DL seems to have seen more possibilities in the Treaty that the Conservative Government which rejected economic and monetary union whilst agreeing to intergovernmental cooperation on a common foreign and security policy and also police, judicial, immigration and asylum policies. Indeed, the DL had held its first conference in June 1992 on the topic of 'Concept and Reality', which focused upon the need for a radical agenda.[12]

Nevertheless, campaigning was not going as well as expected and at the second DL Conference, a Federal Conference held in June 1993 the DL decided to cease existence as a political party and to concentrate upon acting simply as an enabling organisation. Yet this did not seem to arrest the DL's declining support and influence. As a result, the DL Party's Federal Conference of 14 December 1996, its third, was designed as a platform for Steve Munby, author of *Argument Towards a Democratic Left*, who was attempting to encourage the movement towards a more programmatic position. Munby's general argument was that communists of the 1980s must bear the responsibility for encouraging the rise of sectarianism both within the Labour Party and around Tony Benn – a factor seen as important in the split of the Social Democratic Party from the Labour Party in 1981. The general message was that the DL had to have a programme with broad appeal and needed to avoid the sectarianism of the past.[13] In other words, he wanted the DL to veer towards a tight, if broad, programme rather than the loosely based networking strategy it had adopted. Yet this appeal made little difference and within a year there were moves which led to the production of a magazine called *Futures* where individual members gave their views on the problems of the DL and the changes required in what became known as the 'Democratic Left's Second Wave Transformation'.

Between 1997 and December 1999, before its Fourth Federal Conference in June 1999, the DL published nine issues of *Futures*, in anticipation of the changes that were going to be developed. Essentially this publication invited members to write articles of up to 350 words giving their views of DL's future, although by contacting 'Bernard and Nina' they could book a longer, 1,500 word, contribution.

In the first edition of *Futures*, which was produced at the end of 1997 or the beginning of 1998 (no date is provided), a critical Douglas Chalmers, who had been convenor for Scotland for six years, felt that the 1993 decision to change its strategy produced the 'narrow metropolitan vision adopted by our federal officials and committees and their unwillingness to have the hierarchy of their position challenged'.[14] It was this attitude which he felt was responsible for the continued decline of the DL. Others strongly disagreed. John Volleamere, of Liverpool, argued with the Chalmers interpretation but felt that the second conference decision (1993) to cease as a political party meant that the DL lost identity and maintained that the decision to cease being a political party was taken by a minority of delegates because of abstentions.[15] He argued that since 1992 the 'project has been to develop and a cross-party and non [an?], enabling, facilitating, networking organisation'. This was innovative and not easy although it had partly succeeded in Merseyside. Yet the membership of the DL had not been built up as a result. The networking was reasonably successful but often failed to produce members because many supporters of it would not identify with both the Labour Party and the DL. Therefore, Volleamere argued that the real need was to build up membership around the EC proposals and 'to put efforts into greater clarity of our identity'.[16] Martin Jenkins of Ellesmere Port, was even more positive and felt that networking was working by 1998, stating that 'Not being a political party, DL seeks to casually effect the main political parties and establishments by articulating ideas and interests from those radical parts which the main political establishment and parties cannot reach.'[17]

Arthur Mendelsohn (*Futures*, issue 2) was criticised by Mike Waite of Burnley, who questioned the reasons for the existence of DL and demanded that it define its role as a more positive force on the left.[18] Waite rejected the Green Socialist Network for having a very specific manifesto, for developing their 'moving left manifesto' and for likening the Blair Labour government with that of the Tories. Parimel Desai, of London, revealed the true agonies of the movement for the DL was clearly attempting to build up its membership around the re-launched monthly *New Times*, to get 400 new members by the end of 2000 and to gain a circulation of 2,000 for *New Times* by 2001. Yet membership on 4 February 1998 was claimed to be 836. Evidently the EC Biennial Report showed 141 recruits over the previous two years of whom 126 were still members, although two were in arrears, and 15 had lapsed.

None the less, the members of the DL, writing in *Future*, felt changes, however difficult they were, had had to be made after the collapse of the Soviet Union in 1991. Joe Ball, of London, made the obvious point:

> But when the Soviet Union collapsed the central part of philosophy collapsed with it. Many of the old believers were not able to face up to the changes which needed to be made in left-wing politics. It was left to Democratic Left and its counterparts in other countries to take over and advance further the positive role of the previous Communist parties.[19]

The DL was also being forced to change as a result of moves towards devolution in Scotland and Wales. Scottish supporters, quite a powerful group within DL, were particularly active in the late 1990s with the referendum for, and the formation of, a Scottish Parliament. The big problem, of course was that the DL made the decision that Democratic Left Scotland (DLS) would have to constitute itself as an independent organisation to qualify for the settlement. DLS came into existence in May 1998 and a conference was held in June 1998 to approve this change. DLS was committed to a 'holistic approach' to politics in its 'facilitatory' activities to renew radical socialist politics. In particular DL in Scotland looked forward to the proportional representation system being adopted for the Scottish Parliament which meant that the Scottish Green Party, Socialist Alliance and two organisations supported by Scottish DL – the Civil Rights Movement and the Highlands and Islands Alliance – had a good chance of winning seats. The DL was therefore deeply committed to the proportional representation in the case of the Scottish Parliament, for the Welsh Assembly and, it hoped, in the British Parliament with the Roy Jenkins recommendations in 1998.

In the late 1990s, then, the DL was still very much operating what was, increasingly, seen as a faltering 'coalition building approach'. 'GROT, the Respect festivals, Bristol for Democracy, Unions 21, the Police and Racism event, Reconnecting Liverpool and the campaign to reform Westminster's voting system' were all part of its wide-ranging activities.[20] It had organised the 'Getting Real' conferences and attempted to place DL at the centre of efforts to establish a wider modernising left. In effect it was acting as a socialist anti-Conservative front.

The Union 21 campaign was considered to be one of its most successful activities. Organised by Mike Power and Stan Davison it attracted interests from thousands of trade unionists concerned to adapt to the future. Indeed, it had John Monks acting as one of its four trustees and leading government figures spoke on its platform. It was organised from the DL offices and many activists had agreed to promote *New Times*, there being 67 trial subscribers. By December 1999 there were nearly

5,000 names on the Union 21 database, it had an income of £50,000 and operated a substantial publishing and seminar programme.

The DL also worked with the Fabian Society in the 'Getting Real' conference and the *New Times* Student Network grew from no members in October 1997 to 60 by the spring of 1998, as a result of the work of Elizabeth Townsend and Stella Francoise and their close relationship with Labour students. There was also Mike Waite's social exclusion network that emerged in 1998.

Nevertheless, the occasional big campaign and the large number of small local campaigns were never very successful and DL admitted itself that:

> Despite big efforts to involve people and build the membership, the organisation has not been successful at reproducing itself. Indeed, it has blockages which need to be tackled if we are to realise the potential of DL. We must be clear, both to ourselves and to the outside world, that Democratic Left is an open, cross-Party network. We provide a hub for coalition building for people interested in a new politics across the tribal boundaries of parties or with a wider perspective than the one track single issue campaigns. This means letting go of unreal expectations of world revolution but placing higher value on the real change that DL contributes to.[21]

A fundamental change of direction seemed inevitable, a possible move endorsed by the decline of its journal. As already indicated, the DL had inherited its journal *Changes* from the CPGB and re-named it the *New Times*. This was failing in the late 1990s, had 'virtually died on its feet' according to Mike Power, and was to be re-launched as a magazine in 2000.[22]

Even before the DL has arrived at this precarious position it was being written off by academic writers and political commentators. Indeed, Francis Beckett maintained, in his 1995 book on the CPGB, that the DL was presenting a softer image to its potential supporters:

> The DL...now dresses itself in soft blue and mauves, with gentle publicity material designed not to jar the senses. Its soft-focus symbol is three figures holding hands – one green for the environment, one purple for women's rights and one red for socialism. A tasteful blue recruiting leaflet bears the slogan 'caring, sharing, daring'.
>
> The DL does not claim to lead. It claims to enable and empower. It does not aim to be a political party. It is an 'organisation'. One of its new leaders, Mike Waite, explains this in its publication *New Times* (the new name for *Changes*): 'Now DL does not seek to be a "party" alternative to Labour, the Lib Dems, the Scottish Nationalists or anyone else, it can increasingly become a focus for discussion between members of such real political parties about areas of shared concern and interest, which could lead to joint initiatives and campaigns, and to the development of the dialogue and new ideas which political life needs so much.'[23]

With falling membership it is clear that the DL was coming under some considerable strain by the mid-1990s.

At the fourth DL Federal Conference, held at Birmingham on 5 and 6 June 1999, changes were afoot and Nina Temple stressed the need to move away from the idea of 'oppositional' to get the acceptance of left policies and emphasised the need to 'reinforce its pluralism, to keep politics clean and honest and to encourage it to reinforce its manifesto pledges'.[24] The main decision of the 40-odd delegates (of the 50 declared ones – 41 full delegates and 9 consultative delegates) who did attend was:

> ask the new EC to set in train a process to simplify and modernise Democratic Left's constitution and to bring in line with developments in the wider world and in Democratic Left's thinking since our foundation, and to present a report to the next, or special conference.[25]

This was perhaps to be expected given the scaling down of the DL over the years. The writing was on the wall.

At its Executive Meeting in early July 1999 a special conference was called to be held at London on 11 December 1999. This needed to deal with the 'second wave transformation' because it is much more than an internal constitutional amendment, 'it is about the purpose and nature of DL and how it fits into the wider challenge of making the most of the current political opportunities to achieve progressive change'.[26] The idea was to involve all organisations associated with them in this process. The 11 December 1999 conference was thus to be part of the moves to holding a 'Syntegrity style event to be held around Easter 2000'. In addition the *New Times* magazine, with its:

> on side but not always on message theme is helping to establish DL's project amongst the wider circles that we seek to engage in the process. It will engage Labour mid-term, it would question Labour's involvement in Kosova, although Rosemary Bechler, Chair of the Executive of the National Peace Council, was prepared to discuss the pros and cons of Britain being part of the NATO intervention when it was clear that neither the Serbs nor the Albanians were wanting power-sharing.[27]

Were these plans simply pious hopes? There were certainly those who felt so. In June 1999 Michael Weller, of London, reflected that:

> My stint at the call centre and inability to attract other atomised SE London DL members to a local forum on the Jenkins Proportional Representation proposals is failing as a membership organisation. Perhaps DL has been politically 'all dressed up with nowhere to go' since its inception?[28]

For [Weller], and indeed others, the end was nigh for the DL.

The fact is that DL was struggling to survive even as a facilitating organisation. Its membership continued to fall and it lacked any clear identity as an organisation. Its hopes were temporarily revived by the creation of a Scottish Parliament but its membership was still falling and *New Times* was struggling to survive. As a result, the Special 'Transformation Conference' on 11 December 1999 anticipated the end.

The Conference saw DL being dissolved and its reformation as the NPN. Its 'Connecting People and Politics' documents stating that:

> The NPN is an independent political and campaigning think tank concerned specifically with issues relating to democratic renewal and popular participation in politics. We work with a wide range of groups and individuals to provide a forum to look at emerging ideas in society.... Our goal is to provide an independent and innovative debate on the future of politics. Currently, the Network's main areas of activity include:
>
> - Active Citizenship
> - Reform of Public Institutions
> - The Role of Political Parties[29]

The NPN is now run by Peter Facey, the Director, Benjamin Linsley, responsible for communications, publications and research, Caroline Beazley-Long, responsible for membership, events and administration, and Osman Mustafa, responsible for finance. These are people who do not appear to be listed in the list of delegates for the DL conferences of the 1990s. The NPN now disowns its CPGB and DL past and the only significant vestige of that history is its continued use of 6 Cynthia Street, London as its headquarters. Indeed, in offering its brief history it states:

> The New Policy [sic] Network was established in December 1999 following the winding up of the Democratic Left, the organisation that emerged from the remnants of the Communist Party of Great Britain.
> Unlike its predecessor, the Network is politically independent and committed to working with people and organisations from across the political spectrum.[30]

It now publishes a variety of publications such as *Beyond the Classroom*, in which it comments favourably upon the Labour Government's introduction of citizenship into the school curriculum in September 2002, and *Broadening participation – Thinking beyond party membership*, which looks at non-traditional forms of party structures for the future, and *Strong politics, clean politics* which explains how the party looks to improve the health of politics.[31] It works with individuals from all political parties. It inherited two small office buildings in London from the DL which are held by a subsidiary company called Rodell Properties Ltd which provide it with a small but stable income. In 2003 Rodells fixed assets were valued at £1,800,000. In addition, other incomes for NPN comes from its members, supporters and grants from foundations and trusts.[32]

In effect, the NPN might be the direct descendent of the DL and the CPGB but it has nothing to do with the old Marxist–Leninist ideology and traditions of the past, or even the paler versions of Marxism offered by the CPGB in the 1980s. It is now merely one of thousands of political pressure groups, even though it calls itself a party, which demands clean politics, democratic associations and more citizenship – all laudable goals – but lacking in any deep-rooted Marxist instinct. The logic of the changes in the CPGB since 1977 has, in some way, come to fruition. It is therefore, to those groups who left the CPGB because of its Eurocommunism, such as the NCP and the CPB, and Trotskyite organisations that one must look to find the Marxist traditions of the past. The NPN is now an extinct line as far as Marxism is concerned.

New Communist Party of Britain

The NCP was formed as a breakaway from the CPGB in 1977 by Sid French and others, many from the Surrey branch of the CPGB. They split because they objected to the emerging Eurocommunism of the CPGB and its increasing tendency to criticise the Soviet leadership. The NCP gained a reputation for being almost Stalinist in approach. At first it had a few hundred members but it had fallen to about 200 by the mid-1990s. Once the Soviet Union collapsed in 1991 it became strongly supportive, almost worshipful, of China and North Korea and advocated its policies through *The New Worker*. It is still active, its membership may have increased, and, without much concession to grammatical style, claims that:

> The New Communist Party is the Marxist–Leninist party which is fighting for a world without exploitation. A world in which the will of the masses, the workers, the toilers, the people who work in the factories and farms, is carried out. A world in which those who produce the entire wealth of the globe get the fruits of their labour.
>
> This is the world we work for. A socialist society where there are no slums, poverty, or racism. A society where there are no classes, no exploiters, no bigotry and no war. A new and better world – the world Marx and Engels predicted and a world which will surely come to pass. It is already being built in the socialist countries of today. It is being fought for in every continent and every country.
>
> We are part of that struggle.
> This is the century of socialism.
>
> Our weekly newspaper is the 'New Worker'.[33]

Such worldwide aspirations appear bloated out of all proportion, although *The New Worker* has made great play of the situation in Iraq and Iraqi resistance against American attacks around the Imman Ali shrine in Najaf from which it has drawn some support. It also claims support from its policy of advocating the need for new ways of taxing the rich.[34]

It is difficult to find reliable membership figures but the London District of the NCP has ten organised branches.[35] There is also a continuing Surrey branch, although it is not clear whether this is included in the London branches, and also a branch at Brighton.[36] The NCP's London District web page was also full of anti-Blair and pro-Iraq editorials and articles in 2004. It is still organising conferences every two years, the last two, the thirteenth and fourteenth, respectively, occurring in

December 2001 and December 2003. In 2004 it was also raising £3,000 for the *New Worker* Fund, and in the week ending 3 September appears to have raised £253.10 towards it, bringing its running total to £1,846.85. Some of its contributions were coming from individual members in Greater Manchester, Reigate and throughout Surrey.[37]

Although active, with its own web site, it is clear that the NCP of Britain is small, focused very much upon London and Surrey, and lacking in money and resources. It publishes the *New Worker* which is struggling to continue and focuses very much upon the events in Iraq, reporting that 'Iraqui Mass March against the Invaders'.[38] The evidence suggests that it is barely viable as a political party, although that comment would fit many of the Marxist and socialist organisations present in Britain today. In terms of support, however, a more serious contender for the claim to be the true successor of the CPGB is the CPB which wishes that it could use the old name.

Communist Party of Britain

The CPB broke away from the CPGB in 1988 in exasperation at the continuing witch hunt within the Party, the new dissentients joining with older ejects to form this new party. In terms of members and activity it has a stronger claim than most to being the old CPGB, attracting some of the old membership and operating the *Morning Star*. It, like its forbear, was also convinced of the need to build up trade union support as the route way to political success.

In the 1980s and 1990s it was led by Michael Joseph Hicks, a docker and a lifelong communist who was born in 1937 to a Catholic mother and father. Mike Hicks had joined the YCL in 1953, at the age of 16. He worked as a printer and was a member of the print union Society of Graphical and Allied Trades (SOGAT), member of the EC of the CPGB, a full-time union branch official and arrested during the mass demonstrations against the new plant at Wapping set up by Rupert Murdoch. Hicks was expelled from the CPGB after chairing the London District Congress in 1984 and continuing after Gordon McLennan told him to close the meeting. According to Francis Beckett, he was extremely bitter about the events and stated that:

> They knew we could beat them democratically, so they went for the purge. They used the sort of administrative methods which they condemned the Soviet Union for using. If they had not we would have won the National Congress and removed McLennan and that lot. Nina Temple and those people made it clear that they were not Marxist–Leninists. But they stayed on in the Party and therefore had the benefit of money, £4million of it. They were like bees round a honey pot.[39]

In the mid-1990s Hicks remained a powerful trade unionist working for SOGAT whilst continuing to work for the CPB. His Party work was supplemented by others who claimed to work for a working-class party which Harry Pollitt would have recognised.

The CPB is essentially focused upon the need to win trade-union support. In the late 1980s and early 1990s Kevin Halpin, its Industrial Organiser, published, just as

Bert Ramelson did for the CPGB, *Needs of the Hour* every year to tell trade union members what policies they should deliver.[40] Halpin had held a prominent position within the CPGB – had served on the Commission on Inner Party Democracy in 1956 and was a leading figure on the LCDTU – and by the 1990s was retired and putting all his energies into the political activity of the CPB. The Party was at its strongest in the rail union RMT (national union of Rail Maritime and Transport Workers) and, not surprisingly, in the mid-1990s 9 of the 32-member CPB executive were also on the executives of their own union.

In the mid-1990s the CPB claimed to have about 1,500 members, more than the DL claimed at the same time, but has eschewed easy alliances with other dissident groups. Indeed, it never forgave the Straight Left faction for walking out of the London District Congress in 1984 when ordered to do so by McLennan, and so Hicks and his supporters made no alliance. However, Straight Left had ceased by the time the CPGB ceased to exist.

From the beginning the CPB saw itself as a continuation of the CPGB and it called its first conference on 1989 the Thirty-ninth conference, following on from the previous 38 conferences of the CPGB. It also published a new edition of *The British Road to Socialism* in 1989 and another in 1992 'in the light of the enormous changes which had occurred in the former socialist countries of Eastern Europe'.[41] At its 1993 Congress there were about 100 delegates, some very elderly, and at the end Hicks, and the chairman Richard Maybin, a teacher in his fifties, led the delegates in a complete rendering of the Internationale in an endeavour to recapture the spirit of the past. Indeed, it had attracted Andrew Rothstein, the only surviving founding father of the CPGB who remained a member of the CPB until his death in September 1994.

It is clear that in the 1990s there was intense conflict between the DL and the CPB. Nina Temple and Mike Hicks were hostile to each other and adopted conflicting attitudes over many issues, including the Soviet money which flowed into the old CPGB. According to Beckett, Hicks said on the money, that: 'I don't think about the Moscow money but it wouldn't have worried me. The ruling class have always done this sort of thing.' In contrast, Nina Temple thought it corrupt: 'Such substantial secret funds gave vast unaccountable powers to those who held them.' Nevertheless, as Beckett noted, she hung on to every penny and protected the legal position of the DL to the CPGB legacy.[42]

The CPB thought of mounting a court case when the DL was founded to put forwards its claim to the legitimate heir of the CPGB but, says Hicks, 'we decided we would not let a British judge decide the political fate of the Communist Party'. But there was a possibility of another court case. Just before the 1991 Congress which formed the DL, a CPGB member left his money in a will to the CPGB. His executors interpreted this as meaning the CPB, and the DL decided to challenge this in court.

The CPB still has the *Morning Star* as an asset. Although the *Morning Star* claimed to be an independent paper Tony Chater, and most of the staff, were CPB members and the CPB rents office space in the *Morning Star* building – at a commercial rate. However, the relationship presents a serious financial burden.

Until 1991 the *Morning Star* sold 12,000 copies to the Soviet Union, paid for a year in advance until 1988 when the Soviet Union began to pay a year in arrears.[43] In 1991 the order went down to 6,000. Also, in 1992 Soviet hardliners mounted a coup against Gorbachev, the failure of which strengthened the hand of anti-Communists under Boris Yeltsin. As a result, in 1992 Moscow cancelled its *Morning Star* order altogether. After that Chater and the PPPS, which owns the *Morning Star*, have had to survive on plummeting sales and the income derived from the sale of their Farringdon Road building for £2.1 millions in 1987. Chater and Mary Rosser, the Chief Executive at that time, decided to build up a more modest office on the border between Hackney and Islington and new technology enabled them to reduce the number of journalists from 40 to 14. By the mid-1990s the sale of the *Morning* Star was down to about 7,000 per week which meant that the salaries of the small numbers of staff remained low. It was at this point, in 1995, that Tony Chater retired as editor.

In recent years the CPB had undergone a partial change of leadership, if not policy. In 2004 the EC of the CPB re-elected Robert Griffith as general secretary, Anita Halpin as chair, John Foster – the academic historian – as international secretary and Kevin Halpin as Industrial Organiser. They were joined on the PC by John Haylett, Mary Davis, Graham Stevenson, Steve Silver, Martin Levy and Emily Mann.[44]

In 2004 its emphasis upon capturing trade union support remains, and it continues to call for improvement in the wages and conditions of workers. However, there are other issues at stake. It declared its intention to stand a candidate against Tony Blair in the Sedgefield constituency at the next general election in order to expose Blair's 'murderous policies in Iraq' and was obsessed with the desire for Labour unity to replace New Labour.[45] Martin Levy, the Northern District Secretary, was leading a campaign against the proposed assemblies in the Northern, North-West and Yorkshire and Humberside regions because they would not have any legislative or tax-raising powers and might become 'vehicles for privatisation' and 'for the further erosion of local government'.[46] At its EC meeting on 11 January 2004 it endorsed the formation of a European Party of the Left and at its Forty-seventh Congress, held on Saturday, 17 January 2004, it mounted its campaign to defeat New Labour.

Active, committed broadly to the working-class Marxism which existed broadly in the 1970s and 1980s, fond of trade unions and critical of New Labour, the CPB represents the spirit of the old, pre-1977, CPGB better than any other Marxist organisation in Britain. However, its membership and influence are very limited.

Communist Party of Scotland, Scottish Militant and the formation of the Scottish Socialist Party

In contrast to the DL/NPN, the NCP and the CPB, who have disowned their past or failed to develop a significant power base, the move towards a Socialist Alliance, in England, Wales and Scotland have been far more successful. The most successful of these arrangements has been the Socialist Alliance in Scotland which formed the even more successful SSP.

The SSA was formed at Glasgow in April 1996 at a conference attended by 150 delegates after holding several preparatory meetings, one of which, held in Glasgow, had attracted 400 delegates.[47] It was a reaction against the rightward swing in the

British Labour Party and a response to the prospect that a Scottish parliament might be re-established. It was the result of discussions, and a number of preparatory meetings, between a variety of socialist organisations. The Scottish Socialist Movement, which was the 'hard-left' of the Scottish Labour Party, partly led by Allan Green, was deeply involved because of the Labour Party's switch to the right. Green, in fact, became the National Secretary of the Alliance and explained, in 1997, the 'giant leap' taken in 1996 when people disillusioned with New Labour and the SNP joined, 'including the ex-Labour leaders of Dunbarton and Dundee Councils, and the convenor if the SNP in Edinburgh'.[48]

The Communist Party of Scotland, which had been formed in 1991, following the demise of the CPGB and the formation of the DL, also committed itself to the Alliance. A variety of people from international solidarity campaigns, community struggles, women's and gay/lesbian groups, the Green Party were also involved. Some trade unionists were also involved. However, the most powerful body involved was Scottish Militant Labour, a Trotskyite organisation, which included Colin Fox in its leadership.[49] The Scottish Republican Socialist Party (SRSP) was also drawn into the new arrangement.

The SSA quickly became involved in the Save Our Schools and Services Campaign in Glasgow which, after great conflict in 1995 and 1996, forced Glasgow Council to keep open 17 of the 22 schools threatened with closure. It became involved in a variety of campaigns, published a bi-monthly magazine called *Red* from August 1996 and formed Young Socialist Action which brought out a newsletter called *Red Alert*. It produced a more comprehensive programme in May 1996 entitled 'Charter for Socialist Change'. It was at this point that political developments in Scotland moved quickly.

The remarkable development of Scottish Nationalism in the 1980s and 1990s forced Tony Blair's new Labour Government into offering Scottish devolution as an alternative for independence. A referendum was held, the result of which supported Scottish devolution and the creation of a Scottish Parliament, with legislative and financial powers, in 1999. In this climate of rising political opportunity the Scottish Marxist and Socialist organisations made the surprisingly advanced decision to bind themselves into one party – the SSP – which, by the standards of Marxism in Britain, has flourished.

Buoyed up by the way in which the SSA had performed in contesting 16 seats in the 1997 general election, Scottish Militant Labour pushed to form the SSP in September 1998. It immediately declared itself in favour of a free Scottish socialist republic and stated that it was internationalist, anti-imperialist and democratic – 'based upon the principle of one person one vote'.[50] It was to be led by Tommy Sheridan, its great propagandist, and Alan MacCombes, its leading theoretician.

The formation of the SSP was immediately criticised by the International Committee of the Fourth International, whose views were expressed in an article by Chris Marsden.[51] Marsden felt that the decision of Scottish Militant Labour to form the SSP was made despite the opposition of their English comrades and the International movement, and was geared to 'encompass a variety of different political trends on the left, united only by their espousal of Scottish separatism and a vague commitment to reformist policies'.[52] Put bluntly, Marsden and the Fourth International were unhappy with the SSA, 'an umbrella organisation of middle class radicals, ex-Labourists and Stalinists', for its opportunism and its chauvinistic approach. Indeed, Marsden argues that the SSP was formed because of the alleged failure of the Labour Government to be interested in the fate of Scotland and the belief that only a working-class organisation could properly demand and gain independence for Scotland, especially since the SNP was considered to be in the hands of big business. Indeed, he writes critically that:

> Scottish Militant Labour is seeking to rise to prominence on this wave of political disorientation. Rather than arguing for a united struggle by workers throughout Britain against big business and its Labour government, on the basis of a socialist programme, they declare, 'the predominant character of the movement of public opinion in favour of Scottish independence is progressive.' It is, they add, 'made up of a big majority of young people and low paid workers.' Those opposed to independence, they claim, include 'the most right-wing, conservative section of the population, in particular the Scottish ruling class of landowners, financiers and big business interests'.[53]

Marsden doubts the claims of the new SSP, feeling that it has given up the class struggle for quick political gains and that one of its first recruits, Hugh Kerr, a member of the European Parliament who had broken with Labour, had given the game away when he suggested that the SSP could be seen as a left prop for the Blair Labour Government.

Despite flying in the face of international Trotskyism with its blatant appeal to nationalism, the SSP achieved immediate political success. In May 1999 Glasgow Councillor Tommy Sheridan, was elected to the new Scottish Parliament as one of its 129 members (MSPs). It did, however, get fewer votes than Socialist Labour, a United Kingdom-wide party led by Arthur Scargill which consistently refused to countenance the idea of joining forces with the SSP. However, the SSP grew quickly. The SWP in Scotland, another Trotskyite organisation, also agreed to become part of the SSP, although this decision proved controversial. The SSP also attracted to its ranks members from the Labour Party and the SNP.

The SRSP also, by a narrow margin, decided to join the SSP in 1998. Its roots were to be found in the Scottish Republican Socialist Clubs, formed in 1973, to introduce socialism to the SNP and to develop the demand for independence amongst the left-wingers who still wished the retention of the union with the rest of the United Kingdom. The expulsion of the 79 Group from the SNP led the Republican Clubs to form a coherent political party and they formed themselves into the SRSP in 1982. It believed in socialism and independence for Scotland. It therefore organised as a platform within the SSP and called itself the Scottish Republican Socialist Movement (SRSM) and , led by Gerry Cairns, expressed its opposition to any attempt by the SSP to ditch independence by issuing its views through *Scottish Workers' Republic*, which was first published in June 1985.[54]

The diverse nature of the Party has meant that there have been some major internal disagreements. The demand for independence for Scotland, a central policy of the SRSP when it was active, and largely accepted by Scottish Militant Labour, was opposed by the SWP on international grounds. However, the internal party organisation of the SSP almost positively encourages this high level of disagreement in the party by allowing the existence of 'platforms', where different groups support conflicting issues within the Party such as nationalism and internationalism. Effectively, then the SRSP has become the SRSM Platform and the SWP has become the Socialist Workers' Platform.[55]

The SSP has become the foremost far-left force in the Scottish Parliament polling much higher than the Socialist Labour Party (SLP) on 1 May 2003 Scottish Parliamentary elections and it claimed to be 'one of the strongest parties of those left in Europe, with 6 members of the 129 member Scottish Parliament, thousands of individual members, and a network of scores of branches stretching from the Northern Isles to the English border'.[56] The SSP Members of the Scottish Parliament (MSPs) are Tommy Sheridan (Glasgow), Rosie Kane (Glasgow), Colin Fox (Lothians), Frances Curran (West of Scotland), Carolyn Leckie (Central Scotland) and Rosemary Byrne (South of Scotland).

The SSP has been deeply involved in the development of Scottish domestic politics since its formation. In March 2000 it was involved in the march through Glasgow to demand the scrapping of the council tax and its replacement with an alternative income-based 'Scottish Service Tax' designed to make the rich pay more and to cut the bills of most Scots.[57] As with most socialist parties, it opposed racism, demanded decent housing and free school meals, opposed privatisation of public services, welcomed asylum seekers and declared its solidarity with those struggling against injustice in Palestine, Colombia and in many other parts of the world. These views are presented on a daily basis over the internet in the *SSP News*. Its headlines on 2 September 2004 included soldier's mother demanding a withdrawal from Iraq and a SSP republican protest against the official opening of the new Scottish Parliament on 9 October.[58] Many of its articles immediately previous to this focus upon Tommy Sheridan's call for British troops to be brought home from Iraq and his snubbing of the Queen's opening of the new Scottish Parliament building. The SSP also projects its ideas through a weekly newspaper, the *Scottish Socialist Voice*.

Throwing itself into the centre of Scottish politics, the SSP quickly developed a substantial branch system with 7 branches in Central Scotland, 8 branches in Lothians, 8 branches in Mid-Scotland and Fife, 13 branches in Glasgow, 9 branches in the South of Scotland, 12 branches in the Highlands and Islands, 11 branches in north east Scotland and 10 branches in the West of Scotland. Thus in September 2004 the rapidly expanding SSP had 78 branches.[59] It also claimed to have recruited about 3,000 recruits between 1999 and 2003, which, if correct, would suggest that the SSP is undoubtedly the largest hard left socialist or Marxist party in Britain.[60]

By 2004 SNP converts were joining as a result of the 'Time to Go' Appeal of John Sheridan, MSP. Lloyd Quinan, Bill Ramsay, Ken Ferguson and Andy Rossiter – who were on the left of the SNP, in the Scottish Parliament, on the SNP Trade Union Group and active in the SNP heartlands – joined the SSP. Apparently, 'Faced with the gathering move to big business policies in the SNP they have all decided that it is "Time to Go".[61] A contributory factor might well have been the return of Alex Salmond as leader of the SNP since it was felt that it heralds a New SNP which might be closely allied with big business.

There is significant trade union presence developing within the SSP. Bob Crow, RMT general secretary, presented Tommy Sheridan with a cheque of £3,900 for affiliation fees for his union in April 2004. Indeed, with 'With two trades unions affiliated to the SSP, the 70,000-strong RMT and the 4,500-strong Communication Workers Union (CMU) Scotland no. 2 branch and with a full time-workplace organiser, the SSP is committed to giving a voice to trade union members.'[62]

As a result of its rapid growth the SSP opened a new national office, The John Maclean Centre, at 70 Stanley Street in Glasgow on 2 September 2004 – the hundred and twenty-fifth anniversary of the birth of John McLean. It was opened by Allan Green, the Party's national secretary. The SSP has certainly prospered with Scottish devolution and the formation of the Scottish Parliament, although it emphasises that it stands for 'Socialism, Independence and Internationalism' and emphasises that it is an anti-capitalist and democratic party, believing in one person one vote. The picture of success and achievement is not quite so rosy for the Marxist and hard-left organisations in England and Wales, although they are making ripples, if not waves, in British politics.

English and Welsh Socialist Alliances

In the 1950s Ted Grant was part of a tendency within the Fourth International which rejected Trotsky's central conception of the working class as an agency of change. They saw the success of Stalinists in Eastern Europe and China as evidence that 'workers' states' could be established without a conscious revolutionary movement of the working class. It was claimed that Stalinists and reformist bureaucracies would play this role and Militant supporters worked within the Labour Party in order to push it towards nationalisation and welfare reforms. However, under Neil Kinnock the Militant supporters were hounded out of the Labour Party and then under Blair the Labour Party renounced its commitment to social ownership of industry. Some Militant members still wished to work within the Labour Party to bring about social and industrial change but others despaired of the Labour Party and left, provoking a conflict in which Ted Grant was replaced by Peter Taaffe as leader. In 1995 Taaffe declared his support for the creation of a new 'mass socialist party in Britain'.[63] The idea was that there would be a realignment of left groups within the Labour Party, the various fragments of the old Stalinist Communist Party and the smaller left groups like Militant. Indeed, Arthur Scargill's SLP was seen to be party of this process.

The Taaffe group of Militant set up Socialist Alliances throughout Britain as a vehicle for 'regroupment'. The policy emerged in 1995, but was effectively a failure in England by 1995. However, as already indicated, it was a success in Scotland with the SSP in 1998. This provoked the move towards Socialist Alliance in Wales, which has had some limited success, and a revival of the Socialist Alliance idea in England with the proliferation of such organisations in London, Liverpool and other areas. They have achieved some modest success, although nothing on the scale of the SSP.

The Welsh Socialist Alliance (WSA) gained inspiration from the success of the SSP, partly because the conditions of a demand for independence or devolution were similar, if not the same. WSA appears to have become more active in the twenty-first century with branches in Blackwood (2004), Neath, Swansea and many other Welsh towns and cities. By and large these branches take up local issues, such as opposition to the Blackwood by-pass road, the defence of council housing in Swansea and opposition to building an asphalt plant on Neath Abbey wharf near Skewen. It has also been drawn into the work of the First (2003) and Second (2004) Peoples Assembly for Peace and the Second European Forum (November 2003). However, its impact has been minimal in Welsh national politics. It obtained only about 3 per cent of the vote (81 votes) at the Pentywn Council By-Election, Cardiff on 11 September 2003 and in the Welsh Assembly in 2004 gained no success.[64] However, on 13 March a special conference of WSA welcomed the establishment of Respect, the Unity Coalition, which 'is a new political party which stands for peace, social justice and for the principle that everyone should be protected by compassionate public provision from the cradle to the grave'. It emerged from a public demonstration against the invasion of Iraq and was an attempt to unify all British socialists and Socialist Alliance groups.

The English Socialist Alliance (ESA) has similarly made some, if rather limited, impact. The movement began in 1995 and faltered from the start but was revived by the successes in Scotland at the end of the 1990s and through the London Socialist Alliance and other local Socialist Alliances who often stood candidates in elections as United Socialists. Again, like the WSA, it has exerted a very limited impact upon English politics but it brings together a large number of local organisations. Over 200 delegates assembled at Islington to debate the Iraq war at its AGM on 10 May 2003. They were drawn from numerous Socialist Alliance organisations such as Ashfield, Brent and Harrow, Bristol, Cambridgeshire, Colchester, Coventry and Warwickshire, Exeter, Greenwich, Hackney, Islington, Lancashire (with connections in Blackburn, Burnley, Pendle and Preston), Leeds, Leicester, London, Manchester, Middlesbrough, North Derbyshire, Oxford, Plymouth, South Manchester, Southwark, Streatham, Teesside, Telford, Tower Hamlets and York.[65] In addition, Middlesbrough Trades Council, the Fire Brigades Union and several other trade union and radical organisations were attached to them. Many of these have identified with Respect: The Unity Coalition, which was formed in 2003. Indeed, the Lancashire Socialist Alliance noted that the Special Conference of Socialist Alliance held on 13 March 2004 welcomed the establishment of Respect and therefore decided to put its campaigning efforts into supporting the new organisation, placing its details on the Respect North West website.[66] Colchester Socialist Alliance did the same.[67] Others have identified with Respect: The Unity Coalition but not submerged with it, most obviously Hackney which had three Socialist Alliance candidates – Diane Swingler for Northwold ward, Aneta Gluckstein for Springfield ward and Mitch Dublin for Queensbridge ward – for the local contests on 7 June 2004 and Cecilia Prosper as the parliamentary candidate for the Hackney South and Shoreditch parliamentary constituency for the general election of 2005.[68]

Whilst these alliances originally emerged to bring about a realignment of the politics of the hard left in the hope of forcing a change of line by the New Labour Government of Tony Blair it is clear that it was the invasion of Iraq which shaped their activities in 2003 and 2004. In Exeter 800 people, largely socialists, marched in a 'Protest Against the War' on 22 March 2004 and there had been an Exeter Day of Protest Against the War on 20 March 2004. Brent and Hackney organised campaigns against war and against privatisation, and most others have organised marches and protests.

Other Marxist organisations and activities

There are simply scores of Marxist and socialist alliances present, and even active, in England and Wales at the present. Some are remnants from the old CPGB which failed to identify with DL, the NCP and the CPB, and others are simply the Trotskyite organisations which have survived, in various forms, for decades. They are immensely fragmented and have not yet succeeded in achieving the unity shown by the Scottish Marxist movement. The more important ones are referred to below.

(a) Revolutionary Communist Party The RCP of Britain (Marxist–Leninist), known as RCPB(ML), is still active and has operated a website since 1998. Its preoccupation in 2004 was the defence of North Korea against US aggression, the reunification of Korea, opposition to British and US intervention in Sudan and the critical examination of the state of Tony Blair's Britain.[69]

The RCPB(ML) published its *Draft Programme for the Working Class*, on 7 January 1995, its Preamble stating that: 'If the working class is to play its historical role and lead the entire society out of the crisis and open the path to progress, it must have its own independent programme, that is, it must set its immediate and long-term aims.'[70]

Its Immediate Programme was summarised by four principles – recognition of all inviolable rights, more into the economy than is taken out, democratic renewal of the political process, and recognition of the inviolable right of all peoples to determine their own affairs nationally and internationally. It produces this, and its other publications, through the Workers' Publication Centre, 170 Wandsworth Road, London SW8 2LA. It also produced the *Workers' Daily Internet Edition*, a 'Daily On Line Newspaper of the Revolutionary Communist Party of Britain (Marxist–Leninist)', although the last edition issued appears to have been Year 2001, 83, 17 May 2001.[71] It also produces the *Workers' Weekly*.

In the 2001 general election it supported many independent and alternative candidates who were standing for election against the 'Third Way' programme of Tony Blair and against the decline in healthcare standards. These included Roger Nettleship, independent health worker politician candidate, who stood for South Shields, and Salvinder Singh Dhillon, independent candidate for Ealing–Southall, whose main concern was to empower the community. In addition there was Steve Goddard, an ex-firefighter, stood for Birmingham, Erdington, in the West Midlands. A recent defaulted member of the Labour Party, he was on the EC of the Birmingham Trades Council. Caroline Johnson was a prospective candidate for Birmingham Perry

Barr and was active in RAGE, the campaign against the closure of elderly people's homes, and Angela Thompson was the prospective candidate for Dudley South. She worked for the Dudley Nation Heath Service (NHS) and was joint branch secretary of UNISON Dudley Group of Hospitals branch and had been on strike since August 2000 against a private finance initiative scheme to transfer jobs of the Dudley health workers out of the NHS. There was also Helen John who announced her intention to stand against Tony Blair in his Sedgefield constituency. A retired midwife, with 31 previous convictions for criminal damage, she suggested the need to set up a peace camp, like that at Greenham Common, outside the Menwith Hill air base which would be used to track missiles if the 'Son of Star Wars' programme went ahead.

In Greater London, Louise Christian, a leading lawyer, was prospective candidate for Hornsey and Wood Green. She had been a member of the Labour Party from 1976 to 1966 and had been prospective parliamentary candidate for Hendon South in 1987. Until recently she had also been chair of the Civil Liberties Trust. She opposes the attack upon civil liberties and the oppression of asylum seekers and acted for the NUM lawyers during the miners' strike of 1984–5. Also, in the London area were Sally Labern, prospective candidate for Leyton and Wanstead, who was opposed to the privatisation of education services in the Waltham Forest area: 'It is clear that New Labour strategy is to drive big business in through the front door of public services including Education.' Theresa Bennett, prospective parliamentary candidate for Vauxhall, was one of two London Socialist Alliance candidates in the Great London Authority (GLA) elections, saving her deposit with 6,231 votes, or 6.2 per cent of the vote, in Lambeth and Southwark. She had been a welfare rights adviser for more than ten years.

Effectively, the RCPB(ML) supports the Socialist Alliance in England and the WSA who stood about 100 candidates in the 2001 general election. The Socialist Alliance was committed to bringing about fundamental social, political and cultural change through the community, workplace, elections and educational campaigning with the aim of establishing social justice and environmental sustainability.

(b) Socialist Party of Great Britain The SPGB, formed in 1904 in a breakaway from the pre-war Marxist organisation the Social Democratic Federation still retains and the oldest continuing socialist party in Britain, still maintains its limited presence. Committed to publishing as a means of winning converts to Marxism, and prepared to declare the end of Parliament when the SPGB gains a majority in the House of Commons, this organisation presents little real threat to capitalism and continues to attract little interest. It consisted of a few hundred members in London at the beginning of the twentieth century, probably reached a peak of about 500 when it extended its influence into provincial centres such as Leeds in the mid 1970s, but seems to have fallen back since. It prides itself in 'organising democratically and without leaders' and aims to build up a movement towards achieving a socialist state.[72] It continues to advocate its views through the *Socialist Standard*.

(c) Socialist Labour Party Briefly quite effective was the SLP, which was formed on 1 May 1996. In 2004 Paul Hardman was its President, Linda Muir its Vice-President and Arthur Scargill was its general secretary, and it operated from Barnsley. The Party was formed as a left-wing splinter group in reaction to

Tony Blair's policy of taking New Labour to the centre ground of British politics. It supports withdrawal from the European Union, wishes to place Britain in the centre of a new world socialist order, demands equality for women and seeks to support trade unions. It contested parliamentary seats in the 1997 and 2001 general elections without success although Arthur Scargill intends to contest the Hartlepool on the 2005 general election. However, although it remains a small and largely insignificant organisation it has won some support from trade unions.[73]

(d) Others From the welter of other smaller organisations there is Communist Liaison, a loose network of about 150 former Communists in 1995, mostly to be found in London, Liverpool and Newcastle upon Tyne, who did not feel happy with fitting in with the DL or the CPB. There was the Islip Unity Group, which consisted of a few famous trade union names from the CPGB's past trying to salvage something from the past. Their first meeting was in a member's house in Islip Street in Kentish Town. This group included Ken Gill and Jim Mortimer, and Bert Ramelson attended until his death in April 1994. This may well, have disappeared by now but another organisation still active is the CPGB (Provisional Central Committee) formed in the 1990s when *The Leninist* newspaper declared the intention to reforge the old CPGB. And one must not forget the SWP which still produces *Socialist Worker* and maintains its Socialist Worker Student Society.[74]

(e) Marxism and Trade Unionism Within the trade unions too, the Marxist left is coming together to provide an alternative to the policies of New Labour. In the UNISON elections for general secretary in 1996 the Board Left candidate, Roger Bannister, came second to Rodney Bickerstaffe with over 58,000 votes and 20 per cent of the vote. When Bickerstaffe retired in 2000 Bannister obtained a third of the vote, over 71,000 votes, in the subsequent contest. In May 1998, David Rix of the SLP, formed by the ex-Communist and miners' leader Arthur Scargill in 1996, was elected general secretary of the Amalgamated Society of Locomotive Engineers and Firemen.

Conclusion

The Marxist organisations of the 1990s were not very successful and the formation of the NPN, from the failed DL, is a testament to this. It represents an extinct line as far as British Marxism is concerned. Nevertheless, there have been signs since the late 1990s that Marxism and socialism are beginning to revive in Britain. The formation of Socialist Alliances in England and Wales produced a modest, if undistinguished, Marxist presence and brought the CPB, RCPB(ML) and other organisations together in making a token challenge at the general election of 2001. However, the alliance of various Marxist parties represented by the SSP, a predominantly Trotskyite organisation with a dash of old Scottish section of the CPGB support, has gone on further and gained a significant presence in the Scottish Parliament. It may be the peculiar conditions of Scottish politics and the demand for national independence on the left that has paved the way for this success but it does at least raise the possibility of a Marxist revival of types through realignment on the Left. The formation of Respect in 2003, as a result of the invasion of Iraq, and the disenchantment of some Labour MPs at

Re-emergence and reconstruction of Marxism

the foreign policies of the Blair Government, raises another prospect for socialist realignment – although it may be that Respect becomes one of the many innovative casualties of the desperate demand of hard-left socialism in Britain to realign. What is clear is that the Marxism of the old CPGB and Harry Pollitt will not reappear. Whatever occurs, it is clear that the old Stalinist approach is dead as may be, to a lesser extent, the old Trotskyite belief that working-class consciousness can bring about change. The age of socialist realignment amongst the hard left is being attempted, with its emphasis upon social networking, democratic principles, domestic, national and international issues. Whether it will be successful only the future can tell but there is a groundswell of opposition to New Labour which might produce realignment at least as powerful as the CPGB at its height. Gramscian permeation may be more successful than Stalinism and Eurocommunism in the end. As Willie Thompson suggests, it may be inconceivable that a world Communist movement might be recreated, and indeed any Stalinist version would be undesirable, but there may be some prospect of reviving Marxist ideas as freedom in more subtle ways than were adopted in the past.

Conclusion

What can one make of the fortunes of Marxism in Britain, or more particularly the CPGB, since the Second World War? Although each chapter sports its own conclusion three themes have dominated this book. They are the almost constant decline of Marxism in Britain since 1945, the waning influence of Stalinism/Moscow since the late 1960s and the increasing desire of the movement to make contact with other groupings almost to the point of acting as a networking organisation.

Between 1945 and 1991 the membership of the CPGB has fallen from about 45,000 to 4,750, at the historic moment when it dismantled the Party structure in November 1991. The decline was not continuous, for there were periods in the late 1940s, the early 1960s and the early 1970s when membership did recover after periods of rapid loss. However, by and large the onset of the Cold War and the Soviet invasions of Hungary and Czechoslovakia precipitated severe criticism and disillusionment amongst supporters. Other Marxist groups fared little better, although some Trotskyite parties did benefit from the defections from the CPGB and many did particularly well in the political conditions of the 1960s, the 1970s and the early 1980s. And, indeed, since the demise of the CPGB in 1991 it has been the old Trotskyite organisations, particularly through the SSP and the SSA, who have fared best of all. Nevertheless, development elsewhere has been lacking in recent years.

Why did this decline occur? Why has the importance of British Marxism, never a very substantial body in international terms even at its height, shrivelled so quickly? There are some obvious reasons. Ross McKibbin has argued that Marxism never established a niche in the culture and political institutions of the traditional working class. In other words the structural and associational aspects of the working class militated against mass revolutionary organisations.[1] It is possible that the wartime situation, which boosted CPGB membership far beyond the historic level it achieved during the inter-war years, simply exaggerated the decline in its true hard-core support once the renewal of hostility against Marxism occurred again with the Cold War. The organising influence of Stalin and Moscow, whether in discussions that led to *The British Road to Socialism* or the Soviet invasions of 1956 and 1968, did not help matters and proved an impediment to the success of British Marxism. Even when that influence seemed to be on the wane, the Soviet Union continued to help finance the CPGB, albeit secretly, between 1957 and at least 1979.

Nevertheless, there were other deep-seated reasons for the post-war decline of British Marxism. The abandonment of factory branches in favour of the formation of factory committees in 1945 certainly undermined the thriving factory branch movement to a point from which it was never able to recover when the policy was reversed in the late 1940s – despite some recovery in the 1950s and in the early 1960s. Eventually, however, the Party almost abandoned its workplace movement, not holding a workplace conference in the intervening years between 1967 and mid-1976.

In other areas of development some considerable effort was made to extend influence through the Broad Democratic Left Alliance policy, formally adopted in 1968. The CPGB's policy towards the women's movement moved on from tacit support in the 1950s to active participation in the second-wave feminism of the 1970s. However, the desire of the women's section of the CPGB to develop a more socialist–feminist movement narrowed down its vision at a time when the WLM was fragmenting. And the CPGB women's movement was never at ease with the third-wave feminism of the 1980s with its emphasis upon difference and the experience of black women. In any case, the CPGB was declining rapidly in the 1980s and its ability to shape events was diminished.

The influence of Stalin and Moscow was also of primary importance, at least until the late 1960s. As indicated in the introduction, 'realists' and 'essentialists', to use the inappropriate terms applied, have hotly debated the influence of the Comintern, Moscow and Stalinism. Although much of the debate has focused upon events of the 1920s and 1930s it is clear that it has a relevance to the post-war years. What is obvious from this study is that the shape of the politics of the CPGB, if not always the fine detail, was governed by Moscow's wishes in the 1940s and 1950s and early 1960s, although that influenced began to wane from the late 1960s onwards and was the cause of much conflict in the late 1970s and 1980s. There was dedicated pro-Sovietism and faith in the Party in the 1950s and a commitment to a unified line against the demands of free speech within the Party led to the suspension, later resignation, of E. P. Thompson and John Saville. This domination of the pro-Soviet groups was to change gradually. Twenty or so years later, the 'Decisions' television series, 'the fly-on-the wall' documentary on the CPGB filmed in 1977, seems to have caught the CPGB at the cusp of change. Moscow's influence was still evident through the style and domination of Bert Ramelson, although the Eurocommunists were at the gate waiting to force their entry. Even then, democratic centralism lingered on and was used, effectively, by the more right-wing Eurocommunists to expel old, pro-Moscow, supporters who protested at changes in the 1980s. Indeed, the very wrenching away from Moscow's domination produced the enormously divisive internal disputes within the Party in the late 1970s and early 1980s, much of which focused upon control of the *Morning Star*, which retained its faith in a pro-Soviet position. The Eurocommunist-dictated CPGB, which often expressed its views through *Marxism Today*, gained its way in the Special Congress of 1985.

Faced with such a dramatic internal conflict and plunging membership it is not surprising that the Party sought to adapt and change to the point that it sought alliances with numerous protest groups – feminist groups, Green groups and black and anti-racist groups. The natural consequence of this was the redrafting of *The British Road to Socialism* in the form of the 'pick and mix' socialism of *Manifesto for New Times*. Networking became the name of the game and the more federal structure adopted by the DL, the immediate successor to the CPGB.

Thatcherism in Britain and the collapse of Stalinist regimes in Eastern Europe and the Soviet Union in the late 1980s and early 1990s meant the end of the old worldwide context of old communism. The CPGB was forced to adapt to political developments and, indeed, numerous Trotskyite groups needed to do so as well. There are still separatist groups from the old CPGB – such as the NCP and the CPB, who believed that, somehow, the old form of Moscow Marxism might be revived and Trotskyite groups who believe in the possibility of a pure form of Marxism, unsullied by Stalinism, might emerge. Nevertheless, the recent growth of Marxism in Britain is to be found mainly in Scotland where the full spectrum of Marxist groups have allied, although dominated by Trotskyite, within the SSP and the SSA where the immense differences of opinion are accommodated by allowing for different forums to exist for different views. These Scottish organisations have embraced nationalism, despite the internationalism of some of their component groups, and have accepted the need for flexibility and variation. The new arrangement has brought some significant political success in the Scottish Parliament. Although political conditions are different elsewhere, it is possible that this structure of socialist alliances might exert some impact elsewhere in Britain and establish a small viable Marxist political culture in Britain as a whole.

Notes

Introduction to British Marxism since 1945

1 R. McKibbin, 'Why was there no Marxism in Britain', *English Historical Review*, 99, April 1984.
2 Santiago Carrillo, *Eurocommunism and the State*, London, Lawrence and Wishart, 1977 and F. Claudin, *Eurocommunism and Socialism*, Madrid, Siglo Veintiuno, 1977.
3 Look at Chapter 5 for the details.
4 Henry Pelling, *The Communist Party: An Historical Profile*, London, A. and C. Black, 1958.
5 Allan Flanders, *Trade Unions*, London, seventh edition, 1963, p. 160.
6 Nina Fishman, *The British Communist Party and the Trade Unions, 1933–1945*, Aldershot, Scolar Press, 1995.
7 Harriet Jones, 'Is CPGB History Important?', *Labour History Review*, 67.3, December 2002; Alan Campbell and John McIlroy, 'Is the CPGB History Important? A Reply to Harriet Jones', *Labour History Review*, 68.3, December 2003, pp. 385–90.
8 These include Fishman, *The British Communist Party*; Kevin Morgan, *Against Fascism and War: Ruptures and Continuities in British Communist Politics, 1935–41*, Manchester, Manchester University Press, 1989, and, in another vein, Andrew Thorpe, *The British Communist Party and Moscow, 1920–43*, Manchester, Manchester University Press, 2000 and Andrew Thorpe, 'Comintern "control" of the Communist Party of Great Britain, 1920–43', *English Historical Review*, 113, 1998; Matthew Worley, *Class Against Class: The Communist Party of Britain between the Wars*, London, I. B. Tauris, 2002; Matthew Worley, 'Left Turn: A Reassessment of the Communist Party of Great Britain in the Third Period 1928–1933', *Twentieth Century British History*, 1, December 2000.
9 Henry Pelling, *The British Communist Party: An Historical Profile*, London, A. and C. Black, 1958; Leslie J. Macfarlane, *The British Communist Party: Origins and Development until 1929*, London, MacGibbon and Kee, 1966; Walter Kendall, *The Revolutionary Movement in Britain, 1900–1921*, London, Weidenfeld and Nicolson, 1969.
10 I have been asked to comment on this article which will appear in *American Communist History* in 2005.
11 James Eadon and David Renton, *The Communist Party of Great Britain since 1920*, Basingstoke, Palgrave, 2002.
12 Nina Fishman, 'Essentialists and Realists: Reflections on the Historiography of the CPGB', *Communist History Network Newsletter*, Autumn 2001.
13 Ibid. p. 11.
14 Jones, 'Is CPGB History Important?', p. 348. At the April 2001 conference J. McIlroy and A. Campbell presented a paper on Communist trade union leaders, 1949–91, the case of the 'South Wales miners'.
15 'Editorial: New Directions in International Communist Historiography' by John McIlroy and Alan Campbell, *Labour History Review*, Special Issue – International Communism, 68.1, April 2003, p. 3.

In this edition Richard Croucher wrote on the history of German Communism, McIlroy and Campbell wrote on 'Histories of the British Communist Party: A User's Guide'; John Earl Haynes and Harvey Klehr wrote on 'The Historiography of American Communism: An Unsettled Field'; Reiner Tosstorff wrote on 'Moscow versus Amsterdam: Reflections on the History of the Profintern' and John McIlroy, Alan Campbell, Barry McLoughlin and John Halstead wrote 'Forging the Faithful: The British at the International Lenin School'.

16 Ibid. McIlroy and Campbell, 'Histories of the British Communist Party', p. 35.
17 Jones, 'Is CPGB History Important?', pp. 347–54.
18 Ibid. p. 349.
19 Ibid.
20 Campbell and McIlroy, 'Is CPGB History Important? A Reply to Harriet Jones', *Labour History Review*, 68.3, December 2003, pp. 385–90.
21 Jones, 'Is CPGB History Important?', p. 350.
22 John McIlroy and Alan Campbell, 'The Historiography of British Communism: An Alternative Reading' and Kevin Morgan, 'The Historiography of the British Communist Party: Further Consideration and a Response to John McIlroy and Alan Campbell' in *Mitteilungsblatt*, Vol. 31, 2004, pp. 225–41, 243–55, respectively; *Labour History Review*, 69.3, December 2004, and *American Communist Review* in 2005.
23 Brian Behan's letter to the editors about Harry Pollitt and the CPGB in *Labour History Review*, 59, 1994, p. 11.
24 Monty Johnstone letter to the editors, *Labour History Review*, 59.1, 1994, p. 8.
25 McIlroy and Campbell, 'The Historiography of British Communism: An Alternative Reading', p. 242.
26 Ted Grant, *History of British Trotskyism*, London, Well red publications, 2002.
27 Robert Barltrop, *The Monument: The Story of the Socialist Party of Great Britain*, London, Pluto Press, 1975.

1 The Communist Party of Great Britain during the emergence of the Cold War 1945–56

1 N. Branson, *History of the Communist Party of Great Britain 1941–1951*, London, Lawrence & Wishart, 1997, Appendix 1, p. 252.
2 CP/CENT/PC/02/26 contains monthly and quarterly details of membership, transfers, deaths and other details for the end of 1955 and early 1956. Two areas in Scotland, with about 700 members did not report but in March 1956 the total was 33,146 members. London had 8,926 members, Scotland 5,094, Lancashire 3,179, Yorkshire 2,373, the Midlands 1,816 and Wales 1,476. At the other extreme Teesside had 298 members, Devon and Cornwall had 171, the North East 157 and the Channel Islands a mere 35.
3 CP/CENT/EC/01/05, minutes of the EC of the CPGB, 13 and 14 September 1947.
4 Alan Johnson, '"Beyond the Smallness of Self": Oral History and British Trotskyism', *Oral History*, 24.1, Spring 1996, p. 39.
5 CP/CENT/EC/01/05, EC Resolution on the Party, 13 and 14 September 1947.
6 Raphael Samuels, 'The Lost World of British Communism, Part 1', *New Left Review*, 154, 1985 and 'Staying Power: The Lost World of British Communism, Part 2', *New Left Review*, 156, 1986. Also look at Edward Upward, *The Rotten Elements*, 1969.
7 Branson, *Communist Party of Great Britain, 1941–1951*. One, one of the Party faithful, acknowledges that many members of the Party remained faithful to Stalinism until the truth about Stalin's crimes were exposed in 1956.
8 CP/CENT/COMM/09/04, contains YCL material.
9 Labour Party, Minutes, NEC, 27 July 1943.
10 Labour Party, *Annual Report 1943*, London, Labour Party, 1943, pp. 9–16.
11 Rajani Palme Dutt, CP/IND/DUTT/32/18, Central Committee Statement 'Affiliation – Information on the Campaign', indicates that 15 trade union branches and 178

Labour organisations had voted for Communist affiliation and that it had risen to 3,352 organisations by 2 June 1943; Labour Party, *Annual Report 1943*, pp. 162–5.
12 *Tribune*, 17 April 1944.
13 Neil Redfern, 'Winning the Peace: British Communists, the Soviet Union and the General Election of 1945', *Contemporary British History*, Vol. 16.1, Spring, 2002, pp. 29–50.
14 Ibid. p. 30.
15 Ibid. p. 42.
16 Ibid. pp. 43–7.
17 Ibid. pp. 29–30 and quoting Andrew Thorpe. 'Comintern Control of the Communist Party of Great Britain 1920–1943', *English Historical Review*, 113, June 1998, p. 640.
18 Neil Redfern, 'Winning the Peace: British Communists, the Soviet Union and the General Election of 1945', *Contemporary British History*, Vol. 16.1, Spring, 2002, p. 48.
19 J. Callaghan, 'Common Wealth and the Communist Party and the 1945 General Election', *Contemporary Record*, 9, 1995, p. 66, states that: 'The perspective of "lasting amity" between the Allies actually led the Communist Party leaders, in the spring of 1945, to advocate the continuation of the Coalition Government into the peace. They soon reverted, however, to propaganda for a "Labour and electoral alliance" against the Tories, demanding a "popular victory" with an overwhelming majority of Labour and progressive MPs behind it as the election approached.'
20 R. Edmonds, *The Big Three, Churchill, Roosevelt and Stalin in Peace and War*, New York, W. W. Norton, 1991, p. 494.
21 The EC minutes, CP/CENT/EC/01/03, CP/IND/POL/9/6 and CP/IND/POL/P/13 provide evidence of Pollitt arguing for national unity in the wake of Yalta and Walter Hannington leading the opposition to this policy.
22 CP/CENT/EC/01/03, CPGB, EC Minutes, 21 January and 18 February 1945.
23 CPGB, EC Minutes, 18 March 1945, p. 96.
24 Branson, *Communist Party of Great Britain, 1941–1951*, p. 96.
25 Ibid. p. 96.
26 CPGB, EC Minutes, 18 March 1945. Draft of Political Letter on Party discussion, no date but seems to be early 1945.
27 H. Pollitt, *Answers to Questions*, London, CPGB, 1945, p. 45.
28 CP/CENT/EC/ 01/03. Document A.
29 CP/CENT/EC/01, Typed statement.
30 Labour Party Archives, General Secretary Papers, Box 4, Communist Party, GS/COM/HR.
31 Harold J. Laski, *The Secret Battalion: An Examination of the Communist Attitude to the Labour Party*, London, Labour Party, April 1946, p. 3.
32 Ibid. pp. 9, 14.
33 Ibid. p. 15.
34 Ibid. GS/Com/36ii.
35 E. Burns, 'In Perspective', *Communist Review*, July 1946, pp. 3–4.
36 CP/CENT/EC/01/02, EC Minutes, 16 January 1944.
37 John Callaghan and Mark Phythian, 'State Surveillance and the CPGB Leadership: 1920s–1950s' *Labour History Review*, 69.1, April 2004, p. 29.
38 H. Pollitt, 'The Communist Party and the General Election', *Communist Review*, March 1946, p. 7.
39 R. P. Arnot, 'Notes on the Communist Effort for Unity', *Communist Review*, April 1946, pp. 18–23.
40 CP/CENT/EC/01/04, EC Minutes, 28 April 1946.
41 CP/CENT/EC/01/05, EC meeting 19 January 1947 in a confidential statement made by Harry Pollitt.
42 Harry Pollitt, *Looking Ahead*, London, The Communist Party, August 1947, preface.
43 Ibid.

44 Harry Pollitt, *Looking Ahead*, London, The Communist Party, August 1947, preface, p. 85.
45 CP/CENT/EC/01/05, A Report by Harry Pollitt to the Executive Committee of the Communist Party on 12 July 1947, eleven page document.
46 CP/CENT/EC/01/05, 'Why the Communist Party says Reject the Marshall Plan'.
47 CP/CENT/EC/01/07, EC Minutes, 10 September 1949.
48 CP/CENT/EC/01/04, EC Minutes, 13 March 1948.
49 CP/CENT/EC/01/06, EC Minutes, 19 October 1948; Kerrigan gained 4,223 votes compared to the 13,706 gained by the Labour candidate.
50 'Party Intrigue', 8 December 1949, document 886 ab, KV 2/1041 in the National Archives [formerly the PRO], quoted in John Callaghan and Mark Phythian, 'State Surveillance and the CPGB Leadership: 1920s–1950s', *Labour History Review*, 69.1, April, 2004, p. 30.
51 CP/CENT/EC/01/07, EC Minutes, 10 September 1949; draft of the Political Report to the Twenty-First Congress, 26–28 November 1949, section 6.
52 CP/CENT/EC/07, Draft of the General Election Programme, July 1949.
53 Ibid. with attachment on 'For Peace and National Independence', p. 1.
54 *World News and Views*, 27 August 1949; CP/CENT/PC/02/03, four-page copy of 'The Fight for our General Election Programme'. Also a Political Letter entitled 'After the Elections', dated 8 August 1949.
55 CP/CENT/EC/01/07. Letter 2 August 1950, also a letter making much the same point, dated 26 July 1950.
56 CP/CENT/EC/01/07, list of candidates endorsed by PC, 14 October 1950; CP/CENT/EC/02/03, EC Minutes, 8 September 1951; *World News and Views*, 13 October 1951.
57 CP/CENT/EC/03/25, Draft Report to EC on changes needed to *The British Road to Socialism*, July 1956.
58 CP/CENT/EC/02/08, James Klugmann reviewing the Party Congress and outlining the 1952 local election results.
59 CP/CENT/PC/02/34, Report to the PC, 28 June 1956.
60 CP/CENT/EC/03/05, a paper on the *Daily Worker*. No date given but it is in a file for 1956.
61 CP/IND/RAM/06/02, of the Bert Ramelson Papers, Yorkshire District Report, January 1951.
62 Ibid. Yorkshire District Report, p. 7.
63 Ibid. p. 65.
64 Ibid. pp. 7–12.
65 Pollitt, *Looking Ahead*, chapter v on 'Britain's Crisis and the Way Out'.
66 E. Burns, 'The Meaning of the Dollar Crisis', *Communist Review*, October 1947, pp. 291–7.
67 J. Klugmann, 'America's Plan for Britain', *Communist Review*, October 1948, pp. 291–8.
68 CP/CENT/EC/01/05, A Report by Harry Pollitt to the Executive Committee of the Communist Party on 12 July 1947, eleven page document.
69 Ibid. contains a copy.
70 Branson, *Communist Party of Great Britain 1941–1951*, pp. 129–31.
71 CP/IND/MATH/04/04.
72 Branson, *Communist Party of Great Britain 1941–1951*, pp. 132–3.
73 Ibid. pp. 133–40.
74 E. Barnett, 'Nationalization of Transport', *Communist Review*, January 1948, pp. 3–6; M. Hudson, 'The Nationalized Miners', *Communist Review*, September 1948, pp. 277–8.
75 CP/CENT/COBG/05/09, 'Britain's Problems can be solved', Pollitt Report to the CPGB Nineteenth Congress, 1947, p. 17.
76 *Labour Monthly*, July 1949, p. 201.
77 For the rebuttal of these charges see A. Horner, 'Trade Unions and Communism', *Labour Monthly*, February 1948, pp. 41–52, also *Daily Worker*, 6 January 1948.
78 *Daily Worker*, 16 January 1948.

79 Ibid.
80 Ibid. 2 February 1948.
81 Ibid. 10 June 1948.
82 Joseph Melling, 'Red under the Collar? Clive Jenkins, White Collar Unionism and the Politics of the British Left, 1947–1965', *Twentieth Century British History*, 13.4, 2002, p. 419.
83 CP/CENT/CONGRESS/05/08, H. Pollitt, 'For Britain Free and Independent', Pollitt's report to the Twentieth Congress, p. 47.
84 *World News and Views*, 13 October 1951.
85 Peter Kerrigan, 'Harry Pollitt', *Communist Review*, December 1956, pp. 355–61.
86 *Daily Worker*, 30 June 1948.
87 TUC, *Annual Report, 1948*, pp. 78, 274–5; *Daily Worker*, 28 October 1948; H. Pollitt, 'The Margate Conference', *Labour Monthly*, October 1948, pp. 298–303.
88 *Daily Worker*, 15 March 1949.
89 Jim Phillips, 'Labour and the Cold War: The TGWU and the Politics of Anti-Communism, 1945–1955', *Labour History Review*, 64.1, Spring, 1999, p. 48.
90 *Daily Herald*, 18 September 1950.
91 Ibid.
92 CP/CENT/PC/02/04, Report of the London District Committee to the Political Committee of the CPGB, June 1950, presented PC, 18 June 1950.
93 CP/CENT/IND/1/1, which included a copy of *Port Workers' News* incorporating 'Lighterage News', Vol. II, no. 5, February 1951. There are a variety of other printed documents on this issue in this collection.
94 Phillips, 'Labour and the Cold War', p. 56.
95 Richard Stevens, 'Cold-War Politics: Communism and Anti-Communism in Trade Unions' in A. Campbell, N. Fishman and J. McIlroy (eds), *British Trade Unions and Industrial Politics, Volume One: The Post-War Compromise, 1945–64*, Aldershot, Ashgate, 1999.
96 John McIlroy, 'Reds at Work: Communist Factory Organisations in the Cold War, 1947–56', *Labour History Review*, Vol. 65.2, Summer, 2000, p. 188.
97 McIlroy, 'Reds at Work', pp. 181–204.
98 *World News and Views*, 20 December 1947, quotes in McIlroy, 'Reds at Work', p. 182.
99 McIlroy, 'Reds at Work', p. 187.
100 CP/IND/MATH/04/04, 'The Communist Party and the Factories'. This material appears in the collection of George Matthews who was a member of the EC of the CPGB from 1947 until 1979, Assistant Secretary of the Party from 1950–7 and editor of the *Daily Worker/Morning Star* from 1959–74. He was also in charge of the Press and Publicity Department of the CPGB from 1974–9.
101 Ibid. p. 1.
102 CP/CENT/EC/07, Paper presented to the Extended EC Meeting, 4 March 1949.
103 CP/CENT/PC/02/04, Report of the London District Committee, June 1950, pp. 7–9.
104 CP/CENT/EC/07, Paper presented to the Extended EC Meeting, 4 March 1940, p. 2.
105 Ibid. p. 1.
106 McIlroy, 'Reds at Work', pp. 186–7.
107 CP/CENT/EC/02/03, Mollie Guiart, 'The Fight for Peace and Unity', July 1950.
108 CP/IND/MATH/04/07 deals with Party actions in 1953 and contains documents dated 15 April 1953.
109 CP/IND/MATH/O4/97, 'Problems of Trade Union Organisation', 21 December 1953.
110 Ibid. p. 2.
111 CP/CENT/WOM/4/2 carries a three page report of the First National Conference meeting in 1951.
112 In addition to the above reference also look at CP/CENT/WOM/04 for copies of some of the reports of the Women's Advisory Annual and Biennial Conference agendas and reports, 1951–84, including a copy of the 1951 Conference.
113 CP/CENT/PC/02/04, Report of the London District, 1951.

178 Notes

114 CP/ORG/MISC/08/07, dealing with the National Assembly of Women, contains Bulletin no. 12, 10 April 1953, of the National Assembly of Women, various other items and a copy of the *Our Women: Go Forward to the World They Want* magazine or journal, the undated copy of which seems to have been produced in the spring or summer of 1954.
115 Ibid.
116 Ibid. contains copies of *Our Women: Go Forward to the World They Want* magazines. They are not dated but the contents suggests that they were published 1953.
117 CP/CENT/EC Minutes, 21 July 1946.
118 Ibid. Report of the Organization Commission to the Executive Committee, 10 September 1946.
119 EC Minutes 14 September 1947.
120 *World News and Views*, 6 March 1948.
121 EC Minutes, 13 March 1948.
122 CP/CENT/EC/01/07, Political Report to 1949 Conference, section 9.
123 CP/CENT/PC/01/04, Minutes, 18 June 1950, report attached.
124 CP/CENT/COMM/09/04, contains details of the YCL, its campaigning, the Filey Conference and the issue that concerned the membership.
125 J. Duclos article in *Labour Monthly*, August 1945; *World News and Views*, 18 August 1945.
126 H. Pollitt, report to EC, February 1945.
127 *Daily Worker*, 26 November 1945.
128 K. Morgan, *Harry Pollitt*, Manchester, Manchester University Press, 1993, pp. 148–9.
129 K. Cornforth, 'The British Road to Socialism', *Communist Review*, April 1947, pp. 113–18; J. Symons and E. B., 'Britain's Road', *Communist Review*, July 1947, pp. 200–7.
130 Pollitt, *Looking Ahead*, pp. 87–8.
131 H. Pollitt, *Answers to Questions*, pp. 38–42; CP/CENT/COMM/01/01, *The British Road to Socialism*, London, CPGB, January 1951.
132 E. Burns, 'People's Democracy: Britain's Path to Socialism', *Communist Review*, March 1951, pp. 67–71; J. Klugmann, 'Party Education and the British Road to Socialism', *Communist Review*, June 1951, pp. 178–81; M. Morris, 'The Social Services and the British Road to Socialism', *Communist Review*, July 1951, pp. 201–7.
133 CP/CENT/COMM/09/04. This contains a letter setting up the Commission of ten, which included Emile Burns, John Mahon, J. R. Campbell and Tony Cass.
134 CP/CENT/COMM/09/04, Report on the Commission on the Middle Classes.
135 *The Origins of the International Socialists*, London, Pluto Press, 1971 and 1974 contains the open and published letter of Natalia Trotsky announcing her break with the Fourth International whose reformist tendencies, and even entrism, were endangering Trotskyite ideas. Whilst admiring Tito she could not abide the Fourth International's support for *Titoist* bureaucracy in Yugoslavia and was equally at odds with it's the defence of the Stalinist state against the West.
136 John Callaghan, *British Trotskyism: Theory and Practice*, Oxford, Blackwell, 1984, particularly chapter 2.
137 E. Grant, *Against the Theory of State Capitalism*, 1949, amended and reprinted in E. Grant, *The Marxist Theory of the State*, London, Militant Pamphlet, 1980.
138 *The Origins of the International Socialists*, introduction by Duncan Hallas, p. 12. Hallas was born on 23 December 1925 and died 19 September 2002 and his obituary appeared in *The Guardian*, 30 September 2002.
139 *The Guardian*, 30 September includes an obituary on Duncan Hallas who was a member of the Socialist Review Group which ultimately reformed as the International Socialists and finally the Socialist Workers' Party.
140 CP/CENT/EC/03/25 contains a two and a half page summary of Trotskyism in Britain, dated 13 July 1956. It merges and skewers some information but is essentially correct although for greater and more accurate detail consult *The Origins of the International Socialists*, London, Pluto Press, 1971, 1974, particularly p. 95. It also contains articles by

Tony Cliff, Duncan Hallas and Natalia Sedova Trotsky, on her break with the Fourth International.
141 CP/CENT/PC/02/04, Political Committee statement and discussion on Political Vigilance, 25 May 1950.
142 CP/CENT/EC/03/25, file on Trotskyism.
143 G. Healy, *Revolution and Counter-Revolution in Hungary: Stalinism Unmasked*, London, Socialist Labour League, 1957, p. 59.
144 CP/CENT/PC/02/28, copy of article entitled 'The 20th Congress of the CPSU Opens the Final Phase of the Crisis of Stalinism', an article of eight typed pages.
145 Ibid. pp. 6–7.
146 CP/IND/DUTT/17/09, the Dutt Papers includes this file on Trotskyism which is mainly a file of material from 1958 onwards.
147 CP/CENT/PC/02/03, Press Statement to Morning Papers, 17 December 1949.
148 CP/CENT/EC/07, Revised Draft of General Election Programme, July 1949.
149 CP/CENT/PC/02/03, Press Statement by the Political Committee of the CPGB, 17 December 1949.
150 CP/CENT/EC/07, Proposal on Peace Movement agreed by the political Committee, 10 January 1949.
151 James Klugmann, 'Lessons of the Prague Trial', *Communist Review*, March 1953, pp. 79–86.
152 CP/CENT/INT/38/06, *India Newsletter*, no. 1, 26 June 1946. This file also contains the next twenty-eight copies up to 18 July 1947 when a new series began.
153 Ibid. *India Newsletter*, no. 5, 27 April 1946.
154 CP/CENT/INT/39/06, from a paper by V. Balabushevich, 'A New Stage in the National Liberation Struggle of the People of India', produced in 1949, p. 7.
155 CP/CENT/EC/01/05, contains a copy of the EC Minutes for 14 June 1947; CP/CENT/INT/38/06 also contains the twenty-nine issues of *India Newsletter* which appeared between June 1947 and July 1947 before the new series began. The CPGB statement is in *India Newsletter*, 17 June 1947.
156 *India Newsletter*, no. 29, 4 July 1947.
157 Ibid., new series, no. 10, 15 January 1948.
158 CP/CENT/EC/01/06, Programme of the Twentieth Party Congress, EC 10 April 1948.
159 CP/CENT/INT/39/06, contains a typed document by V. Balabushevich entitled 'A New Stage in the National Liberation Struggle of the Peoples of India' and this contains the information on the peasant revolts on p. 13.
160 CP/CENT/PC/02/26, W. Gallacher, 'The Problem of Leadership', to the Political Committee, 2 February 1956.
161 CP/CENT/EC/03/25, 17-page draft following discussion of EC Resolution, 13 July 1956, dealing with the 'Cult of the Individual'; and the need for changes in Party policy.
162 CP/CENT/EC/07, Proposals on the Peace Movement, 10 January 1949.
163 CP/IND/DUTT/17/09, a file from the papers of R. P. Dutt filed as 'Trotskyism' contains a clipping from various newspapers and journals.
164 Eric Hobsbawm in *Marxism Today*, November 1986, p. 16. Also CP/CENT/PC/02/28 deals with the June 1956 discussions by the Political Committee on Krushchev. Apart from containing a copy of E. P. Thompson's article 'Winter Wheat in Omsk', which is referred to later, it also includes an extract from the *Daily Worker*, 22 June 1956 that the PC of the CPGB had stated that 'in the absence of an official denial an official text, the U.S. version of the Krushchev report on Stalin be taken as more or less authentic'.
165 *Daily Express*, 14 May 1956.
166 Morgan, *Pollitt*, pp. 171–2.
167 *Daily Express*, 14 May 1956. For an in-depth description of the Twentieth CSPU Congress and its effect on the CPGB, see J. Saville, 'The Exit Congress and the British Communist Party', *Socialist Register*, 1976, pp. 1–23.
168 CP/CENT/EC/03/24, Pollitt's resignation letter.

Notes

169 CP/CENT/EC/03/24, draft of EC Resolution for Executive Committee, 12 and 13 May 1956.
170 Ibid.
171 Ibid. p. 5.
172 John Callaghan, 'The Road to 1945', *Socialist History*, November 1995, pp. 3–21.
173 CP/CENT/EC/03/25, Minutes of the EC meeting 14–15 July 1956.
174 CP/CENT/EC/03/25 contains extracts from *World News*, 21 July 1956 and various reports and drafts connected with the EC of the CPGB discussion of the 'Cult of the Individual'; on 13 July 1956.
175 K. Laybourn and D. Murphy, *Under the Red Flag: A History of Communism in Britain*, Stroud, Sutton, 1999, pp. 144–5. Also look at CP/CENT/02/28 which contains a copy of E. P. Thompson's article to *World News and Views* and a copy of the article 'Winter Wheat in Omsk'.
176 CP/CENT/02/28, in a letter from E. P. Thompson to James Klugmann, 15 March 1956.
177 Ibid. letter from Thompson to Klugmann, 22 March 1956.
178 Ibid. letter from Thompson to Klugmann, 2 May 1956.
179 Ibid. letter from Klugmann to Thompson, 20 March 1956.
180 Ibid. letter from E. P. Thompson to Bert Ramelson, 28 May 1956.
181 Ibid. letters from E. P. Thompson to editor of *World News and Views*, 31 May and 8 June 1956.
182 CP/CENT/PC/02/23, PC files, June 1956.
183 CP/CENT/ORG/18/03, copies of the first, July, edition and the third, November, edition of *The Reasoner*.
184 CP/CENT/EC/03/26, EC Minutes 8–9 September 1956.
185 Resolutions of the Communist Party EC, 'Lessons of the 20th Congress of the CPSU', *Marxist Quarterly*, July 1956.
186 CP/CENT/ORG/18/04, letter from E. P. Thompson to Howard [Hill], 9 November 1956.
187 CP/CENT/PC/02/30, Report on Working Class Unity presented to the PC of 30 August 1956.
188 *Yorkshire Post*, 15 November 1956.
189 CP/CENT/ORG/18/04 letter from E. P. Thompson to Howard Hill, 9 November 1956.
190 CP/CENT/EC/04/01, EC Minutes, 10–11 November 1956.
191 CP/CENT/ORG/18/05 contains upwards of 100 letters from districts and branches.
192 Ibid. letter from Bert Ramelson, no date.
193 CP/CENT/04/02, Resolutions of branches to EC, 15 December 1956.
194 CP/CENT/ORG/18/05, letter from R. Cocker, Halifax branch to EC.
195 *Yorkshire Post*, 19 November 1956.
196 CP/CENT/PC/02/01, 'Some Thought About Intellectuals' presented to the Political Committee meeting, 17 January 1957.
197 Sandor Kopacsi, *In the Name of the Working Class*, London, Fontana, 1989.
198 CP/IND/GOLL/02/06, Gollan Papers.
199 Ibid. notes on EC meeting, 3 November 1956; J. Saville, 'The XXth Congress and the British Communist Party', *Socialist Register*, 1976, pp. 1–23.
200 CP/CENT/EC/04/01, from George Matthews notes of the Extended EC, 3 November 1956.
201 M. MacEwan, 'The Day the Party had to Stop', *Socialist Register*, 1976, pp. 24–42.
202 CP/IND/GOLL/02/06, Gollan Papers.
203 Brian Behan, letter to editors about Harry Pollitt and the CPB in *Labour History Review* 59.1, 1994, p. 11. A fuller version of this is quoted in the Introduction.
204 *Marxism Today*, November 1986, p. 21.
205 CP/CENT/EC/04/01, Draft Resolution 'Stop the War in Egypt' and 'Draft Resolution on Hungary'.
206 CP/CENT/PC/02/03, George Matthews hand written notes, PC meeting, 15 November 1956.
207 Ibid.
208 CP/IND/GOLL/02/06, Gollan Papers.

209 *Yorkshire Post*, 14 November 1956.
210 CP/CENT/EC/04/02, EC Minutes, 10–11 November 1956.
211 Ibid. letter from P. J. Wexler, secretary of the Manchester University of Graduate Branch of the CPGB.
212 *Yorkshire Post*, 15 November 1956.
213 W. Thompson, *The Good Old Cause: British Communism 1929–1991*, London, Pluto Press, 1992, pp. 126–7.
214 CP/CENT/COMM/09/08, *The Report of the Commission on Inner Party Democracy*, 25th (Special), Congress of the Communist Party, April 19–22, 1957, Hammersmith Town Hall. This 58-page report, which was still subject to amendments before 22 March 1957, lists the membership as Emile Burns, Kevin Halpin, Christopher Hill, Nora Jeffrey, James Klugmann, William Lauchlan, Malcolm MacEwan, John Mahon, Betty Reid, Joan Bellamy (a member of eleven years from Yorkshire who was appointed by the Party Districts), Harry Bourne, Peter Cadogan, Joe Cheek, Alex Clark and Charles Miles.
215 CP/CENT/COMM/09/08, *The Report of the Commission on Inner Party Democracy* (as above), Minority Report, pp. 45–59, particularly pp. 47, 54 and 59.
216 CP/CENT/EC/04/03, Report to the Executive Committee on Inner Party Democracy, p. 153.

2 The emergence of the Broad Left 1957–70

1 The KGB released this information in November 1991, indicating that the sums fell in the 1970s and disappeared altogether in 1979. Reuban Falber published an unrepentant article in *Change*, 15 November 1991, indicating that this information had been kept from Nina Temple, the new General Secretary. The Political Committee then condemned the action.
2 CP/IND/RAM/06/01, Yorkshire District papers 1955 to 1968 submitted under the name of Bert Ramelson; Yorkshire District CP Report, 1955.
3 Ibid. 1958 Report.
4 Ibid. Report to the 12th York(shire) District Congress.
5 Ibid. Report to the 12th Congress of the York(shire) District (1968?), p. 12.
6 Ibid. p. 19.
7 W. Lauchlan, 'The Communist Party and the Daily Worker', *Marxism Today*, June 1959.
8 CP/IND/MATH/04/09 contains *newspaper* clippings on the details of the case probably taken from *The Times*.
9 CP/IND/MATH/03/09 contains the copy of a substantial statement made by Frank Leslie Haxell, presumably to the Court.
10 *The Spectator*, 4 August 1961 in an article entitled 'Light and Liberty: The Story of the ETU Case', pp. 164–6, particularly p. 164.
11 Ibid. p. 165.
12 Ibid.
13 CP/IND/MATH/04/09, newspaper cuttings on the ETU for 1961 including a cutting from *The Times*, 17 April 1961 reporting on the Queen's Bench Division case of Byrne and another v Foulkes and Others.
14 CP/IND/MATH/03/09 contains a detailed CPGB examination of the findings of the case.
15 Thompson, *The Good Old Cause*, pp. 126–7.
16 CP/IND/MATH/04/02, copy of the circular from Byrne to the ETU branches circulated on 13 July 1962 following a meeting of the EWTU Executive Council, 12 July 1964.
17 CP/IND/MATH/04/02, page 6 of a six-page untitled CPGB statement.
18 CP/IND/MATH/9/02 contains editorials from a variety of newspapers on 13 and 14 July 1964, including ones from the *Daily Express*.
19 Ibid. a one-sheet list of CPGB officials. It includes Gus Cole (Liverpool), Eric Elsom (Sheffield), Albert Gray and Sid Maitland (Middlesex), Arthur Stride (London), George Tilbury (Surrey), Turner (Lancashire) Frank Turner (Cheshire), Ted Ward

(Hammersmith), Bert Bachelor (Beckenham, Kent), Bobby Black (Scotland), J. Feathers (Belfast), Frank Morgan (Manchester), Bob McLennan (Hayes, Kent) and Fred Gore (Hounslow).

20 Ben Pimlott, *Harold Wilson*, London, HarperCollins, 1992, quoting from the Barbara Castle Dairy, 12 May 1966, p. 126.
21 Ibid. p. 406 suggests that this meeting was held on 17 June 1966, although the Communist press suggests the 17 June.
22 Ibid.
23 CP/IND/GOLL/04/07, the John Gollan papers includes this item on the points made by Harold Wilson in the House of Commons, 20 June 1966. Also, look at *The Times*, 21 October 1966 for a full report.
24 Pimlott, *Harold Wilson*, p. 406.
25 *Morning Star*, 20 May 1966.
26 CP/CENT/PC/09/05 contains the full draft of the PC Statement. It also has a slightly different version of the report from the *Morning Star* asking its members 'to do all in their power to mobilize maximum solidarity with the seamen who are at this moment in the vanguard of the struggle...'.
27 Ibid. 23 May 1966.
28 Ibid.
29 *Morning Star*, 25 June 1966.
30 *Daily Telegraph*, 23 June 1966.
31 *Red Flag*, 1 July 1966.
32 CP/CENT/IND/1/2, National Factory Conference, 1966.
33 Ibid. quoted in a PC meeting 29 February 1968.
34 Ibid. contained in an eight-page document.
35 Ibid. contains an eight-page pamphlet entitled *The Communist Party in the Factories*.
36 Thornton and Thompson, 'Scottish Communists, 1956–57', pp. 78–9, 90–1.
37 CP/IND/RAM/06/02, a miscellaneous collection of papers.
38 CP/CENT/PC/10/08, Political Committee, 1 August 1968, statement on Government Incomes Policy and the Prices and Incomes Act.
39 CP/CENT/PC/10/10, PC, 17 October 1968, Draft Report of the Lancashire and Cheshire District Committee.
40 CP/CENT/EC/12/07, EC, 9–10 March 1968, report from Peter Kerrigan.
41 Ibid. Draft Report on Branch Life to the EC, 21 October 1968.
42 *Sunday Telegraph*, 30 June 1968.
43 Johnson, 'Beyond the Smallness of Self', pp. 39–48 examines the experience of many of these organisations, their conflicts and the problems posed by the alleged 'Stalinism' of Gerry Healy.
44 CP/IND/DUTT/17/09 contains [Some Notes about the *Universities and Left Review* for Comrade Eric Hobsbaum -sic], information for the National Executive Committee, 10 May 1958.
45 Ibid.
46 Brian Behan letter in *Labour History Review*, 59.1, Spring 1994, p. 11.
47 CP/IND/DUTT/17/09, particularly articles in *The Socialist Leader*, 21 November 1958 and 9 February 1960, both written by Walter Kendall.
48 Johnson, 'Beyond the Smallness of Self', p. 45.
49 *Socialist Leader*, 9 September 1961.
50 Johnson, 'Beyond the Smallness of Self', p. 45.
51 CP/IND/DUTT/17/09 contains a cutting on this statement.
52 Ibid. contains a copy of the publicity for the *International Socialist Journal*.
53 Ibid. contains a cutting dated 10 May 1968, although it is not clear from which paper it is taken.
54 *Red Flag*, July–August, 1963 which contains a detailed article which deals with the second to the coming seventh world congress of the Fourth International, meeting in 1948, 1951, 1954, 1957, 1960 and 1964.

55 Ibid. September–October and November–December 1963.
56 Ibid. 16 December 1966.
57 Ibid. October 1966.
58 Ibid. 25 July 1967.
59 *Daily Worker*, 14 August 1962.
60 *Marxism Today*, September and October 1962.
61 Michael McCreery, *Destroy the Old to Build the New!*, Scarborough, Committee to Defeat Revisionism for Communist Unity, November 1963.
62 CP/CENT/EC, Minutes, 11–12 May 1968, Comments on the British Draft Towards Socialism.
63 B. Reid, 'Trotskyism in Britain Today', *Marxism Today*, September 1964, pp. 274–83.
64 *The Newsletter*, 25 April 1964.
65 CP/CENT/EC/12/07, Executive Committee, 11–12 May 1968; 'Rebellion, the Left and the Ultra-Left Report', 12 May 1968; Report by J. Klugmann and Betty Reid listing.
66 *The Listener*, 2 March 1961.
67 *The Newsletter*, 1 June 1968.
68 CP/CENT/PC/10/05, Report on May Day Conference, 27–28 April 1968.
69 The circular from Raymond Williams on A National Convention of the Left, circulated in March 1969 and organised by the Preparatory Commission, 11 Fitzroy Square, London, W1.
70 *The Times*, 13 June 1968.
71 *Morning Star*, 27 July 1968.
72 CP/CENT/PC/10/07, PC, Draft Report on Eastern Europe, 11 July 1968 and 25 July 1968.
73 CP/CENT/PC/10/08, PC, 8 August 1968.
74 CP/CENT/EC/12/111, various letters to EC, CP/CENT/EC/12/12.
75 PC, 29 August 1968.
76 CP/CENT/PC/10/09, PC, 12 September 1968.
77 Gollan Papers, CP/IND/GOLL/02/01, CPSU statement, 13 September material.
78 Gollan Papers, CP/IND/GOLL/03/07, news cuttings of the PC statement. This contains numerous notes, files and the rafts of statements on Czechoslovakian position as it developed throughout the summer months. It contains *Pravda* material and much from *Soviet News*.
79 Ibid. YCL of GB statement.
80 CP/CENT/PC/10/10, Resolution to be presented to the London District Committee, 16–17 November 1968.
81 *Red Flag*, 10 March 1969.
82 CP/CENT/WOM/04/02, 'Resolutions passed at C.P. National Congresses on Women' (1961–1983).

3 The Red Seventies: industrial conflict and the emergence of Eurocommunism 1971–9

1 CP/CENT/COMM/09/07, a 14-page statement from John Baruch of Bradford, p. 6.
2 *The Times*, 25 July 1978.
3 R. Barber, *Trade Unions and the Tories*, London, Bow Group, 1976, p. 2.
4 Francis Beckett, *Enemy Within: The Rise and Fall of the British Communist Party*, London, John Murray, 1995, p. 179.
5 CP/IND/MATH/05/09 (George Matthews Collection), list of 'Trade Unionists to be invited to Functions', dated 8 May 1973.
6 CP/IND/MATH/05/09, The document was signed by Bert, presumably Bert Ramelson.
7 Beckett, *Enemy Within*, p. 178.
8 CP/IND/MATH/05/02, 'Needs of the Hour', 31 October 1973.
9 *World News and Views*, 10 August 1978.
10 A. Taylor, *Trade Unions and the Labour Party*, London, Croom Helm, 1987, p. 5.

184 Notes

11 A. Taylor, *Trade Unions and the Labour Party*, London, Croom Helm, 1987, p. 5.
12 CP/IND/MATH/05/02, 'Needs of the Hour', 31 October 1973.
13 CP/IND/MATH/05/02, report by Mick Costello entitled 'Community Work in Industry'.
14 Ibid. p. 3.
15 Ibid.
16 Ibid.
17 Ibid. p. 5.
18 Ibid. p. 6.
19 CP/IND/MATH/05/02, handwritten letter from George Matthews to Mick Costello, 3 February 1978.
20 Ibid.
21 CP/IND/MATH/05/02, in a note to the Political Committee by Mick Costello.
22 Stevi Jackson and Sue Scott, 'Sexual Skirmishes and Feminist Factions' in *Feminism and Sexuality: A Reader*, Edinburgh, Edinburgh University Press, 1996, fn. 43, p. 29.
23 Christine Collette and Keith Laybourn (eds), *Modern Britain since 1979*, London, I. B. Tauris, 2003, chapter 8 on 'Feminist Debates and the Changing Position of Women in British Society', pp. 208–44.
24 CP/CENT/WOM/02/06 contains a full set of *Link*.
25 CP/CENT/WOM/02/05 contains copies of the bulletin *Women in Action*.
26 CP/CENT/WOM/04/02, Betty Matthews manuscript, p. 10.
27 Ibid. Report to the 1971 Conference of 24 July 1971, dated 24 April 1971.
28 CP/CENT/WOM/04/02, National Half-Yearly Meeting 9–10 June 1973, dealt with tax credits and family allowances and operated alongside the Housewives' Union, Shelter, Child Poverty Action Group, the Married Women's Association and the Labour Party in petitioning for family allowances to cover the first child.
29 CP/CENT/WOM/02/06 contains the spring 1973 issue of *Link*. This issue contains the editorial of which this quote is part.
30 *Link*, no. 3, Autumn 1973.
31 Ibid. no. 4, Winter 1973.
32 Ibid. no. 7, Autumn 1974, 'An Equal Chance to Serve' by Abbott, pp. 3–4.
33 Ibid. no. 10, Summer 1975, 'Speed up the Struggle' by Jean Styles, p. 11.
34 Ibid. no. 12, Winter 1975, 'How it all Started' by Wendy James, p. 3.
35 Ibid. no. 12, Winter 1975, 'The TUC Charter' by Barbara Switzer, p. 12.
36 Ibid. no. 13, Spring 1976, 'Is the Women's Movement Necessary', by Judith Hunt, pp. 3–5.
37 Ibid. no. 20, Spring 1978.
38 CP/CENT/WOM/03/01, *Link*, 24, Spring 1979.
39 CP/CENT/WOM/04/02, in the section indicates as 'Resolutions passed at C. P. National Congresses on Women' (1961–83).
40 Ibid.
41 CP/CENT/WOM/04/01, Minutes of the National Women's Advisory Committee, 10 March 1978.
42 Ibid. National Women's Advisory Committee, minutes, 9 May 1978.
43 Ibid. Minutes, 15 March 1979.
44 Ibid.
45 CP/CENT/WOM/03/01/, *Link*, 25, Summer 1979, pp. 3–4.
46 *Link*, 24, Spring 1979.
47 CP/CENT/WOM/04/02, Report on the 7th Biennial Conference on Work Among Women, p. 10.
48 CP/IND/MATH/05/02, the note of Mick Costello to the Political Committee.
49 CP/IND/MATH/06/16 contains numerous cuttings and letters on the issue, including one letter from Monty Johnstone to George Matthews, dated 6 September 1978, and cuttings from the *Tribune* and also from *Marxism Today*, 6 October 1976.
50 *Morning Star*, 22 July 1978.
51 *World Times*, 10 August 1978, p. 5.

52 Ibid.
53 CP/IND/MATH/06/08 contains numerous cuttings and documents relating to the 'Decisions' programme. Some of this is taken from 'The British Road Map' cutting, for which no reference is given.
54 Ibid.
55 *Socialist Challenge*, no. 58, July 1978.
56 Ibid. p. 5.
57 CP/IND/MATH/06/08, the three-page long 'DECISION – rules for filming'.
58 CP/IND/MATH/06/08, *Decision: British Communism*, Manchester, Granada, 1978, pp. 11–15. Also look at *World Times*, Thursday, 10 August 1978.
59 F. Claudin, *Eurocommunism and Socialism*, London, NLB, 1978, pp. 7–9.
60 CP/CENT/COMM/09/05-09.
61 Ibid. meeting 27–28 January 1979.
62 CP/CENT/COMM/09/06, 46-page document on *Inner Party Democracy*, pp. 2–4.
63 CP/CENT/COMM/09/07 contains much correspondence to the Commission on Inner Party Democracy.
64 Ibid.
65 Ibid.
66 Ibid.
67 Ibid.
68 Ibid. 14-page statement by John Baruch.
69 Ibid. p. 11.
70 CP/CENT/COMM/09/07, letter from Sunderland branch of the CPGB.
71 Ibid. letter from Willie Thompson.
72 Ibid. letter from Betty England.
73 Ferdinand Claudin, *Eurocommunism and Socialism*, first published by Singlo Veintiuno, Madrid, 1977, and then by London, NLB, 1978, p. 7. Claudin suggests that the term was first used in 1970. However, H. T. Willetts, 'The USSR and Eurocommunism' in Richard Kindersley (ed.), *In Search of Communism*, London, Macmillan, 1981, pp. 1–2, suggests that the term was first coined by France Barbeiri in *Giornale Nuova*, 26 June 1975.
74 Claudin, *Eurocommunism and Socialism*, p. 7.
75 Ibid. p. 7.
76 Ibid. p. 8; Santiago Carrillo, *Eurocommunism and the State*, London, Lawrence & Wishart, 1977.
77 Claudin, *Eurocommunism and Socialism*, p. 8.
78 Ibid.
79 Ibid. p. 7. Also look at Carrillo, 'Analysis of the Soviet Union' in *Socialist Europe: Communist Journal of Soviet and East European Studies*, no. 3 (1977).
80 Willie Thompson, *The Communist Movement since 1945*, Oxford, Blackwell, 1945, pp. 166–70.
81 Carillo, *Eurocommunism and the State*, chapter on 'The Historical Roots of Eurocommunism', p. 111.
82 CP/CENT/EC/15/16, referring to the *Morning Star's* publications between February and July 1977.
83 CP/CENT/INT/45/01 contains a copy of Gerard Streiff's article.
84 Ibid. contains a discussion paper on Eurocommunism by Gerry Pocock. Look at page 6.
85 *Morning Star*, 4 July 1977, an interview on page 2 of Gordon McLennan by Peter Avis entitled 'Britain, Socialism and Euro-Communism'. This is also contained in CP/CENT/INT/45/01.
86 Beckett, *Enemy Within*, p. 163.
87 CP/CENT/EC/17/07, EC, 10–11 March 1979.
88 Edmund and Ruth Frow, *The Liquidation of the Communist Party of Great Britain: A Contribution to the Discussion*, Salford, Jubilee House, 1996, pp. 12–13.

89 Internal Policy review, in CP/CENT/EC/17/10, July 1980, p. 8.
90 Ibid.
91 Ibid. p. 11.
92 Letter from Reuben Falber, Assistant General Secretary, to members of the Executive Committee of the Communist Party of Great Britain, CP/CENT/EC/15/14, 18 July 1977, dealing with the formation of the breakaway New Communist Party.
93 Beckett, *Enemy Within*, pp. 196, 227.
94 Ibid. pp. 184–5.
95 Ibid. p. 172.
96 Johnson, 'Beyond Smallness of Self', p. 45.
97 Beckett, *Enemy Within*, p. 185.
98 Ibid. chapter 12.

4 The challenge of Thatcherism, the triumph of Eurocommunism and the collapse of 'Stalinism', 1980–91

1 Beckett, *Enemy Within*, p. 191.
2 Frow and Frow, *Liquidation*, p. 3.
3 T. Lane, 'The Union caught on the Ebb Tide', *Marxism Today*, September 1982, p. 13.
4 Frow and Frow, *Liquidation*, p. 23.
5 CP/CENT/PC/14/15, Draft Report on the *Morning Star*, 1 September 1978, p. 14.
6 CPGB, Statement for the Executive Committee, *The Morning Star*, 1978, p. 14.
7 *The Guardian*, 6 February 1981.
8 Beckett, *Enemy Within*, p. 195.
9 *Morning Star*, 26 August 1982.
10 Quoted in Beckett, *The Enemy Within*, p. 195.
11 CP/CENT/EC/19/02, Letter from Tony Lane to EC, 26 August 1982.
12 Beckett, *Enemy Within*, p. 195.
13 CP/CENT/EC/15/14, Martin Jacques replaced James Klugmann, who had edited *Marxism Today* for twenty years, at the Executive Committee meeting, 12–13 March 1977.
14 CP/CENT/EC/11/01, Statement of EC, 12 September 1982.
15 *Morning Star*, 7 October 1982.
16 Frow and Frow, *Liquidation*, p. 14; Thompson, *The Good Old Cause*, p. 185. Of course, the *Morning Star* did not have to consult the CPGB about its appointments.
17 Beckett, *The Enemy Within*, p. 195.
18 CP/CENT/EC/19/05, EC, 12–13 March 1983.
19 CP/CENT/EC/20/06, copy of letter from Beatrix Campbell.
20 Beckett, *The Enemy Within*, p. 198.
21 CP/CENT/EC/19/05, 'Report to EC', *Marxism Today*, 12–13 March 1983.
22 CP/CENT/EC/19/05.
23 CP/CENT/EC/01/01, 'Factional & other Unprincipled Activity in the 38th Congress'.
24 CP/CENT/EC/20/06, East Midland Report, 1984 and the Carlisle branch letter, 17 January 1984.
25 *The Guardian*, 15 March 1984.
26 TUC, *Annual Report, 1984*, London, TUC, 1984, pp. 399–400, 403, appendix 5.
27 Beckett, *Enemy Within*, p. 206.
28 Jon Blomfield, 'Crossed Lines: Communists in Search of an Identity', *Marxism Today*, April 1984, 27; Dave Cook, 'No Private Drama', *Marxism Today*, February 1985, pp. 25–9.
29 H. Francis, 'Mining: The Popular Front', *Marxism Today*, February 1985, pp. 12–15.
30 Quoted in the *Morning Star*, 11 June 1985.
31 Quoted in Beckett, *Enemy Within*, p. 205.
32 Beckett, *Enemy Within*, p. 206.

33 Ibid. p. 207.
34 Ibid. p. 208.
35 *Link*, no. 29, Summer 1980 issue.
36 Ibid. no. 31, Winter 1980 issue.
37 Ibid. no. 33, Summer 1981 issue. The editorial group at this time consisted of Mary Davis, Jean French, Caroline Rowan, Linda Smith, Jean Styles, Margaret Bowden and Jane Mace.
38 Ibid.
39 Ibid.
40 Ibid. no. 34, Autumn 1981, pp. 12–13.
41 Ibid. no. 35, Winter 1981/2, p. 14.
42 CP/CENT/WOM/04/01, minutes of the National Women's Advisory Committee, 28 July 1984.
43 Ibid. no. 39, winter 1982/3 and no. 40, Spring 1983.
44 Link, no. 40. Spring 1983 and no. 41, Summer 1983.
45 CP/CENT/WOM/05/01, letter dated 29 May 1991 on the National Aggregate Meeting of Black Members.
46 CP/CENT/WOM/05/03, National Women's Advisory Bulletin on the National Demonstration and Gala, 11 August 1984.
47 CP/CENT/WOM/04/01, minutes of the National Women's Advisory Committee, 28 July 1984.
48 CP/CENT/WOM/05/02, Women Against Pit Closures, Report and Statement, 1985.
49 Ibid.
50 CP/CENT/WOM/04/02, Communist Party Women's Conference, 2–3 October 1982.
51 Ibid. Women's Conference 1–2 October 1983, held at St. John's Street, London, various conference papers including Mary McIntosh, 'Why we don't want an "Alternative Family Policy"', 21 September 1983.
52 CP/CENT/WOM/04/02, Jean Turner, 'Women and the Peace Movement' September 1983.
53 CP/CENT/WOM/04/02, poster on the Women's Conference of 10 December 1983; CP/CENT/WOM/04/01, minutes of the National Women's Advisory Committee, 28 July 1984.
54 CP/CENT/WOM/04/02, Tricia Davis three-page paper on Unemployed Workers Centre.
55 CP/CENT/WOM/04/02, papers by Angela Mason, August 1982 on 'Wages and Income', by Susannah Lash on 'Training', by Philippa Clark on 'Training' and by Alex Gordon on 'Apprenticeship and Training'.
56 CP/CENT/WOM/04/02, Resolutions passed at C.P. National Congresses on Women (1961–83).
57 CP/CENT/WOM/04/02, a one-page sheet on 'Common Women's Day'.
58 CP/CENT/WOM/04/02, letter from Soviet Women, 12 May 1984.
59 CP/CENT/WOM/04/02, material connected with Greenham Common.
60 Beckett, *Enemy Within*, p. 201.
61 CP/CENT/EC/21/06, Report of the London District Congress, 24 November 1984, by Gordon McLennan, see also Frow and Frow, *Liquidation*, pp. 21–2.
62 CP/CENT/21/06, Minutes of Special Executive Committee, 30 November 1984.
63 Frow and Frow, *Liquidation*, pp. 20–1.
64 Ibid. p. 22.
65 *Morning Star*, 12 May 1985.
66 Ibid. 20 May 1985.
67 Blomfield, 'Crossed Lines', p. 27; Cook, 'No Private Drama', pp. 25–9.
68 CP/CENT/PC/16/08, Report of the Political Committee, 15 December 1984.
69 J. Grahl and B. Rowthorne, 'Dodging the Taxing Questions', *Marxism Today*, November 1986, 24–5.
70 B. Rowthorne, in *The Guardian*, 14 January 1987.

71 CP/CENT/PC/17/04, Letter from Gordon McLennan to the Political Committee, 24 March 1988.
72 CP/CENT/PC/16/18, PC, 2 February 1987.
73 CP/CENT/EC/22/07, Report to EC, 11–12 January 1986.
74 Ibid. notes submitted to the PC, 14 February 1987.
75 CP/CENT/EC/23/03, EC Meeting, 14–15 November 1987.
76 CP/CENT/EC/13/05, Minutes from a Special Emergency Executive Committee Meeting, 28 June 1987, 'Some points of discussion from Nina Temple'.
77 *Morning Star*, 18 July 1987.
78 *7 Days*, 12 December 1987, article by Ian McKay, National Organiser of the CPGB, who was later a candidate for the post of General Secretary of the CPGB.
79 *Morning Star*, 11 November 1987.
80 CP/CENT/PC/16/18, letter from Graham Taylor, Secretary of Brent North branch, 8 February 1987.
81 Beckett, *Enemy Within*, p. 202.
82 Ibid. p. 223.
83 *Changes*, 2–15 February 1991, article by Mike Power, editor of *Changes* and a fervent supporter of Nina Fishman and the CPGB. *7 Days* (1985–90) was replaced by *Changes* (1991–2) and then by *New Times* (1992–2000). *Changes* described itself as a fortnightly committed 'towards renewing and developing the politics of progress: red, green, democratic, feminist, anti-racist and internationalist'. Copies can be found in the records of the Democratic Left.
84 *Changes*, 2–15 February 1991.
85 CP/CENT/EC/24/01 includes the views of Nina Temple in this respect.
86 *Labour Party Conference Report, 1985*, London, Labour Party, 1985, p. 128.
87 *Observer*, 6 October 1986.
88 P. Taaffe, *The Rise of Militant*, London, Militant Publications, November 1995, pp. 248–50, 257–69, 298–306.
89 *Daily Telegraph*, 10 January 1990.
90 Beckett, *Enemy Within*, p. 216.
91 CP/CENT/EC/24/01, Tony McNally, 'In Support of a Special Congress to Transform the Communist Party into a Broad Eco-Socialist Movement'.
92 Martin Jacques found that his power base shrunk as the Party withdrew its subsidy of £50,000 per year to *Marxism Today* which then sought finance outside the Party.
93 CP/CENT/EC/24/01, letter from David Green to EC, 6 January 1990.
94 Thompson, *The Good Old Cause*, p. 200.
95 *Changes*, 15–21 December 1990.
96 Ibid.
97 Ibid.
98 Ibid. The following were elected, with their district and the number of votes. * indicates retiring from previous EC. Rosemary Belcher, London, 89; Tessa Bid good, Midlands, 107; George Bolton, Scotland, 125*; Peter Carter, London, 69; Trevor Carter, London, 126*; Doug Chalmers, Scotland, 133*; Malcolm Cowle, North Western, 88*; John Cox, Wales, 117; Marian Darke, Surrey, 135*; Sarah Gasquoine, London, 74*; Asquith Gibbes, London, 127*; Joanna de Groot, Yorkshire, 92*; Stuart Hill, Northern, 84*; Steve Howell, Yorkshire, 67*; Kate Hudson, London, 82; Bill Innes, Yorkshire, 125*; Lou Lewis, London, 101*; Joe Marshall, London, 68; Steve Mathewson, Scotland, 88*; Ian McKay, London, 141*; Tom McNally, Midlands, 105*; Steve Munby, Merseyside/Cheshire, 103*; Frieda Park, Scotland, 71*; David Parker, Yorkshire, 78*; Ann Pocock, Eastern, 132*; Gerry Pocock, Eastern, 132*; Lorna Reith, London, 98*; Gordon Samson, Scotland, 86*; Les Skeates, Wales, 86; Mhairi Stewart, Scotland, 12*; Helen Taylor, Merseyside/Cheshire, 70; Nina Temple, London, 137*; Lynn White, Merseyside/Cheshire, 86*; Terry Wilde, Yorkshire, 89* and Margaret Woddis, Eastern, 123.
99 CP/CENT/CONG/25/06, Draft Constitution.

100 *Changes*, 11–24 May 1991, issue 15.
101 Ibid. 8–21 June 1991.
102 Ibid. 12–25 October 1991, Garry Haywood 'Party Name Questionnaire – First Returns'.
103 CP/CENT/PC/17/18, PC, 23 September 1991.
104 CP/CENT/EC/24/15, letter from Dave Priscott to EC, 26 October 1991.
105 Beckett, *Enemy Within*, pp. 217–19.
106 CP/CONT/CONG/25/06, *New Times: The Journal of the Democratic Left*, no. 1, 30 November 1991, report of Forty-third Congress debate.
107 Ibid.
108 *Changes*, 8–21 June 1991.

5 Postscript: the re-emergence and recontruction of Marxism in Britain or 'All dressed up with nowhere to go?'

1 Thompson, *The Communist Movement since 1945*, p. 213.
2 Beckett, *Enemy Within*, p. 227.
3 Ibid.
4 Democratic Left archive, box 5, although this may be changed when the collection is fully archived. This contains copies of some of *New Times* and certainly issues 1, 2 and 3, dated 28 December 1991, 11 January 1992 and 25 January 1992, respectively, as well as some other issues.
5 *New Times: The Journal of the Democratic Left*, no. 7, 21 March 1992.
6 Ibid. no. 8, 4 April 1991.
7 Ibid.
8 Ibid. but no date given although it presumably must be from an issue in 1994.
9 Democratic Left archive, *Report of Democratic Left's 4th Federal Conference at the Birmingham and Midlands Institute on the 5th & 6th June 1999*, p. 12.
10 *New Times*, no. 4, 8 February 1992, article by John Volleamere, of Liverpool, entitled 'New Times Trade Unions in the 1990s'.
11 Ibid. no. 18, 5 September 1992.
12 Ibid. no. 16, 25 July is when it was announced.
13 Kevin Morgan, *Newsheet* located in the Labour History Archive and Study Centre, John Rylands University Library, University of Manchester.
14 Democratic Left archive was not properly listed and the vast majority of items were unavailable at the time of the examination and subject to a time limit before they become available. *Futures*, issue 1 is in the collection and contains an article by Douglas Chalmers. *Futures* is undated but was probably published in 1997 or early 1998.
15 Democratic Left archive, *Futures*, issue 3, which appears to have been published in 1998.
16 Ibid.
17 Ibid.
18 Ibid. There are copies of *Futures*, issue 2, and *Futures*, issue 4, in the accessible part of this archive. The problem with them, and much of the DL material, is that the dates of publication are missing and that bit is not always easy to establish the timing and pattern of events. The Waite and Mendolsohn material cane be found in issue 3.
19 Ibid.
20 This is taken from a one-sheet piece on the 'Democratic Left's Second Wave Transformation', launched at a meeting in London on 11 December 1999, located in the Democratic Left archive in the Labour History Archive and Study Centre, John Rylands University Library, University of Manchester. From the scattered records it would appear that the DL held its First Conference in 1992, a Federal Conference in 1993, when it ceased to be a party and became a facilitating organisation. A third conference (Federal) was held in 1996 and the fourth held in 1999. A special 'Transformation' conference was held on 11 December 1999.
21 Democratic Left archive, *Futures*, issue 3.

22 Democratic Left archive, *Futures*, issue 4 (final), published in November/December 1999.
23 Beckett, *Enemy Within*, p. 222.
24 Democratic Left archive, *Report of Democratic Left's 4th Federal Conference at the Birmingham and Midlands Institute on the 5th & 6th June 1999*, p. 4. The delegates included Stuart Hall and Linda Hoffman from Northern England and Yorkshire, along with Hetty Bechler, Nina Fishman, Nina Temple and Mike Power from London.
25 Democratic Left archive, 'Democratic Left's Second Wave Transformation'.
26 Ibid.
27 Ibid. *Futures*, issue 4 (final), published in 1999.
28 Ibid. *Futures*, issue 4 (final), published November/December 1999.
29 http://www.new-politics.net/, accessed 2 September 2004.
30 Ibid.
31 http://politics.guardian.co.uk/thinktank/page/0,10538,1092273,oo.html, accessed 2 September 2004.
32 http://www.cleanpolitix.com/faq/index.asp.page+NewPol, accessed 2 September 2004.
33 http://www.newworker.org/homepage.htm, accessed 2 September 2004.
34 http://www.newworker.org/newwork.htm, accessed 2 September 2004.
35 http://www.londoncommunists.org/28008/index.html, accessed 2 September 2004.
36 http://www.londoncommunists.org/51226.html, accessed 2 September 2004.
37 Ibid.
38 *The New Worker*, 27 August 2004, in http://www.newworker.org.newwork.htm
39 Beckett, *Enemy Within*, p. 222.
40 Ibid. p. 224.
41 Ibid. p. 225.
42 Ibid.
43 Ibid. p. 226.
44 http://www.communist-party.org.uk/, accessed on 2 September 2004.
45 Ibid.
46 Ibid.
47 http://www.greenleft.org.au/back/1996/242/241p22.htm
48 http://www.greenleft.org.au/back/1997/264/264p21.htm
49 http://www.greenleft.org.au/back/1996/242/242p22.htm, which was consulted on 9 September 2004 and contains an article, written by Stuart Russell, entitled 'Socialist Alliance formed in Scotland'.
50 http://www.scottishsocialistparty.org, accessed 2 September 2004.
51 http://www.wsws.org/polemics/1998/oct1998/ssp-024.shtml, accessed 2 September 2004. This article, published on the World Socialist Web Site was written by Chris Marsden and dated 24 October 1998.
52 Ibid. Marsden article, p. 1.
53 Ibid. p. 2, quoting from *Scottish Socialist Voice*, June 1997.
54 http://srsm.port5.com/swr/, which was accessed on 9 September 2004 and http://www.fact-index.com/s/sc/scottish-republican-socialist-party.html, also accessed 9 September 2004.
55 http://www.fact-index.com/s/sc/scottishsocialistparty.html, accessed 2 September 2004.
56 http://www.scottishsocialistparty.org, accessed 2 September 2004.
57 Ibid.
58 http://www.scottishsocialistparty.info, accessed 2 September 2004.
59 http://www.scottishsocialistparty.org/pages,branches.html, accessed 2 September 2004. Central Scotland; Aidrie, Coat bridge & Shotts branch, Bellshill and Motherwell, Cumbernauld & Kilsyth, East Kilbride, Falkirk, Hamilton and Blantyre, Kilmarnock: Lothians: Edinburgh Central, Edinburgh East & Musselburgh; Edinburgh North & Leith, Edinburgh South, Edinburgh Pentlands, Edinburgh West, Midlothian, West Lothian; Mid Scotland & Fife: Cupa and Howe of Fife, Dunfermline, Glenroathes, Kirkcaldy,

Perth, St. Andrews, Stirling, Tay Coast; Glasgow: Anniesland & Knightswood; Baillieston; Campsie; Cathcart; Drumchapel & Blairdardie; Govan, Kelvin, Maryhill, Pollok, Pollokshshaws Rd, Rutherglen, Shettleston, Springburn; South of Scotland: Annandale, Borders, Clydesdale, Cumnock, Dumfries, East Lothian, Galloway, Irvine, South Ayrshire; Highlands and Islands: Caithness, Dingwall & District; Easter Ross/Sutherland, Elgin, Forres, Inverness, Lochaber; Oban and Lorn, Orkney, Shetland, Ullapool, Western Isles; North East Scotland: Aberdeen North & Central, Oban and Lorn, Orkney, Shetland, Ullapool, Western Isles; North East Scotland: Aberdeen North & Central, Aberdeen South, Angus, Buchan, Deeside, Dundee East, Dundee Central, Dundee West, Inverurue, Keith/Huntley, Kincardine; West of Scotland; Arran, Bute, Clydebank, Dumbarton, Dunoon, Helensburgh, Inverclyde, Port Glasgow, Renfrewshire and Saltcoats & Ardrossan.
60 http:// www. Socialist-alliance.org/conf/2003-5/2003-ssp.shtml, accessed 9 September 2004.
61 http://www.scottishsocialistparty.org, accessed 2 September 2004.
62 Ibid.
63 Marsden, 'Scottish Socialist Party fosters nationalist divisions', published in 1998 and accessed 2 September 2004, http:www.wsws.org/polemics/1998/oct1998/ssp-o24.shtml .
64 http://www.welshsocialistalliance.org.uk; Alan Thomson (Swansea East) 133 votes, Leigh Richards (Swansea West) 272; Huw Pudner (Neath) 410; Raja Gul Raiz (Cardiff Central) 541; Richard Morse (Newport West) 198.
65 There are a variety of websites for these including http://www. exetersocialistalliance.org.uk/ and http://www.lancsocialistalliance.org.uk/. Some of the websites remain although many have joined Respect; The Unity Coalition and now record their events on the Respect national website.
66 http://lancsocialistalliance.org.uk/, accessed 9 September 2004.
67 http://www.geocities.com/colchester-socialist alliance/main.html, accessed 9 September 2004.
68 http://www.hackneysa.org.uk/front.html, accessed 9 September 2004.
69 http://www.rcpblml.org.uk, accessed 2 September 2004.
70 http://www.recpml.org.uk.draftpro.htm, accessed 2 September 2004.
71 http://www.wwne.demon.co.uk/ww2001/d01-83.htm, accessed 2 September 2004.
72 http://www.worldsocialism.org.spgb.about.html
73 http://www.socialist-labour party org.uk/arty1mainframe.htm
74 http://www.swp.org.uk, accessed 9 September 2004 and, for a copy of *Socialist Worker* look at http://www.socialistworkers.co.uk also, accessed 9 September 2004.

Conclusion

1 Ross McKibbin, 'Why was there no Marxism in Britain?', *English Historical Review*, Vol. 99 (April 1984).

Bibliography

Primary sources

Manuscripts

In the Labour History Archive and Study Centre: John Rylands University Library, University of Manchester:
Bert Ramelson Papers
Communist Party of Great Britain archives
Democratic Left archive (most access is denied)
R. P. Dutt Papers
George Mathews Papers
J. Gollan Papers
Harry Pollitt Papers
Labour Party archives

Books, pamphlets, reports and printed contemporary material

Barber, R., *Trade Unions and the Tories*, London, Bow Group, 1976.
The British Road to Socialism, London, CPGB, 1951.
Carrillo, S., *Eurocommunism and the State*, London, Lawrence and Wishart, 1977.
Carrillo, S., 'Analysis of the Soviet Union', *Socialist Europe: Communist Journal of Soviet and East European Studies*, no. 3, 1977.
Claudin, F., *Eurocommunism and Socialism*, Madrid, Siglo Veintiuno, 1977.
Hudson, M., 'The Nationalized Miners', *Communist Review*, September 1948, pp. 277–8.
Klugmann, J., 'America's Plan for Britain', *Communist Review*, October 1948, pp. 291–8.
Labour Party, *Annual Reports* (a full collection can be found in the Labour History Archive and Study Centre: John Rylands, University Library, University of Manchester), 1943.
Laski, Harold J., *The Secret Battalion: An Examination of the Communist Attitude to the Labour Party*, London, Labour Party, 1946.
McCreery, M., *Destroy the Old to Build the New!*, Scarborough, Committee to Defeat Revisionism for Communist Unity, November 1963.
Pollitt, H., *Answers to Questions*, London, CPGB, 1945.
Pollitt, H., *Looking Ahead*, London, The Communist Party, August 1947.
The Report of the Commission on Inner Party Democracy, London, CPGB, 1957.
TUC, *Annual Reports*, 1984.

Articles

Arnot, R. P., 'Notes on the Communist Effort for Unity', *Communist Review*, April 1946, pp. 18–23.
Barnett, E., 'Nationalization of Transport', *Communist Review*, January 1948, pp. 3–6.
Blomfield, J., 'Crossed Lines: Communists in Search of an Identity', *Marxism Today*, April 1984, p. 27.
Burns, E., 'In Perspective', *Communist Review*, July 1946, pp. 3–4.
Burns, E., 'The Meaning of the Dollar Crisis', *Communist Review*, October 1947, pp. 291–7.
Burns, E., 'People's Democracy: Britain's Path to Socialism', *Communist Review*, March 1951, pp. 67–71.
Cook, D., 'No Private Drama', *Marxism Today*, February 1985, pp. 25–9.
Cornforth, K., 'The British Road to Socialism', *Communist Review*, April 1947, pp. 113–18.
Francis, H., 'Mining: The Popular Front', *Marxism Today*, February 1985, pp. 12–15.
Grahl, J. and Rownhorne, B., 'Dodging the Taxing Questions', *Marxism Today*, November 1986, pp. 24–5.
Healy, G., *Revolution and Counter-Revolution in Hungary: Stalinism Unmasked*, London, Socialist Labour League, 1957.
Horner, A., 'Trade Unions and Communism', *Labour Monthly*, February 1948, pp. 41–52.
Kerrigan, P., 'Harry Pollitt', *Communist Review*, December 1956, pp. 355–61.
Klugmann, J., 'America's Plan for Britain', *Communist Review*, October 1946, pp. 291–8.
Klugmann, J., 'Party Education and the British Road to Socialism', *Communist Review*, June 1951, pp. 178–81.
Lane, T., 'The Union Caught on the Ebb Tide', *Marxism Today*, September 1982, p. 13.
Lauchlan, W., 'The Communist Party and the Daily Worker', *Marxism Today*, June 1959.
MacEwan, M., 'The Day the Party had to Stop', *Socialist Register*, 1976, pp. 24–42.
Morris, M., 'The Social Services and the British Road to Socialism', *Communist Review*, July 1951, pp. 201–7.
Pollitt, H., 'The Margate Conference', *Labour Monthly*, October 1948.
Reid, B., 'Trotskyism in Britain Today', *Marxism Today*, September 1964, pp. 274–83.
Report of Democratic Left's Fourth Federal Conference at Birmingham and Midlands Institute on the 5 and 6 June 1999.
Saville, J., 'The Exit Congress and the British Communist Party', *Socialist Register*, 1976.
Saville, J., 'The XXth Congress and the British Communist Party', *Socialist Register*, 1976.
Symons, J. and E. B., 'Britain's Road', *Communist Review*, July 1947, pp. 200–7.
Volleamere, J., 'New Times Trade Unions in the 1990s', *New Times*, 4.8, February 1992.

Newspapers and journals

7 Days
Changes
Communist Review
Daily Express
Daily Herald
Daily Telegraph
Daily Worker
Futures
The Guardian

India Newsletter
Labour Monthly
Link
The Listener
Marxism Today
Morning Star
New Times: The Journal of the Democratic Left
Newsletter
The New Worker
Observer
Our Women: Go Forward to the World They Want
Red Flag
Socialist Challenge
Socialist Leader
Socialist Register
Socialist Worker
The Spectator
Sunday Telegraph
The Times
Tribune
World News and Views
World Times
Yorkshire Post

Internet sources and websites

http://srsm.port.com/swr/, accessed 9 September 2004.
http://www.cleanpolitix.com/faq/index.asp?page+NewPol, accessed 2 September 2004.
http://www.communist-party.org.uk/, accessed 2 September 2004.
http://www.exetersocialistalliance.org.uk, accessed 9 September 2004.
http://www.fact-index.com/s/sc/scottish-republican-socialist-party.html, accessed 2, 9 September 2004.
http://www.geocities.com/colchester, accessed 9 September 2004.
http://www.greenleft.org.au/back/1996/242/241p22.htm, accessed 9 September 2004.
http://www.greenleft.org.au/back/1996/242/242p22.htm, accessed 9 September 2004.
http://www.greenleft.org.au/back/1997/264/264p21.htm, accessed 9 September 2004.
http://www.hackneysa.org.uk/front.html, accessed 9 September 2004.
http://www.lancsocialistalliance.org.uk, accessed 9 September 2004.
http://www.londoncommunists.org/28008/index.html, accessed 2 September 2004.
http://www.londoncommunists.org.51226.html, accessed 2 September 2004.
http://www.new-politics.net/(New Politics Network), accessed 2 September 2004.
http://www.newworker,org/homepage.htm, accessed 2 September 2004.
http://www.newworker.org.newwork.htm, accessed 2 September 2004.
http://politics,guardian.co.uk/thinktank/page/0,10538,1092273,oo.html, accessed 2 September 2004.
http://www.recpml.uk.drdtpro.htm, accessed 2 September 2004.
http://www.repblm.org.uk, accessed 2 September 2004.
http://www.scottishsocialistparty.info, accessed 2 September 2004.
http://www.scottishsocialistparty.org, accessed 2 September 2004.

http://www.scottishsocialistparty.org.pages.branches.html, accessed 2 September 2004.
http://www.socialist-labour party.org.uk/arty1mainframe.htm, accessed 2 September 2004.
http://www.socialistworkers.co.uk, accessed 9 September 2004.
http://www.swp.org.uk, accessed 9 September 2004.
http://www.welshsocialist-alliance.org.uk, accessed 9 September 2004.
http://www.worldsocialism.org.spgb.about.html, accessed 9 September 2004.
http://www.wsws.org/polemics/1998/oct1998.sssp-024.shtml, accessed 2 September 2004.
http://www.wsws.org/polemics/1998/oct1998/ssp-024.shtml, accessed 2 September 2004.
http://www.wwne.demon.co.uk/ww2001/d01-83-htm, accessed 2 September 2004.

Secondary sources

Books

Barltrop, R., *The Monument: The Story of the Socialist Party of Great Britain*, London, Pluto Press, 1975.
Beckett, F., *Enemy Within: The Rise and Fall of the British Communist Party*, London, John Murray, 1995.
Branson, N., *History of the Communist Party of Great Britain 1941–1951*, London, Lawrence & Wishart, 1997.
Callaghan, J., *British Trotskyism: Theory and Practice*, Oxford, Blackwell, 1984.
Campbell, A. Fishman, N. and McIlroy, J. (eds), *British Trade Unions and Industrial Politics, Volume One: The Post-War Compromise, 1945–64*, Aldershot, Ashgate, 1999.
Collette, C. and Laybourn, K., *Modern Britain since 1979*, London, I.B. Tauris, 2003.
Duncan Hallas, Introduction to *The Origins of International Socialists*, London, Pluto Press, 1971 and 1974.
Eadon, J. and Renton, D., *The Communist Party of Great Britain since 1920*, Basingstoke, Palgrave, 2002.
Edmonds, R., *The Big Three, Churchill, Roosevelt and Stalin in Peace and War*, New York, W.W. Norton, 1991.
Fishman, N., *The British Communist Party and the Trade Unions, 1933–1945*, Aldershot, Scolar Press, 1995.
Flanders, A., *Trade Unions*, London, Hutchinson's University Library, seventh edition, 1963.
Frow, E. and Frow, R., *The Liquidation of the Communist Party of Great Britain: A Contribution to the Discussion*, Salford, Jubilee House, 1996.
Grant, E., *The Marxist Theory of the State*, London, Militant Pamphlet, 1980.
Grant, Ted, *History of British Trotskyism*, London, Well red publications, 2002.
Jackson, S. and Scott, S., 'Sexual Skirmishes and Feminist Factions', in *Feminism and Sexuality: A Reader*, Edinburgh, Edinburgh University Press, 1996.
Kendall, W., *The Revolutionary Movement in Britain 1900–1921*, London, Weidenfeld and Nicolson, 1969.
Kopasci, S., *In the Name of the Working Class*, London, Fontana, 1989.
Laybourn, K. and Murphy, D., *Under the Red Flag: A History of Communism in Britain*, Stroud, Sutton, 1999.
McDermott, K. and Agnew, J., *The Comintern: A History of International Communism from Lenin to Stalin*, London, Macmillan, 1996.
Macfarlane, L. J., *The British Communist Party: Origins and Development until 1929*, London, MacGibbin and Kee, 1966.

McIlroy, J. and Campbell, A. (eds), *Labour History Review*, Special Issue – International Communism, 68.1, April 2003.
Morgan, K., *Against Fascism and War: Ruptures and Continuities in British Communist Politics, 1935–41*, Manchester, Manchester University Press, 1989.
Morgan, K., *Harry Pollitt*, Manchester, Manchester University Press, 1993.
Pelling, H., *The British Communist Party: An Historical Profile*, London, A and C. Black, 1958.
Pimlott, B., *Harold Wilson*, London, HarperCollins, 1992.
Taaffe, P., *The Rise of Militant*, London, Militant Publications, 1995.
Taylor, A., *Trade Unions and the Labour Party*, London, Croom Helm, 1987.
Thompson, W., *The Good Old Cause: British Communism 1921–1991*, London, Pluto Press, 1992.
Thompson, W., *The Communist Movement since 1945*, Oxford, Blackwell, 1998.
Thorpe, A., *The British Communist Party, and Moscow, 1920–43*, Manchester, Manchester University Press, 2000.
Upward, E., *The Rotten Elements*, Middlesex, Penguin Books.
Willets, H. T., 'The USSR and Eurocommunism', in Richard Kindersley (ed.), *In Search of Communism*, London, Macmillan, 1981.
Worley, M., *Class Against Class: The Communist Party of Britain between the Wars*, London, I.B. Tauris, 2002.

Articles

Behan, B., letter to editor, *Labour History Review*, 59.1, 1994, p. 11.
Callaghan, J., 'Common Wealth and the Communist Party and the 1945 General Election', *Contemporary Record*, 9, 1995, p. 66.
Callaghan, J., 'The Road to 1945', *Socialist History*, November 1995, pp. 3–21.
Callaghan, J. and Phythian, M., 'State Surveillance and the CPGB Leadership: 1920s–1950s', *Labour History Review*, 69.1, April 2004, p. 29.
Campbell, A. and McIlroy, J., 'Is the CPGB History Important? A Reply to Harriet Jones', *Labour History Review*, 68.3, December 2003, pp. 385–90.
Fishman, N., 'Essentialists and Realists: Reflections on the Historiography of the CPGB', *Communist History Network Newsletter*, Autumn 2001.
Johnson, A. '"Beyond the Smallness of Self": Oral History and British Trotskyism', *Oral History*, 24.1, Spring 1996, pp. 39–48.
Johnstone, M., letter to editors, *Labour History Review*, 59.1, 1994, p. 8.
Johnstone, M., 'The CPGB, the Comintern and the War, 1939–41: Filling in the Blackspots', *Science and Society*, 61.1, 1997.
Jones, H., 'Is CPGB History Important?', *Labour History Review*, 67.3, December 2002, pp. 347–53.
McIlroy, J., 'Reds at Work: Communist Factory Organisations in the Cold War, 1947–56', *Labour History Review*, 65.2, Summer, 2000, pp. 181–201.
McIlroy, J. and Campbell, A., 'Editorial: New Directions in International Communist Historiography', *Labour History Review*, Special Issue – International Communism, 68.1, April 2003, pp. 3–5.
McIlroy, J. and Campbell, A., 'Histories of the British Communist Party: A User's Guide', *Labour History Review*, 68.1, April 2003, pp. 33–59.
McIlroy, J. and Campbell, A., The Historiography of British Communism: An alternative reading.

McKibbin, R., 'Why was there no Marxism in Britain', *English Historical Review*, 99, April 1984, pp. 297–331.

Melling, J., 'Red under the Collar? Clive Jenkins, White Collar Unionism and the Politics of the British Left, 1947–1965', *Twentieth Century British History*, 13, no. 4 , 2002, p. 419.

Morgan, Kevin, The Historiography of the British Communist Party, further consideration and response to John McIlroy and Allan Campbell in *Mittelungsblatt*, 2004, *Labour History Review*, December 2004 and *American Communist Review*, 2005.

Phillips, J., 'Labour and the Cold War: the TGWU and the Politics of Anti-Communism in Trade Unions', *Labour History Review*, 6.1, Spring 1999, pp. 44–61.

Redfern, N. 'Winning the Peace: British Communists, the Soviet Union and the General Election of 1945', *Contemporary British History*, 16, no. 1, Spring, 2002, pp. 29–50.

Samuels, R., 'The Lost World of British Communism', Part 1, *New Left Review*, 154, 1985.

Samuels, R., 'Staying Power: The Lost World of British Communism', Part 2, *New Left Review*, 156, 1986.

Stevens, R., 'Cold-War Politics: Communism and Anti-Communism in Trade Unions', in A. Campbell, N. Fishman and J. McIlroy (eds), *British Trade Unions and Industrial Politics, Volume One: The Post-War Compromise, 1945–64*, Aldershot, Ashgate, 1999.

Thornton and Thompson, 'Scottish Communists, 1956–57', *Science and Society*, 61.1, pp. 68–93.

Thorpe, A., 'Comintern "Control" of the Communist Party of Great Britain, 1920–43', *English Historical Review*, 113, 1998, p. 640.

Worley, M., 'Left Turn: A Reassessment of the Communist Party of Great Britain in the Third Period 1928–1933', *Twentieth Century British History*, 1 December 2000.

Index

Adams, Shelley 128
Afghanistan 109–14
Ainley, David 58, 144
Airey, Margaret 33
Alexander, A. V. 44
Alexander, Ken 51
Ali, Tariq 9, 73, 111
Allaun, Frank 72
All Britain Anti-Poll Tax 140
All-India Peasant Association 45
All-India Trades Union Congress (AITUC) 45
Amalgamated Engineering Union (AEU) 26, 42, 58, 84, 86
Ambrose, Les 26
American Communist Review 4, 7
American Loan 21, 24
Arnot, Robin Page 20
Associated Society of Locomotive Engineers and Firemen (ASLEF) 59
Association of Supervisory Staffs and Executive Technicians (ASSET) 26
Attlee, Clem 11, 13–14, 20–1, 24, 26–7, 36–7, 39, 44; *see also* Labour governments

Banda, Michael 70
Barltrop, R. 9; *The Monument* 9
Barrow, Sion 142
Baruch, John 104–5
Beavis, Ian 131
Bechler, Rosemary 151, 155
Beckett, Francis 113, 118, 123, 154, 158–9
Behan, Brian 7, 53, 70
Bellamy, Joan 24
Bellamy, Ron 137
Benn, Tony 109, 112, 139, 152; Bennites 109, 112
Bennett, Kate 128

Bennett, Mick 22, 54
Beuchamp, Kay 94
Bevan, Aneurin 14; Bevanites 57, 59
Bevin, Ernest 22, 26–7, 43, 46
Bickerstaffe, Rodney 86, 168
Black Dwarf 9, 73
Blair, Tony 153, 157, 160–2, 164, 166–9
Bolton, George 120
Bornstein, S. 42
Bowden, Margaret 92
Bowler, Lorraine 128
Branson, Noreen 15, 94
Brennan, Irene 91, 99, 101
British Empire 3, 44, 46
Broadside 88
Browder, Earl 36, 47
Brown, Isobel 94
Building Workers' Charter 88
Bulgaria 43, 128
Burns, Emile 19
Byrne, John 60–2, 71
Byrne, Rosemary 163

Cadogan, Peter 55, 70, 78
Cairns, Gerry 162
Callaghan, James 89, 109
Callaghan, John 16
Campaign for Nuclear Disarmament (CND) 58, 78, 135, 138, 143
Campbell, Alan 4–6, 8
Campbell, Beatrix 96, 119
Campbell, John R. 18, 48
Cannon, Les 60, 62
Carrillo, Santiago 2, 81, 106; *Eurocommunism and the State* 2, 106
Carter, Peter 123
Cartwright, Margaret 96
Castle, Barbara 63, 69; *In Place of Strife* 69, 77, 88

Index

Challinor, Raymond 72
Chalmers, Douglas 152
Chalmers, Frank 116
Chapple, Frank 60, 62
Chater, Tony 107–8, 116–20, 122, 131, 145; Chaterites 116–20, 131, 135, 140, 159–60; 'Wimpy Bar meeting' 117
China 2, 40, 57, 74, 110, 157, 164; Great Leap Forward 2, 74
Churchill, Winston 11, 15, 20, 22, 43, 46
Claudin, F. 2, 81; *Eurocommunism and Socialism* 2
Clay Cross Labour Council 86
Cliff, Tony 39–40, 70, 72, 76; 'Russia: A Marxist Analysis' 39–40
The Club 40
coal miners' strikes: (1972) 84–5; (1974) 84–5; (1984–5) 114, 121–3
Coates, Ken 72–3
Cold War 1, 3, 11–56, 130, 170
Cominform 13, 26, 38, 48, 55
Comintern 7, 10, 13–16, 20, 36, 106, 171; Seventh Congress (1935) 36, 106
The Committee of 100 78
Committee to Defeat Revisionism for Communist Unity 75
Commonwealth 3, 15, 43–7
Common Wealth Party 15, 18
Communist Campaign Group 2, 135–6
Communist History Network Newsletter 5
Communist League of Great Britain 9; *Combat* 9; *Compass* 9; *Intercom* 9
Communist Party of Britain (CPB) 3, 7, 131, 136–7, 146, 158–60, 168, 172; *Communist Review* 9; communist unity conference 136; *Needs of the Hour* 136, 159; *The Weekly Worker* 3; see also *Morning Star*
Communist Party of Great Britain (CPGB) i, 1–7, 9–172; *7 Days* 133–4, 142; *The Attack upon the Party from the so-called 'Extreme Left'* (1964) 75; *Britain for the People: Proposals for Post-War Policy* (1944) 19; *The British Road to Socialism* 11, 35–8, 41, 46–7, 49, 56, 69, 75, 78, 81, 88, 97–9, 101–2, 106–7, 129, 135–7, 170, 172; *Broad Left* 88; Broad Left approach/Broad Democratic Alliance 57–9, 63, 88, 100, 108, 135, 171; *Changes* 144, 150, 154; *City Limits* 119; Class Against Class 36; *Comment* 89; Commission on Inner Party Democracy (1956–7) 41, 51, 55–7; Commission on Inner Party Democracy (1977–8) 101–6, 109; *Communist* 101; *Communist Focus* 119–20; communist membership 28; 'Communist Party and the Factories' 29; *Communist Party and the Factories* 30; *The Communist Review* 38; *Congress Truth* 120; Congresses, Seventeenth (1944) 19, 34–6; *The Crisis in Our Communist Party: Cause, Effect and Cure* 119; *Daily Worker* 40, 43, 53, 58–9, 74; Decisions 81, 98–100; democratic centralism 7, 49–52, 97–106; Eighteenth (1945) 34–6; Empire Conference (1947) 3; factory organisation 27–30, 34–5, 66; feminism 4, 25, 31–4, 80–1, 89–97; First National Conference of Communist Women (1951) 31–2; Forty-Third Congress (1991) 115, 145; History Group 103; India 43; *Labour Monthly* 59; Lancashire and Cheshire District 68; *Link* 4, 34, 90–3, 95–6, 101, 103, 124–8; London district 17, 29–30, 32, 35, 131, 136; *Manifesto for New Times* 38, 131, 137–8, 140; *Marxism Today* 59, 75, 89, 98–9, 108, 115, 117–18, 122–3, 133, 135, 138, 140, 142, 171; membership i, 1, 7, 11–12, 31, 35, 49, 57–9, 80–2, 97, 133, 139; Moscow money 114; municipal results 23, 60, 68; National Aggregate Meeting of Black members (1991) 127; National Peace Council 43; National Women's Advisory Committee 4, 11, 92–3, 95, 103, 124, 127; National Women's Conferences 94, 97, 128; 'Needs of the Hour, 1973' 85; new revisionist history 4–8; Nineteenth (1947) 25; North-West District 131–2; Organisation Commission (1944–6) 34; 'For Peace and National Independence' 21; Political Committee 17; *The Reasoner* 7, 41, 49, 51–2, 56; *Restore the Unity of the International Communist Movement* 75; *For Soviet Britain* (1935) 20; Special Congress, Forty-Second Congress (1990) 140–2; *Straight Left* 119; Straight Left/ists 118–20, 131, 140, 159; Thirty-Fifth Congress (1978) 101; Thirty-Sixth Congress (1985) 132; trade unions 3, 11, 84–9; Twentieth (1948) 25–6, 35; Twenty-Eighth Congress (1963) 63; Twenty-Fifth Congress (1957) 56; Twenty-Second (1951) 22, 37; Twenty-Third Congress (1954) 48–9; wage restraint (1948) 26; *Why the Communist Party says Reject the Marshall*

Plan 21, 24; *Women in Action* 9;
Women's National Biennial Conferences,
Women Conference on Racism (1984)
126; Women's Network 127; *The Worker*
15; workplace organisation 27–30, 89;
World News and Views 36, 50–1;
Yorkshire District 24–5, 58–9
Communist Party of India (CPI) 44–6
Communist Party of Scotland 149, 160–1
Communist Party of the Soviet Union
(CPSU) 8, 11, 13, 42, 47–8, 99
Communist Party of the United
States 36, 47
The Communist Review 38
Confederation of Shipbuilding and
Engineering Unions 31
Congress (1956) 8, 11, 40, 42, 47–8, 53
Conservative government (1970–4) 81–4,
111–12
Conservative Party 15, 17, 38, 47, 54, 80,
82–5, 112, 150–3
Cook, Dave 116, 135
Coote, Anna 127–8; *Family in the Firing
Line* 128
Cornforth, Kitty 37
Costello, Mick 87–9, 96, 100, 116–20,
122–3, 145; 'Wimpy Bar meeting' 117
Coussins, Jean 128; *Family in the Firing
Line* 128
Cowan, Jim 122
Cox, Idris 53
Cripps, Stafford 44
Croft, Andy 143
Curran, Frances 163
Czechoslovakia 1–2, 7, 10, 12, 43,
57–8, 78–80, 98–9, 107, 170;
Soviet invasion 78–81

Daily Express 63
Daily Herald 14, 18
Daily Mirror 117
Daily Worker 23–4, 27, 41, 43, 48, 50,
53–5, 58, 67, 72, 75
Daly, Lawrence 67, 85
Davis, George 136
Davis, Mary 96, 126–7, 136, 160
Davis, Tricia 120, 127, 129
Davison, Stan 153
Deakin, Arthur 27–8
Delmont, Gloria 130
Democratic Left (DL) 2, 115, 144, 149–58,
171; *Futures* 152–3; membership 149;
New Times 150, 153–5
Democratic Left Scotland (DLS) 153

Desai, Parimel 153
Devine, Pat 102
Dock Strike (1951) 3, 12, 28
Donovan Commission 68
Dubcek, Alexandra 78
Dutt, Rajani Palme 3, 21, 25, 42, 44–5,
59, 70, 75; *Freedom for India* 44; *India
Newsletter* 44–5; *Labour Monthly* 59

Eadon, James 5
Egan, Ellen 127–8
Electrical Trade Union (ETU) 3–4, 26–7,
60–3, 71
Empire (British) i, 3
Engineering and Allied Trades Shop
Stewards' National Council 25; *The Metal
Worker* 25; *The New Propeller* 25
Engineering Gazette 88
English Socialist Alliance 3, 165, 167
Eurocommunism/ists 1–2, 9–10, 81–2, 89,
97–9, 100–1, 106–10, 116, 124, 131–2,
135–6, 145–7, 157, 169

Facey, Peter 156
Falber, Helen 94
Falber, Reuban 58, 102, 110, 138, 144
Falklands War 129
Fancy, William 72
Feather, Vic 12
Felton, Monica 33
feminism 4, 25, 31–4, 80–1, 89–97, 103,
123–31; bi-sexual 90; black 90, 96, 125,
128; Black Women's Centre, Brixton
125; Black Women's Group 125; first
National Black Women's Conference
(1978) 126; gay 90, 127; 'queer theory'
90; *see also* Greenham Common
Fields, Terry 138–9
Fife Socialist League 67–8
Filling, Brian 119
Fire Brigade's Union 27, 54, 165
First World War 1–2
Fischer, Mark 3
Fishman, Nina 3–6, 142
Flashlight 88
Foot, Michael 28, 138–9
Foot, Paul 72
Foster, John 132, 160
Foulkes, Frank 60, 62
Fourth International, Third World
Congress of 8, 40
Fox, Colin 161, 163
Francis, Hywel 140, 154, 158
Fraser, John Norman 61

French, Jean 91, 96, 107
French, Sid 79, 98, 107, 110, 157
Frow, Eddie 115–16; *The Liquidation of the Communist Party of Great Britain* 109, 115
Frow, Edmund 108–9, 115–16; *The Liquidation of the Communist Party of Great Britain* 109, 115
Frow, Ruth 108, 115–16; *The Liquidation of the Communist Party of Great Britain* 115–16
Fryer, Peter 41, 70–1; *Newsletter* 70, 72, 76
Fyrth, Jim 143

Gallacher, Willie 12, 18, 36–7, 46
Gandhi, M. K. 46
general election (1945) 12, 15, 18, 20
  (1966) 60
Germany, Eastern 12, 44; German rearmament 32
Gill, Ken 86, 117, 119, 132, 137, 168; 'The Alternative Economic Strategy' 86
Glasgow Forward 14
Gollan, John 21, 37, 44, 47, 49, 52–4, 56–9, 63, 65–6, 70, 114, 144, 149; 'Some Thoughts About Intellectuals' 52, 114
Gorbachev, Mikhail 133, 138, 160
Gorbals, parliamentary by-election (1948) 21, 33
Graef, Robert 98–100
Grahl, John 133
Grant, Ted 8, 39–40, 73, 111, 164; *History of British Trotskyism* 8
Green, Dave 139, 142
Greenham Common 90, 130–1
Green Party 141, 171
Griffiths, Robert 160
Groot, Joanna de 94, 96
Grunwick 86
The Guardian 116, 117, 133, 145
Guiar, Mollie 30
Gunn, Uian 136
Gunter, Ray 63–4

Hall, Stuart 76
Halpin, Anita 160
Halpin, Kevin 55
Halverson, Ron 120
Hancock, Florence 27
Hannington, Walter 16, 26, 36
Hardman, Paul 167
Hatton, Derek 139
Haxell, Frank Leslie 60–1, 71
Haylett, John 160

Haywood, Jackie 127
Healy, Gerry 8, 39–42, 70–1, 75, 111, 139; see also Labour Party, *Labour Review*
Heath, Edward 80, 81–2, 111
Heathfield, Betty 4
Heathfield, Peter 128
Hicks, Mike 131–2, 136, 145, 158–9
Hill, Christopher 55
Hill, Howard 52
Hinton, James 15
Hitler, A. 1, 7; Stalin–Hitler Pact 7
Hobsbawm, Eric 6
Hodgson, Charles 65
Holman, John 67
Hood, Nicholas 72
Horner, Arthur 12, 26
Horner, John 54
Hughes, Emrys 14
Hungary i, 2, 7, 10–12, 41, 52–6, 70, 76, 80–1, 107, 123, 170; Nagy Government 53–4
Hunt, Judith 93
Hyland, Anthony 3

Independent Labour Party 18
India 3, 43–4; Indian Congress 44–5; Indian Independence Day 45
Industrial Relations Act/Bill (1971) 82–6, 88, 112
International Charter for Women 33; International Women's Day (1952) 32; International Women's Day Committee 4; see also National Assembly of Women
International Communist Party of the Fourth International 3
International Group (IG) 73
International Marxist Group 9, 73, 82, 111; see also *Black Dwarf*
International Marxist groups/Socialist League 9; *International* 9; *Red Mole* 9; *Red Weekly* 9; *Socialist Action* 9
International Socialists 9, 39, 71–2, 76; *International Socialist Journal* 72; see also Socialist Workers' Party (SWP)
Islip Unity Group 168

Jack, Digby 78
Jackson, Frank 25
Jacques, Martin 97, 99, 108, 115, 117–18, 140–2, 145, 148
Jenkins, Clive 26
Johnson, Alan 111
Johnstone, Monty 7–8, 51, 98, 133

Index

Jones, Harriet 6
Jones, Jack 84, 86

Kane, Rosie 163
Kautsky, Karl 9
Kelsey, Stan 3
Kemp, Tom 70, 72
Kendall, Walter 4, 8, 71
Kenny, Joe 65
Kerrigan, Peter 21–2, 34, 53, 59, 62, 70, 72
Kettle, Arnold 53
Keys, Bill 86, 123
Klugmann, James 7–8, 24, 44, 53, 58, 75, 108; 'Lessons of the Prague Trial' 44
Korean War 32–3, 43
Kruschev, N. 11, 46–8, 50

Labour governments (1945–50) 3, 11–14, 17, 20, 37, 39, 43, 46; (1950–1) 37, 39, 43; (1964–70) 63, 80; (1974–9) 84, 86, 88; Social Contract 86–7; 'Winter of Discontent' 87
Labour History Review 4–7
Labour Monthly 25
Labour Party 3, 12–20, 25–6, 37, 39, 43, 46, 49, 56, 73, 90, 97, 135, 138–9, 164, 168–9; affiliation of CPGB vote (1943) 14; affiliation of CPGB vote (1946) 19; *Britain Will Win with Labour* (1974) 86; *The Communist Party and the War – A Record of Hypocrisy and Treachery to the Workers of Europe* 14; Conference (1944) 14; Conference (1946) 18; Conference (1985) 139; *Economic Policy and the Cost of Living Statement* 86; *Get Britain Back to Work* (1974) 86; Howdenshire Constituency Labour Party 18; *Labour Review* 42, 71; National Executive Committee 18; New Labour 160, 168–9; *The Secret Battalion* (1946) 18; TUC–Labour Party Liaison Committee 86; Young Socialists (LPYS) 73
Lane, Tony 115, 117
Laski, Harold 18–19; *The Secret Battalion* (1946) 18
Laughlin, Bill 151
Lawrence, John 8, 40–1
Leckie, Carolyn 163
Lenin, V. I. 37, 39, 93–4
The Leninist 168
Lessing, Doris 69
Levy, Martin 160

Liaison Committee for the Defence of Trade Unions (LCDTU) 68, 84, 88
Liberals 17
Lilburne, Ann 127
Linsley, Benjamin 156
London Trades Council Women's Charter 92–3
London Women's Conference 32
London Women's Peace Council 32
Longdon, Bill 25

McCreery, Michael 75; *Destroy the Old to Build the New* 75; *Vanguard* 75
McCrindle, Jean 128
MacEwan, Malcolm 55
Macfarlane, L. J. 4
McGahey, Mick 85–6, 122–3, 149
McGregor, Ian 121
McIlhone, Bob 29
McIlroy, John 4–6, 8, 28–30
McIntosh, Mary 128; *Anti-Socialist Family* 128
Macintyre, Alistair 72
McKay, Ian 131, 138
McKibbin, Ross 2, 170
McLennan, Gordon 114, 118–19, 131, 158
McNally, Tony 140
McShane, Harry 42, 47; McShane Group 41–2, 47
Mandal, Ernest 72
Mann, Emily 160
Maoist/s 75
Marsden, Chris 162
Marsh, Charlotte 32
Marx, Karl 9, 37, 115
Marxism/Marxist and Marxist–Leninism *passim*
Marxist Leninist Organisations in Britain 9; *Class Against Class* 9; principles 117, 136
Matthews, Betty 91
Matthews, George 43, 81–2, 88–9, 98, 118, 149
May Day Manifesto 76–7
Medvediv, Roy 117
Mendolsohn, Arthur 143, 152
MI5 20, 22
Middleton, J. S. 13–14
Miliband, Ralph 72
Militant Tendency (MT) 39, 73, 111, 138, 164; *Militant* 38, 39, 73
Mitchell, H. 120
Moffatt, Abe 26
Moffit, Alex 54

Morgan, Kevin 5, 15
Morning Star 9, 58, 78, 81, 97, 100–1, 107–9, 116–20, 122–4, 135–7, 140, 144, 159–60, 171
Moroney, Jill 130
Morrison, Herbert 21, 24
Mortimer, Jim 72, 168
Moscow 2, 4, 6–7, 10, 13, 16, 20, 56, 98, 118, 133, 171
Mountbatten (Lord) 45; Mountbatten Plan 45
Muir, Linda 167
Munby, Steve 152; *Argument Towards a Democratic Left* 151
Municipal and General Workers' Union 85
Myant, Chris 116, 119–20

National and Local Government Officers Association (NALGO) 143
National Assembly of Women 4, 32–5, 43; First Assembly (1952) 32; *Our Women* 33; Second Assembly (1953) 33; Third Assembly (1954) 33
National Association of Teachers in Further and Higher Education (NATFHE) 143
National Coal Board 121–3
National Federation of Building Operatives 26
National Hospital campaigns 20
National Industrial Relations Court 82–6
National Peace Conference (1952) 43
National Seamen's Union 63–6
National Unemployed Workers' Movement 26
National Union of Mineworkers 12, 26 121–3, 127; Scottish NUM 26
National Union of Students (NUS) 78
National Union of Teachers (NUT) 143
Nehru, Pandit 44–6
Nellist, Dave 139
New Builder's Leader 25
New Communist Party (NCP) 2, 98, 107, 110, 136–7, 145, 157–8, 166, 168; *The New Worker* 110, 157–8; 'tankists' 98
New Left 76–7; *May Day Manifesto* (1968) 76; New Left May Day Manifesto Group 76; *New Left Review* 76
New Politics Network (NPN) 2, 156; *Beyond the Classroom* 156; *Broadening Participation – Thinking beyond party membership* 156; *Strong politicsm clean politics* 156
The Newsletter 76
New Times 108

Newton, Harry 115
Nicholson, Fergus 119
North Atlantic Treaty Organisation (NATO) 22, 43, 79
North Korea 129

Observer 123
Ollerton 121
Operation Barbarossa 11
Orgreave 121

Pablo, Michael 40; 'The Rise and Decline of Stalinism' 40
Pakistan 44
Palmer, John 72
Papworth, Bert 26
Paynter, Will 59–60
Pearson, Lord 63; Court of Inquiry 1966 63
Pelling, Henry 4
Pentonville Five 83, 85
People's Printing Press Society (PPPS) 116, 119, 132
Pethwick-Lawrence, Frederick W. 44
Phillips, Morgan 4, 18–19, 26
Piratin, Phil 12, 18, 53
In Place of Strife (1969) 88
Pocock, Gerry 107, 132
Pollitt, Harry 7, 13–14, 16–18, 20–1, 31, 36–7, 47–9, 108, 149; *Looking Ahead* 21, 24, 37, 108, 158, 169
Popular Front 36
Posadas, J. 9, 74
Post Office Workers' strike (1971) 85
Powell, Len 25
Power, Mike 136, 142
Prescott, John 6
Priscott, Dave 102–3, 118, 132–4

RAGE 167
Rail, Maritime and Transport Workers (RMR) 159
Ramelson, Bert 49–50, 54, 65, 72, 84–5, 87–8, 98–9, 101, 123, 158, 168, 171
Redfearn, Neil 14–17
Reid, Betty 55, 75–6
Reid, Jimmy 65, 82, 84, 97, 112
Renton, David 5
Revolutionary Communist Party (RCP) 9, 11, 38–40, 73, 166; The Club 40; The Group 39; *The Next Step* 9; *Socialist Appeal* 39; *Socialist Outlook* 39
Revolutionary Communist Party of Britain (Marxist Leninist) (RCP ML) 166, 168; *Draft Programme for the Working Class* 166

Revolutionary Marxist Tendency of the Fourth International 9; *International Marxist Review* 9
Revolutionary Socialist League (RSL) 39, 41, 111
Revolutionary Workers' Party 9, 66, 74, 113; *Red Flag* 9, 66, 74
Rix, David 168
Robinson, Ron 137
Rooney, Alan 73
Roosevelt, F. D. 15, 20
Rowthorne, Bob 133
Rust, William 16, 36–7

Salmond, Alex 163
Samuels, Raphael 13
Sassoon, Donald 6
Saville, John 41, 50–2, 171
Scanlon, Hugh 84, 86
Scargill, Ann 4, 122, 127–8
Scargill, Arthur 121–3, 128, 139, 162, 164, 167
Scotland 1; *Alert Scotland* 3
Scottish Green Party 153
Scottish Militant Labour 140, 161–2
Scottish National Party (SNP) 150, 163
Scottish Parliament 3
Scottish Republican Socialist Movement (SRSM) 161, 163; *Scottish Workers' Republic* 163
Scottish Republican Socialist Party (SRSP) 161, 163
Scottish Socialist Alliance (SSA) 1, 3, 153, 160–1, 172
Scottish Socialist Party (SSP) 1, 3, 160–5, 168, 172; *Scottish Socialist Voice* 163; *SSP News* 163
Seamen's Strike (1966) 4, 63–8; *Seamen's Charter* 88
Second World War 1, 3, 7, 11, 13, 19–20, 36, 112
Sedgewick, Peter 72
Sheridan, Tommy 140, 163
Shop Steward's National Council, conference 25
Silver, Steve 160
Simpson, Renate 98
Skipton parliamentary by-election (1944) 15
Slansky, Rudolf 44
Slater, Jim 86
Slaughter, Cliff 70
Small, Rosemary 91, 96, 103; *Women: The Road to Equality and Socialism* 91
Smith, Ned 123

Social Democratic Federation (SDF) 9
Socialist Labour League (SLL) 39–42, 70, 72–6, 111; see also *The Newsletter*
Socialist Labour Party (SLP) 162–3, 167
The Socialist Leader 71
Socialist Outlook 40–1
Socialist Party of Great Britain (SPGB) 8, 74, 167; *Socialist Standard* 9, 74, 167
Socialist Review Group 39, 40; *Socialist Review* 40; see also Socialist Workers' Party
Socialist Workers' Party (SWP) 39, 71, 72–4, 82, 100, 110–11, 163; *The Socialist Worker* 111
SOGAT (Society of Graphical and Allied Trades) 136, 158
South Africa 86
Soviet Union 1, 3–4, 6–7, 11, 14–15, 17, 20, 34, 38, 49–50, 52, 74, 78–80, 98–9, 101, 107, 116, 146, 158–9, 170
Soviet Women's Anti-Fascist Committee 34
Stalin, J. 7–8, 11, 13, 14, 16, 20, 35–7, 42, 46, 48–9, 98, 138; Stalin–Hitler Pact 7
Stalinism/ist/s 1–2, 4–8, 13, 50, 52, 72, 108, 114–20, 147–8, 164, 169–71
Stevens, Walter 26
Stevenson, Steve 160
Stockholm Peace Appeal 129
strikes 27–8
student revolt 69, 77–8
Styles, Jean 91–3, 96, 103
Sunday Telegraph 77
Sunday Times 144

Taaffe, Pat 164
TASS 86, 117, 132, 137
Tatchell, Peter 137
Taylor, Helen 150–1
Teheran agreement/conference (1943) 13, 15–16, 20
Temple, Nina 134–6, 138–45, 149–51, 158–9
Tewson, Vincent 27
Thatcherism 9, 14, 89, 114, 120, 134; Margaret Thatcher 9, 89, 114, 120, 123, 129, 135
Thompson, E. P. 8, 41, 50–2, 76; 'Winter Wheat in Omsk' 50
Thompson, Willie 6, 15, 118, 144–5, 148, 169
Thorpe, Andrew 15
Tito 38, 43, 55
Tobacco Workers and Foundry Workers 27

Tonge, Margaret 125
Topham, Tony 73
Trades Union Congress (TUC) 24, 26–8, 61, 63–4, 83–6, 137; 'A Warning to Trade Unionists' 27; *Defend Democracy* (1948) 27; *The Tactics of Disruption* (1949) 27
Trade unions 3, 24–31, 114
Transport and General Workers' Union (TGWU) 26–8, 31, 83–4
Trevitt, Eric 136–7
Tribune 40, 98; Tribune Group 82
Trotsky, Leon 38
Trotskyism 1, 8–9, 38–43
Trotskyite i, 1, 3, 8–9, 11–12, 38–43, 47, 57, 69–76, 110–11, 138–9, 147–8, 164, 169; Fourth International 39–40, 73; Fourth World Congress of the Fourth International 40; International Secretariat of the Fourth International (ISFI) 39; Third World Congress of the Fourth International 40
Turner, Jean 129, 136

UNISON 168
United States 13, 24, 30, 43
Universities and Left Review (ULR) 42–3, 69
Upper Clyde Shipbuilders 85

Vietnam 66, 68–9, 78, 85, 91
Volleamere, John 152

Waite, Mike 152–3
Wall, Pat 139
Walshe, Denise 103

Warsaw Treaty Powers 75, 79
Weller, Michael 155
Welmark, Jenny 96
Welsh Socialist Alliance 3, 164–5
Whitelaw, Willie 123
Whitfield, David 117–18, 132
Williams, Raymond 76–7; *see also* May Day Manifesto
Wilson, Harold 63–5, 72, 80, 86
Women 25, 31–4, 80, 89–97
Women Against Pit Closures (WAPC) 4, 122, 127–8
Women in Action 90, 96; Women in Action 90, 96
Women's Liberation Movement 80–1, 89–97
Women's Today 32
Women's Trades Union Congress 93; 'The TUC Charter for Women Workers' 93
Woodcock, George 65, 83
Woods, Charlie 119–20
Workers' International League (WIL) 11, 39
Workers' Revolutionary Party (WRP) 111
Working Women's Charter 92

Yalta agreement (1945) 13, 15–16, 20, 36
Yeo, Stephen 76
Young, K. 128
Young Communist League (YCL) 13, 23, 35, 58, 79, 138; *Challenge* 58
Yugoslavia 2, 7, 40, 43, 55

Zabie, Neehm 126

eBooks – at www.eBookstore.tandf.co.uk

A library at your fingertips!

eBooks are electronic versions of printed books. You can store them on your PC/laptop or browse them online.

They have advantages for anyone needing rapid access to a wide variety of published, copyright information.

eBooks can help your research by enabling you to bookmark chapters, annotate text and use instant searches to find specific words or phrases. Several eBook files would fit on even a small laptop or PDA.

NEW: Save money by eSubscribing: cheap, online access to any eBook for as long as you need it.

Annual subscription packages

We now offer special low-cost bulk subscriptions to packages of eBooks in certain subject areas. These are available to libraries or to individuals.

For more information please contact webmaster.ebooks@tandf.co.uk

We're continually developing the eBook concept, so keep up to date by visiting the website.

www.eBookstore.tandf.co.uk